1800 STAMPS

OF THE WORLD

A stunning visual directory of rare and familiar issues, organized country by country with 1800 images of collectables from more than 150 countries

Includes charity seals, wartime issues, bogus stamps, famous flaws, modern innovations, important commemoratives and beautiful pictorial stamps

Dr James Mackay

southwater

Author's Dedication: **For my granddaughter, Sophie**

This edition is published by Southwater

Southwater is an imprint of Anness Publishing Ltd
Hermes House, 88–89 Blackfriars Road, London SE1 8HA
tel. 020 7401 2077; fax 020 7633 9499
www.southwaterbooks.com; www.annesspublishing.com

If you like the images in this book and would like to investigate using them for
publishing, promotions or advertising, please visit our website www.practicalpictures.com
for more information.

© Anness Publishing Ltd 2007

UK agent: The Manning Partnership Ltd
tel. 01225 478444; fax 01225 478440; sales@manning-partnership.co.uk
UK distributor: Grantham Book Services Ltd
tel. 01476 541080; fax 01476 541061; orders@gbs.tbs-ltd.co.uk
North American agent/distributor: National Book Network
tel. 301 459 3366; fax 301 429 5746; www.nbnbooks.com
Australian agent/distributor: Pan Macmillan Australia
tel. 1300 135 113; fax 1300 135 103; customer.service@macmillan.com.au
New Zealand agent/distributor: David Bateman Ltd
tel. (09) 415 7664; fax (09) 415 8892

A CIP catalogue record for this book is available from the British Library.

Publisher: Joanna Lorenz
Editorial Director: Helen Sudell
Editors: Catherine Stuart and Elizabeth Woodland
Copy-editor: Beverley Jollands
Designer: Nigel Partridge
Photography: Martyn Milner and Malcolm Craik
Production Manager: Steve Lang

Note
The stamps reproduced in this book do not appear at their actual size. A small defacing
bar has been added to mint issues, where applicable, to indicate that they are a
reproduction.

Ethical Trading Policy
At Anness Publishing we believe that business should be conducted in an ethical and
ecologically sustainable way, with respect for the environment and a proper regard to the
replacement of the natural resources we employ. As a publisher, we use a lot of wood pulp
to make high-quality paper for printing, and that wood commonly comes from spruce
trees. We are therefore currently growing more than 500,000 trees in two Scottish forest
plantations near Aberdeen – Berrymoss (130 hectares/320 acres) and West Touxhill (125
hectares/305 acres). The forests we manage contain twice the number of trees employed
each year in paper-making for our books. Because of this ongoing ecological investment
programme, you, as our customer, can have the pleasure and reassurance of knowing that
a tree is being cultivated on your behalf to naturally replace the materials used to make the
book you are holding. Our forestry programme is run in accordance with the UK
Woodland Assurance Scheme (UKWAS) and will be certified by the internationally
recognized Forest Stewardship Council (FSC). The FSC is a non-government organization
dedicated to promoting responsible management of the world's forests. Certification
ensures forests are managed in an environmentally sustainable and socially responsible
basis. For further information about this scheme, go to www.annesspublishing.com/trees

Previously published as part of a larger volume, *The World Encyclopedia of Stamps
& Stamp Collecting*

CONTENTS

INTRODUCING STAMPS AND PHILATELY

Philately, to give stamp collecting its proper name, has been called "the king of hobbies and the hobby of kings" – alluding to the fact that George V and Edward VIII of Britain, Carol of Romania, Alfonso XIII of Spain and Farouk of Egypt were all enthusiasts. The most famous non-royal head of state who was a lifelong philatelist was Franklin Delano Roosevelt.

Stamps function rather like miniature posters: they reflect what a country thinks of itself, or how it wishes to be seen by the world.

Left: A 1947 stamp from Monaco showing Roosevelt at his stamp collection. It was designed by Pierre Gandon and does not set a good example for stamp collectors, for its subject is about to scuff the stamps with the cuff of his shirt. It must be presumed that Gandon exercised some artistic licence.

Every country in the modern world has produced stamps at some time. At present there are some 240 countries that issue distinctive stamps, and there are at least three times that number of "dead" countries, which no longer exist as political entities or have changed their name, but which have left their mark in the stamp album.

In the following pages you will find a survey of the stamps from around the whole world from 1840 to the present day.

This comprehensive directory provides a survey of all the existing countries that currently issue stamps, as well as many obsolete entities – former German, Italian and Indian states,

for example – that issued them. Some countries are grouped according to common links in their political and philatelic histories, while others stand alone in the extent of their contribution to philately.

Each section covers the stamps of a particular continent, and, within these parameters, the stamps of individual countries, or a group of nations that are related politically or geographically. The United States, for example, has remained remarkably stable since the inception of its stamps, yet even in this instance the Civil War gave rise to the separate issues of the Confederate States. At the other extreme are countries that

Above: A multi-tiered collectable bearing an Egyptian stamp, a contemporary Army Post stamp and a cancellation made by British field post handstamp E 602 in 1940.

Right: Definitive sets of mounted stamps are widely available to purchase, and are often favoured by collectors who organize their stamps by country.

Left: A stockbook, with transparent strips and clear interleaving, is useful for storing stamps awaiting mounting.

Below: The great hurricane that struck Samoa in 1889 destroyed the British, American and German warships anchored at Apia. The islanders, who resented foreign interference, regarded it as an act of God.

have frequently changed their political status (such as Albania, which has been a principality, a republic, an independent kingdom, an Italian colony, a people's republic and now a democracy), or have changed their name (such as Southern Rhodesia, which became Rhodesia and is now Zimbabwe). There are stamps that reflect the economic upheavals of the past century and a half and those that mark civil wars, or were issued by occupying forces in wartime or as part of plebiscites to decide a country's future. The book includes thematic features illustrating stamps that reflect the culture, art or history of a particular region. In addition to tracing the cultural and economic shifts of the modern world, these intricately designed pieces of paper are a testament to the sheer volume of material available to today's collector.

Above: A historic Madras War Fund charity label produced during World War I to raise funds for a hospital ship.

Left: These stamps issued in 1992 were among the first independent issues by the former Soviet Central Asian states Turkmenistan and Uzbekistan.

Below: A strip of five Australian stamps issued on January 26, 1988, showed the arrival of the First English Fleet in 1788.

AMERICA

The American continent was quick to follow Britain in introducing adhesive stamps during the 1840s, and America took the lead in adopting pictorial stamps from the 1850s onwards. The continent's vast size and scattered population encouraged the early development of airmail.

CANADA

One of the world's largest countries, Canada was colonized by the French after 1534. Britain acquired Hudson's Bay, Newfoundland and Nova Scotia in 1713 and gained control of New France in 1763 after a decisive victory at Quebec in 1759. Thereafter, exploration and settlement extended British influence from coast to coast. Upper and Lower Canada (Ontario and Quebec) acquired self-government in 1837. They joined with New Brunswick and Nova Scotia in 1867 to form the Confederation of Canada; British Columbia (1871) and Prince Edward Island (1873) joined later, but Newfoundland was not admitted until 1949. Until recently all Canadian stamps were printed by the intaglio process.

Left: This stamp of 1927, celebrating the 60th anniversary of the Confederation of Canada, shows how much its territory had grown over the period since the union was formed.

BRITISH NORTH AMERICA

Before confederation, the individual British colonies issued their own stamps. Canada led the way in 1851 by separating its postal services from the General Post Office in London. In the 1860s stamps were produced for use on both Vancouver's Island and British Columbia [1], but these were followed by separate issues due to differences in the value of their currency [2]. New Brunswick's diamond-shaped stamps (1851) were followed in 1860 by a pictorial series that was quasi-commemorative, the 1c stamp celebrating the opening of the railway [3].

Newfoundland's first stamps were issued in 1857 [4], with square, upright rectangular and triangular stamps featuring the heraldic flowers of the United Kingdom. Pictorial stamps, with a penchant for royal portraiture [5], followed in 1865, and from 1898 onwards there were long scenic sets. Newfoundland's last issues (1947) before joining Canada celebrated the

21st birthday of Princess Elizabeth and the 400th anniversary of Cabot's sighting of "the new found land" [6].

Nova Scotia issued the world's first diamond-shaped stamps in 1851, beating New Brunswick by four days. The advent of the dollar in 1860 resulted in a series issued by the American Bank Note Company of New York with a full-face portrait of Queen Victoria [7]. By contrast, most of Prince Edward Island's stamps were rather crudely typographed in London [8].

A LITTLE BIT OF FRANCE IN NORTH AMERICA

When France ceded all its territory on the mainland to the British it retained the two tiny islands of St Pierre and Miquelon, off the coast of Newfoundland, as a base for fishing on the Grand Banks. French colonial general issues were followed by distinctive stamps in 1885, most of them with motifs alluding to the fishing industry [9]. In more recent times a wider range of subjects, such as scenery [10] and bird life, have been covered, reflecting the growing importance of tourism.

CONFEDERATION

The stamps of Canada introduced in 1851 were extended to the rest of the confederation from 1867 onwards. The dominion favoured portraits of Queen Victoria in a wide range that showed her at different stages throughout her long life. Her diamond jubilee in 1897 was the occasion for a set of 16, from 1/2c to $5, showing the Chalon portrait of 1837 and Von Angeli's bust of the 1890s [11]. The advent of imperial penny postage in 1898 gave rise to the world's first Christmas stamp [12] showing a world map with the territories of the British Empire coloured red. The history of Canada was charted by commemoratives, including a single stamp of 1917 for the golden jubilee of confederation [13]: this motif was reprised ten years later, along with others, for the 60th anniversary.

As with the issues of Newfoundland, a strong thread running through Canadian stamps is royal portraiture, notably for coronations, jubilees and royal visits [14]; to Canada belongs the only stamp ever to refer to Elizabeth II as Duchess of Edinburgh [15].

Stamps of 1951 and 1991 reproduced Canada's first stamp, the Threepenny Beaver. A long-running series consisted of pairs portraying former prime ministers [16]. Canada and the USA issued identical stamps for the opening of the St Lawrence Seaway in 1959, one of the earliest joint issues,

Below: Canada's first stamp inscribed solely in French marked the occasion of the Montreal Jazz Festival in 2004.

Works of Art

Since 1988 Canada has issued a large stamp each year reproducing an outstanding painting by a Canadian artist. These stamps are greatly enhanced by the use of gold or silver foil frames. The stamps have been produced in small sheets with descriptive text in the sheet margins, encouraging philatelists to collect them entire.

while the US bicentennial yielded a stamp portraying Benjamin Franklin, a reminder that he had been Deputy Postmaster General for the whole of North America [18].

Like the USA, Canada includes at least one stamp in the definitive range showing the national flag in various settings [17] but also has an alternative stamp at the basic domestic rate portraying Elizabeth II. Modern stamps are imperforate and produced in self-adhesive booklets. Canadian stamps were originally inscribed only in English, but from 1927 onwards they were regularly inscribed in French as well. Now stamps are captioned solely in French where relevant.

While it was once a conservative country with regard to stamp production, Canada broke new ground in 1994 with the world's first customized stamps, which offered the customer a choice of different circular labels to add to the basic stamp.

10

11

12

13

14

15

16

17

18

1

2

3

4

5

6

7

8

9

10

11

12

UNITED STATES DEFINITIVES

Although a New York private post had a stamp by 1842, and postmasters were authorized to issue their own stamps in 1845, it was not until 1847 that the US Post Office adopted stamps nationwide. At this time 5c and 10c stamps sufficed, and the USA chose portraits of Benjamin Franklin,

the first Postmaster General of the United States, and George Washington, the "Father of His Country". Every definitive series from then until the 1970s portrayed George Washington, and he has seldom been far from the scene since. Benjamin Franklin was included in every series up to the set of 1970–4.

Left: George Washington on America's "Penny Black", the 10c stamp of 1847, based on a portrait by Gilbert Stuart.

DEAD PRESIDENTS
Thomas Jefferson, the third president, was also the third man to appear on US stamps, on the 5c stamp of 1856, but in the series of 1860–1 he had to vie with Franklin on two values and Washington on the other five. The necessity for a 2c stamp in 1863, for local letters, led to the admission of Andrew Jackson on one of the oddest American stamps of all time, with a full-face portrait that seems to overflow the confines of the design [2]. A 15c in grey-black was added in 1866 and portrayed Abraham Lincoln within months of his assassination [1].

BROADENING THE SCOPE
Franklin [3], Washington and Lincoln graced the 1869 series, which introduced the concept of pictorial motifs [4], including creditable attempts to reproduce historical paintings of the landing of Columbus (15c) and the Declaration of Independence (24c). This novelty was short-lived, and the following year reverted to the portrait gallery approach, with images of politicians Edwin Stanton and Henry Clay, Daniel Webster, General Winfield Scott, the lexicographer Alexander Hamilton and Commodore Perry.

ADVENT OF PHOTOGRAPHY
All the 1870 stamps bore profiles sculpted like classical busts, but in 1875 a 5c stamp was added to the series that

bore a facing portrait of General Zachary Taylor taken from a daguerreotype. James Garfield, assassinated the previous year, was the subject of a 5c stamp in 1882, also derived from a photograph. Thereafter the classical profile gradually died out. In the series of 1890 only the three lowest values (1–3c) showing Franklin, Washington [5] and Jackson [6] and the two top values featuring Jefferson (30c) and Perry (90c) retained that style, while the six middle values (4–15c) were based on photographs. The only newcomers to this line-up were Ulysses Grant [7] and General Sherman on the 5c and 8c stamps. In 1894–5 the designs were modified and the opportunity was taken to add the fourth president, James Madison ($2) and the jurist John Marshall ($5), whose portraits were based on oil paintings.

For the new century definitive design took a backward step, setting the portraits [8] in very fussy frames, though the designs repay a second glance as Franklin on the 1c was flanked by allegorical figures holding electric light bulbs aloft. Newcomers included Admiral Farragut, hero of the recent Spanish–American War, and Martha Washington, the original First Lady, and first woman to appear [9].

There seems to have been a reaction against this surfeit of the great and good, for the definitives of 1912–22 were confined to profiles of Franklin

Non-portrait Definitives

Apart from portraiture, the series of 1975–81 (combining landmarks and symbols of the American Revolution with an assortment of musical instruments) and the coil series of 1985–93 (transportation from the Conestoga wagon to the school bus) have a strong thematic appeal.

and Washington. But by 1922 the public were ready for some variety and the series, which eventually ran to 23 stamps, ranged from the ¹/₂c [10] showing Nathan Hale (executed by the British as a spy in the War of Independence) to middle values portraying Teddy Roosevelt, William McKinley, James Monroe, Rutherford B. Hayes and Grover Cleveland [11], all of whom had died by that time.

The concept of portraying dead presidents reached its climax with the series of 1938–54, which portrayed every deceased holder of the highest office [12]. Furthermore, up to the 22c value, each president was portrayed on a stamp whose denomination accorded with his number. Above that, the presidents were shown in chronological order with their dates in office, ending with Calvin Coolidge on the $5 stamp. No doubt these stamps helped people to remember which president was which. Fractional values portrayed Franklin, Martha Washington and the White House.

PROMINENT AMERICANS

Dead presidents continued to dominate the 1954–65 series [13–14] but newcomers included General Pershing [15], Paul Revere [16] and Robert E. Lee, and from then on the presidential preference waned. To be sure, later series included Kennedy (1967) and Eisenhower (1970), but from that time

the themes would be Prominent Americans (1965–81) [17–19], Great Americans (1980–94) [20–22] and the current series of celebrities that began in 2000 [23–24].

Since May 1978 the US Post Office has issued undenominated stamps at times when the domestic first-class rate is being increased, to cover an anticipated shortage of stamps showing the new rate. The earliest featured a stylized eagle and were lettered A–D (up to 1985) but later stamps had distinctive motifs whose initial letter followed the same code. Thus the increase to 25c in 1988 was covered by a stamp showing the Earth. When the rate rose to 29c in 1991 a Flower stamp was accompanied by a "make-up" stamp inscribed: "This US stamp along with 25c of additional US postage is equivalent to the F stamp rate."

Above: Old images of Washington and Jackson were re-used in a diamond format on the $5 stamp in the 1990s.

13

14

15

16

17

18

19

20

21

22

23

24

1

2

3

4

5

6

7

8

9

10

11

UNITED STATES COMMEMORATIVE AND SPECIAL ISSUES

The first set of adhesive stamps intended for temporary sale, as opposed to the permanent or definitive series, was issued in January 1893, partly to commemorate the quatercentenary of Columbus's arrival in the New World

and partly to publicize the Columbian Exposition in Chicago. The set consisted of 16 values from 1c to $5 and cost over $16 in total, a colossal sum for that period.

Left: The Columbian series traced the volatile career of Christopher Columbus.

EXPOSITION PUBLICITY

The Trans-Mississippi Exposition at Omaha in 1898 had a more modest nine stamps up to the $2 value [1], while the Pan-American Exposition at Buffalo in 1901 [2] had a mere six stamps, the highest value being 10c. The St Louis International Exposition, doubling up with the centenary of the Louisiana Purchase in 1904, rated five stamps (1c–10c); by the time of the Panama–Pacific Exposition in 1913 four low-value stamps sufficed [3].

The Jamestown Exposition (1907) rated only three stamps while the Alaska–Yukon–Pacific Exposition of 1909 had to be content with a single 2c stamp. Thereafter, most commemorative and special issues were singles [4], and the occasion had to be very special to merit more. In the 1930s there was a rash of small-format stamps celebrating the major anniversaries of the oldest colonies [5]. A return to expensive issues, last seen in the 1890s, came with the release in 1930 of three high-value stamps commemorating the Europe–Pan-American flight of the *Graf Zeppelin*, while the most prolific issue since the Columbian Exposition was a set of 12 for the bicentenary of the birth of Washington in 1932.

FARLEY'S FOLLIES

Most special issues before World War II took note of historic anniversaries or major current events, but in 1934 a set

of ten featured scenery in some of the national parks [6]. The issue was quasi-commemorative as it coincided with National Parks Year, although this was not actually mentioned on the stamps.

This was also the era of the Farley Follies, when Postmaster General James Farley, currying favour with Franklin D. Roosevelt (an ardent philatelist), presented him with imperforate blocks of commemoratives. When word got out, collectors clamoured that what was good enough for the president was good enough for them also, and Farley was forced to release special printings. The 1935 American Philatelic Society Convention in Atlantic City was favoured with sheets of six of the stamp showing Mirror Lake and Mount Rainier. In 1936 the third International Philatelic Exhibition in New York saw a miniature sheet of four recent commemoratives in an imperforate block.

COMMEMORATIVE THEMES

A more frankly thematic approach was evident in the four stamps of 1937 showing scenery and landmarks in US territories [8] and reached its climax in the sets of five honouring heroes of the Army and Navy [9]. Sets of five in 1940 honoured famous Americans: authors, poets, educationalists, scientists, composers and artists – a series of 35 in all [7]. This concept was put to good use in the 1943–4 set of 13 showing flags of the oppressed nations [12].

Above: Imperforate stamps of 1934–7, released on the authority of Postmaster General James Farley, were nicknamed Farley's Follies by collectors, whose protests forced the US Post Office to make them generally available.

SOCIAL FOCUS

In the immediate postwar era single stamps were the norm [11], but their frequency accelerated and reached a peak in 1948 [13]. Stamps were issued not only to mark historic anniversaries and contemporary events [10] but, increasingly, to focus attention on social issues and groups – from gold-star mothers [15] to newspaper boys. Different aspects of the American way of life were the pretext for numerous stamps through the 1950s and beyond [14], and this notion of using stamps to raise awareness of important social issues continues to this day, from the "Register and Vote" campaign to concern for victims of AIDS and breast cancer in recent years.

As everywhere else in the world, a topical slant has entered the new issue policy [16–17]. The 1956 trio showing wild animals may have had the laudable objective of making the public conservation conscious but its thematic appeal was overwhelming. Similarly the set of six in 1960–1 showing quotations and autographs attracted topical collectors, although at the height of the Cold War its political message was its main objective. Sometimes the approach was more subtle: the stamp marking the Red Cross centenary in 1963 showed the Red Cross flag over the SS *Morning Light* – the ship that repatriated participants in the Bay of Pigs invasion of Cuba [18]. Most special issues are now self-adhesive [19].

Black Heritage

Protests that Black Americans had been neglected in US stamps led to the introduction of an annual stamp devoted to Black Heritage. Beginning in 1978 with Harriet Tubman, organizer of the "underground railway" for runaway slaves, the series has ranged from the civil rights activist Ida B. Wells to Jan Ernst Matzeliger, the inventor of the shoe-lasting machine, and W.E.B. Du Bois, founder of the Niagara Movement, precursor of the National Association for the Advancement of Colored People.

12

13

14

15

16

17

18

19

1

2

3

4

5

6

7

8

9

10

11

12

13

UNITED STATES POSSESSIONS AND TERRITORIES

A number of administrations, from mainland states and institutions to off-shore territories, formerly had their own stamps but are now part of the United States of America and employ the latter's issues. This includes even the extra-territorial post office of the United Nations, located in the headquarters building at the eastern side of mid-town Manhattan, New York

City. It should be noted that many similar stamps, inscribed in French or German, are used at the other UN post offices in Geneva and Vienna.

Left: To celebrate the 55th anniversary of the founding of the United Nations, stamps were issued in 2000 showing the headquarters building, both while under construction and at the present day. This stamp presents an unusual view looking southwards, with the East River on the left and Brooklyn in the distance.

CONFEDERATE STATES OF AMERICA

Eleven states seceded from the Union in 1861 over the vexed question of states' rights, with particular regard to slavery, and formed a federal republic under the title of the Confederate States of America. At first it was left to individual postmasters to furnish stamps to their own design. Many, such as the 2c stamp produced in Memphis, Tennessee, bore the name of the postmaster rather than the town [1]. Other stamps, many unique or extremely rare, were crudely handstamped.

The first issues for general use were 5c and 10c stamps, printed by Hoyer & Ludwig of Richmond, Virginia; they portrayed Jefferson Davis [2] and Thomas Jefferson respectively. A supply of stamps was procured from De La Rue of London [3] – the only stamps of continental USA produced outside the country. Later stamps portrayed Jefferson Davis [4] and George Washington [5], a reminder that the Father of His Country had been a slave-owning Southern gentleman.

HAWAII

The Polynesian kingdom of Hawaii in the north central Pacific introduced stamps in 1851. Crudely typeset, they

are popularly known as Missionaries as most of them were used by Christian missionaries to send mail back to New England: some stamps bore the inscription "H.I. & U.S. Postage". Stamps portraying Kamehameha III appeared in 1853, followed by a veritable portrait gallery of Hawaiian royalty, including Kamehameha IV [6], Kamehameha V [7] and Princess Victoria Kamamalu [8].

In 1887 King David Kalakaua [9] was forced to accept a Western-style constitution that curbed native power. When his successor, Queen Liliuokalani, attempted a coup to restore the old laws, American business interests overthrew the monarchy and proclaimed a provisional government. On 4 July 1894, the Republic of Hawaii was proclaimed [11]. The islands were annexed by the USA on 12 August 1898. During this interim period (1899–1900) Hawaii's very last stamp portrayed the statue of Kamehameha I [10]. Ordinary US stamps have been used in Hawaii since 14 June 1900.

SPANISH–AMERICAN WAR

During the war between Spain and the United States in 1898 the US occupied the Spanish territories of Cuba and the Philippines. American stamps were overprinted for use during the period of military administration, after which the islands were handed over to the indigenous authorities.

The USA also captured the islands of Guam in the Pacific and Puerto Rico in the Caribbean, both of which were ceded to it by Spain. Apart from occupation by the Japanese in 1941–4, Guam was under the control of the US Navy until 1950. American stamps were overprinted from 1899 to 1901 [12] and ordinary US stamps have been in use since then.

Puerto Rico used Spanish colonial keytypes in the latter part of the 19th century [13–14]. Having been ceded to the US on 10 December 1898, it was under military administration until 1900. Contemporary US stamps were at first overprinted "Porto Rico" [15], followed by the correct spelling in 1900 [16]. Ordinary US stamps have been used since April 1900.

UNITED NATIONS

Distinctive stamps for the use of the United Nations Secretariat in New York City were introduced on October 24 – United Nations Day – 1951. Since then the UN has produced a prodigious number of stamps, mainly publicizing the work of its specialized agencies and promoting causes of international concern. The UN building itself appeared in the first series [17] and has been the subject of many stamps since then, either in splendid isolation [18] or in relation to the neighbouring skyscrapers of Manhattan [19]. Several stamps feature the interior [20] or the gardens, statuary and stained glass windows. Stamps of 1952 [21] and 1995 [22] commemorated the signing of the UN Charter in San Francisco, and featured the Veterans' War Memorial Building in that city.

In the early years a valiant attempt was made to inscribe every stamp in the five major languages of the world – English, French, Spanish, Russian and Chinese – but by the mid-1960s this had been quietly dropped and English predominated in the stamps issued by the office in New York.

By 1967 a more thematic approach was evident, and a long-running series was devoted to works of art donated by member countries. In 1980 the UN embarked on a series depicting the flags of the member countries. These were released in sheetlets of 16, each containing four different flags. This marathon series came to an end in 1989, the final flag being that of the UN itself, but the accession of new countries in the 1990s as a result of the fall of communism led to the issue of a further 24 flag stamps between 1997 and 1999. The latest series is devoted to endangered species of the world.

Below: In recent years the UN has featured sites on its stamps, and the set of 2004 focused on Greece to coincide with the Athens Olympics.

CONFEDERATE STATES OF AMERICA

14

15

16

17

18

19

20

21

22

1

2

3

4

5

6

7

8

9

10

UNITED STATES TRUST TERRITORIES IN THE PACIFIC

Germany acquired a number of Pacific island groups towards the end of the 19th century. The first were the Marshall Islands, which it colonized in 1855, and in 1899, at the end of the Spanish–American War, Spain sold the Caroline Islands to Germany. At the same time, the Mariana Islands, which had been administered by the Philippines, were transferred by the United States to Germany in November 1899. All three groups remained under German control until 1914, when the Caroline and Mariana Islands were occupied by the Japanese. The Marshall Islands were captured by New Zealand forces but transferred to Japan at the end of World War I. The Marianas were captured by US forces in 1944 and the other two island groups fell into American hands at the end of World War II. All three were declared the United States Trust Territory of the Pacific Islands by the United Nations on 18 July 1947.

Self-government was introduced in 1979 in the Marshall and Caroline Islands. The former group retained its original name but the latter was renamed the Federated States of Micronesia. The following year the Palau group in the western Carolines separated from Micronesia and became a republic in January 1981. In 1986 all three territories entered into the Compact of Free Association with the United States, which remained responsible for defence and external relations.

Left: A joint issue of stamps by the Marshall Islands and Micronesia in October 1996 celebrated the tenth anniversary of the Compact of Free Association; both designs featured a sailing boat alongside their respective flags.

In the Caroline and Mariana islands, which were under German rule from 1899 until 1914, stamps were issued in the contemporary colonial keytypes [1–2]. The Marshall Islands used ordinary German stamps until 1897, when overprinted stamps were adopted. These were followed by the Yacht stamps in 1901 [3]. Ordinary Japanese stamps were later used, followed by American stamps from 1945 onwards, and examples of these with identifiable postmarks of the islands are now much sought-after.

MARSHALL ISLANDS

Postal independence was inaugurated in May 1984 with a celebratory block of four stamps, followed shortly afterwards by a definitive series featuring maps of the various atolls. Subsequent issues have been strongly thematic, with fish, birds and ships [5] featured. In the early years of the Marshall Islands' independence commemorative stamps were issued relatively infrequently and, in fact, stamps relating purely to the islands are few in number [4; 6]. This was more than balanced by the stamps that increasingly looked to the outside world.

In 1989 an ambitious programme was launched chronicling all the major campaigns and battles of World War II. The series eventually ran to 157 stamps, including portraits of the leading figures on both sides of the war [7]. More recent issues include a sheet of 50 showing American warships, from the USS *Alabama* to the USS *Wyoming* – one for each state – and stamps showing solidarity with the United States in the aftermath of 9/11 [8]. Historic ships are a recurring theme [9] for stamps, while figures such as Winston Churchill and Tsar Nicholas II have also been portrayed.

MICRONESIA

The inaugural issue consisted of a block of four showing maps of Yap, Truk, Pohnpei and Kosrae, the groups making up the Federated States of Micronesia, all formerly part of the Caroline Islands. At the same time a definitive series portrayed explorers and island scenes, notably the famous stone money of Yap [11]. A moderate policy of new issues was pursued at first, with most of the stamps devoted to subjects of island interest [10] or commemorating salient events in the islands' recent history [13].

In the early period the stamps were designed and marketed by the Crown Agents in England, and this was reflected in the use of British designers and European printers. In 1991, however, the contract passed to the Unicover Corporation of Cheyenne, Wyoming, which was already printing the stamps of the Marshall Islands. Unicover had its own printing facilities and employed mainly American designers, notably the father-and-son team of Paul and Chris Calle. This inaugurated an era in which popular themes such as fish, butterflies and flowers were the subjects of long sets, often released in sheets of up to 25 different stamps side by side. In 1993 Micronesia introduced a series devoted to pioneers of aviation portrayed alongside their aircraft [14], from the Wright Brothers to heroes of World War II. These stamps were issued in *se-tenant* blocks of eight and continued to appear at regular intervals until 1996.

In the following year the contract passed to the Inter-Governmental Philatelic Corporation of New York, and since then a much more prolific policy has been pursued. There is now a greater focus on events and personalities of worldwide significance, from Elvis Presley to Princess Diana.

Caught in the Act

To mark the Ameripex stamp show in Chicago (1986) Micronesia issued five stamps illustrating the life and crimes of Bully Hayes. In addition to murder and mayhem, he forged rare stamps of Hawaii, as shown on the 33c stamp. Incidentally, the forgery, like the genuine stamp, did not have perforations (as shown below right).

Bully Hayes 1829–77   *Forgery of Hawaiian 5c Blue*

PALAU

This republic had a head start on the others, adopting its own stamps in March 1983. It has maintained a more prolific policy ever since. Successive definitive sets have featured marine life [12], flowers [15], birds [16] and insects. As a popular destination for Japanese tourists visiting the war graves, Palau has made a number of issues relating to its links with Japan [17], and its connection with the USA has yielded stamps featuring Ronald Reagan [18] and Operation Desert Storm [19]. Many sheets vividly illustrated every phase of World War II in the Pacific, notably the fighting over Peleliu in 1944. A self-adhesive die-cut stamp in the form of a Bai gable marked the republic's tenth anniversary.

Palau has been a client of the Inter-Governmental Philatelic Corporation since its inception, and although the flow of new issues was relatively modest in the early years it has greatly increased recently. Sheets of 25–40 different stamps have been prevalent from 1986 onwards, with increasing emphasis on stamps with immense appeal to collectors worldwide, from Disney characters to footballers.

11

12

13

14

15

16

17

18

19

NORTH AMERICAN INDIANS IN STAMPS

When Europeans penetrated North America at the beginning of the 16th century there were probably about a million Native Americans spread across what is now Canada, the USA and Mexico. By the end of the 19th century that figure had been halved, but after 1910 the Native American population began to recover. Driven off their ancestral lands by the encroachment of Europeans, many tribes ended up living on large reservations in areas of little interest or apparent use to the incomers, such as the Dakotas and the arid regions of the South-west.

The first Native American to appear on a US stamp was Minnehaha, the heroine of Longfellow's epic poem *Hiawatha* – and as that was the $60 newspaper stamp of 1875 it is unlikely to figure in most pictorial collections devoted to this theme.

The earliest stamp to show indigenous people in their own right was the 4c value of the set of 1898 publicizing the Trans-Mississippi Exposition. The first Indians to be identified by name on stamps were Powhatan and his

Below: Blocks of four showing Pueblo decorated pots, 1977 (left) and shamanistic masks, 1979 (right).

daughter Pocahontas, whose microscopic effigies were worked into the framework of the 1c stamp of 1907 portraying Captain John Smith, marking the tercentenary of Jamestown. Pocahontas herself was portrayed on the 5c stamp, all dressed up in the height of Jacobean fashion as Smith paraded her in London.

While the low values of the 1922–32 US definitive series focused on famous Americans, and especially presidents, the 14c showed an unnamed American Indian in feather war bonnet. It later transpired that the image was derived from a photograph of Hollow Horn Bear, chief of the Brule Sioux. After

Above: Chief Hollow Horn Bear of the Brule Sioux (left) and an Indian Head cent on the definitive 13c stamp of 1978 (right).

Right: Pocahontas appears in Jacobean dress on a stamp of 1907.

Hopi: Heard Museum Phoenix
Pueblo Art USA 13c

Acoma: School of American Research
Pueblo Art USA 13c

Heiltsuk, Bella Bella
Indian Art USA 15c

Chilkat Tlingit
Indian Art USA 15c

Zia: Museum of New Mexico
Pueblo Art USA 13c

San Ildefonso: Denver Art Museum
Pueblo Art USA 13c

Tlingit
Indian Art USA 15c

Bella Coola
Indian Art USA 15c

Above: Crazy Horse, Sequoyah, Sitting Bull and Red Cloud in the Great Americans definitive series, 1980–94.

that, Native Americans had a very low profile and appeared as minuscule subsidiary figures, such as the Indian woman standing respectfully behind the intrepid explorers on the Lewis and Clark Expedition stamp of 1954.

The turning point came in 1961 with the advent of multicolour intaglio. The first stamp to make use of the new Giori presses marked the centenary of Frederic Remington's birth by reproducing his famous painting *The Smoke Signal*. The first example of Native American art was a totem pole carved by the Tlingit of southern Alaska, chosen as the motif for the 1967 stamp marking the centenary of the purchase of Alaska from Russia.

In 1970 one of the four stamps in the set celebrating the centenary of the American Natural History Museum showed a Haida ceremonial canoe. The Haida, like the Tlingit, settled on the north-western Pacific seaboard, a reminder of the fact that the continent's indigenous races had originally come from eastern Asia across the land bridge up to 30,000 years ago. A 50c stamp of 1991 showed some of the earliest emigrants from Siberia arriving in Alaska.

In 1977 the first set devoted to American folk art concentrated on the applied arts of the Pueblo Indians, featuring decorated pots produced by the Zia, San Ildefonso, Hopi and Acoma peoples. In 1979 the series returned to Native American art with shamanistic masks of the Heiltsuk branch of the Bella Bella, Chilkat Tlingit, mainstream Tlingit and Bella Coola tribes of the north-west Pacific coast.

Two stamps of 1989 showed pre-Columbian carvings, a Mimbres ritual figure and the "Key Marco Cat" carved by Calusa Indians. In 1990 a booklet of five stamps featured war bonnets of the Cheyenne, Flathead, Comanche, Shoshone and Assiniboine tribes.

The first Great Americans definitive series of 1980–8 included Crazy Horse, the Sioux leader, and the Cherokee chief Sequoyah, who appeared on the 13c and 19c stamps. The second series (1985–94) portrayed Red Cloud of the Oglala Sioux (10c) and Sitting Bull of the Hunkpapa Sioux (28c). The first Indian woman since Pocahontas to appear on an

Above: Traditional dances and beadwork patterns were featured in a booklet of five 32c stamps in 1996.

American stamp was Sacagawea, on a 29c stamp in the sheet of 20 showing Legends of the West, released in 1994. Chief Joseph of the Nez Perce and the Apache leader Geronimo were also featured in this issue as well as a stamp showing a montage representing Native American culture.

In 1996 a set of five in a *se-tenant* strip focused on Native American dances without assigning them to any particular tribes. In August 2004 a 2c definitive showed a silver and turquoise Navajo necklace, and in the same month a sheet of ten stamps was devoted to Native American art from the 11th century to about 1969.

Left: Indian paddling Father Jacques Marquette's canoe, 1968.

Below: Indian carved figure, 1989 (left) and Remington's The Smoke Signal *(right).*

1

2

3

4

5

6

7

8

BAHAMAS, BERMUDA AND WEST INDIES

It is a popular fallacy that the Bahamas and Bermuda are in the West Indies: they actually lie well to the north of the Caribbean but philatelists put them in the same category as those islands. It appears that the first land sighted by Columbus in the New World was in the Bahamas, as celebrated by sets of stamps in 1942 and 1992. Of the islands grouped here, most are or were under British administration, but some – Curaçao, Aruba and the Netherlands Antilles – came under Dutch rule, while Guadeloupe and Martinique are now French overseas departments. The Danes sold their possessions in the West Indies to the United States in 1917 and they are now known as the American Virgin Islands.

Left: Although the Netherlands were overrun by the Germans in World War II, Curaçao remained in Dutch hands and issued stamps showing Queen Wilhelmina, Princess Juliana and Prince Bernhard with their daughters.

BAHAMAS

The Bahamas were a crown colony before attaining self-government in 1964 and becoming an independent member of the Commonwealth in 1973. Unlike most other colonies, the islands had distinctive stamps from their inception in 1859, including some pictorial designs from 1901. A favoured venue for political summit conferences between Britain and the USA [1], the islands have also become very popular tourist destinations and this is reflected in many issues of recent years highlighting everything from birdwatching to beaches [2–3]. The Bahamas contributed a squadron of Spitfires in World War II, recorded on several issues since 1990 [4].

BARBADOS

This crown colony, settled in the early 17th century, enjoyed autonomy from early times. Its first stamps, reproduced on centennial commemoratives in 1952, showed Britannia seated on sugar bags, a motif also used by Mauritius and Trinidad [7]. The old-world charm of Barbados comes across in designs using ancient landmarks [5], but its relaxed atmosphere is neatly conveyed by the Christmas stamps of 2003 [6].

BERMUDA

This island lies about 1060km/660 miles east of North Carolina. Like the Bahamas and Barbados it has long been a very popular resort for Americans. Stamps were introduced as early as 1848 and were struck by hand by the postmasters of Hamilton and St George's. More conventional stamps, printed in London, were adopted in 1865, but they did not conform to the usual colonial keytypes, except for the high values of 1918–52, portraying George V or George VI. This design, with the profile of Queen Elizabeth substituted, was revived for a $22 stamp in 1996 [8]. Modern issues are very much tourist-orientated, such as the series showing island souvenirs [9] or the idyllic scenery [10]. Many stamps issued since the 1950s have alluded to the settlement of the island by shipwrecked sailors.

TRINIDAD AND TOBAGO

Both islands had their own stamps until 1913. British stamps were used in Tobago until 1879, when a series portraying Queen Victoria was introduced [11], but Trinidad's *Lady McLeod* steamship stamp of 1847 was the first from any British colony in the Western

Bottle-shaped Stamps

Trinidad and Tobago issue very few stamps, but none was so spectacular as the set released in January 2000 to celebrate the 175th anniversary of angostura bitters, distilled from an aromatic bark and a popular ingredient of cocktails. The stamps, produced by Southern Colour Print of New Zealand, were self-adhesive and shaped like the bitters bottles.

Hemisphere, followed by the Britannia design in 1851 [7]. Bicoloured intaglio in the 1930s and 1940s [13] has now given way to multicolour lithography for stamps that illustrate island occupations and, of course, the local passion for cricket [14].

EUROPEAN COLONIES

The Danish West Indies consisted of the islands of St Croix and St Thomas and had stamps mainly in the prevailing Danish designs [12]. They remained valid for a few months after the islands were sold to the USA, and covers with mixed franking of DWI and US stamps are much sought-after.

The Netherlands Antilles comprised the islands of Curaçao and Bonaire, near to coastal Venezuela, together with the Leeward islands of St Estatius, Saba and part of St Maarten, the rest of which formed part of the French colony of Guadeloupe. Stamps inscribed "Curaçao" [15] were used throughout the Dutch islands until 1948, when the term "Netherlands Antilles" was adopted. A stamp of 1959 showed the sea-water distillation plant installed by Weir's of Cathcart, Scotland [16]. Until 1986 Aruba was part of the Netherlands Antilles but since then has enjoyed autonomy and

its own stamps, which convey an unhurried lifestyle [17] as well as its popularity with cruise ships [18].

In the 17th and 18th centuries France and Britain fought for control of the Caribbean, and islands frequently changed hands until the end of the Napoleonic Wars. All that then remained in French hands were Guadeloupe and Martinique, two groups of islands in the Lesser Antilles. Guadeloupe comprised two large islands, Basse-Terre and Grande-Terre, together with some smaller islands and the northern part of St Martin (the rest of the island being in the Netherlands Antilles). Martinique was administered as a separate colony.

Originally both territories used the general stamps of the French colonies, but the first distinctive stamps appeared in the 1880s and consisted of provisional surcharges identified by the initials GPE or MQE respectively. In 1946 both colonies became overseas departments of France and their stamps were phased out two years later. They have used French stamps ever since.

Above: Island women and coastal scenery dominated the last definitive series of Guadeloupe (1947).

Below: Government House at Fort-de-France appeared on stamps of Martinique from 1933 to 1945.

1

2

3

4

5

6

7

8

9

CUBA, HISPANIOLA AND JAMAICA

The three largest islands of the Caribbean comprise the republics of Cuba and Jamaica, with Hispaniola shared by Haiti and the Dominican Republic. Associated with Jamaica are its former dependencies, the Cayman Islands and the Turks and Caicos Islands. All these islands were originally under Spanish rule, but the French later colonized the western part of Hispaniola, while the British captured Jamaica in 1655. Dominican rebels tried to join Bolivar's Greater Colombia in 1821 but were thwarted by the Haitians, who invaded the eastern part of the island and occupied it until 1843. Cuba remained in Spanish hands until the war with the United States in 1898. After a period under American military administration (1899–1902) Cuba became an independent republic, though the USA retained Guantanamo Bay as a military base. Cuba became a socialist state on 1 January 1959, and a centre for Marxist subversion throughout Latin America.

Left: Major Ernesto "Che" Guevara, born in Argentina, trained as a doctor but joined Castro's revolutionary movement in Cuba, becoming finance minister. He left to organize revolutions all over Latin America, but was captured and shot in Bolivia in 1967. This stamp, celebrating Day of the Guerrilla, shows a map of Latin America, highlighting Bolivia.

CUBA

From 1855 to 1898 Cuban stamps conformed to Spanish colonial keytypes [1]. US stamps were briefly overprinted before a definitive series appeared in 1899 [2]. Many republican stamps honoured José Martí, father of Cuban independence [3]. After the rebels, led by Fidel Castro, seized power, stamps became heavily politicized, often making common cause with Vietnam or promoting Marxist ideology, an exception being the set of 1963 honouring Ernest Hemingway [4]. Stamps celebrated anniversaries of the abortive invasion of Playa de Giron, known in the US as the Bay of Pigs [5]. In recent years, however, the Marxist hard line has been played down and stamps have been much more thematic in character.

DOMINICAN REPUBLIC

Occupying the eastern and much larger part of Hispaniola, this republic almost went to war with neighbouring Haiti when the latter protested at the way the map had been redrawn on the definitive stamps of 1900 [6]. The boundary dispute was not settled until 1935, when Dominica's dictator General Rafael Trujillo brokered a deal [7].

The republic was an early exponent of bicoloured stamps, including a set of 1939 for the New York World's Fair, one of which showed the Trylon and Perisphere together with a projected lighthouse to mark the 450th anniversary, in 1942, of Columbus's arrival in the New World [8]. Like other Latin American countries, Dominica regularly issued compulsory tax stamps to raise funds for public works [9]. Since Trujillo's fall in 1961, stamps have become increasingly thematic.

HAITI

The world's first black republic was founded just after the French Revolution but was suppressed by Napoleon. With British help the Haitians threw out the French, and Jean-Jacques Dessalines proclaimed

Presidential Gallery

To mark the bicentenary of the US constitution in 1987 the Turks and Caicos Islands produced a series of sheetlets portraying every American president with a scene representing his time in office. Whereas presidents such as George Washington, Abraham Lincoln and John F. Kennedy have tended to hog the philatelic limelight, these little islands at last gave prominence to Millard Fillmore, Rutherford B. Hayes and others who had been largely forgotten.

himself emperor. Following his murder in 1806 the country split into a kingdom under Henri Christophe and a republic under Alexander Petion.

Stamps were introduced in 1881; the first, showing the head of Liberty, was followed by the national arms [10]. The centenary of independence was celebrated by two sets of 1904 portraying Toussaint l'Ouverture [11] and other patriots, and many later stamps depicted the impressive citadel of Christophe [12]. In recent years restrained intaglio has given way to gaudy lithography [13].

JAMAICA

The largest colony in the British West Indies, Jamaica had a postal service from 1671, using British stamps until 1860, when distinctive issues appeared. They followed the British colonial pattern, although a pictorial 1d stamp appeared as early as 1900. The definitives of 1919–21 took the colourful history of the island as their subject. Self-government was granted in 1945 and independence in 1962 [14], with Elizabeth II remaining head of state. Since then stamps have become much more colourful – not only the small-format definitives but also the special issues marking events of specifically Jamaican importance [16–17]. Even Christmas stamps are used to get across vital public messages [18]. The Jamaican dollar, adopted in 1969, remained fairly stable until the 1990s when it depreciated heavily. As a result, stamps since 1996 have been denominated in as many dollars as they were formerly in cents.

The Cayman Islands used Jamaican stamps until 1900, when distinctive issues were produced. Though best known today as a financial centre, the islands also rely heavily on tourism, reflected in the stamps. Stamps were issued by the Turks Islands from 1867 until 1900 [15] when they joined with the Caicos group (formerly under the Bahamas). Although stamps in joint names are still current, the Caicos Islands have occasionally had distinctive stamps since 1981.

Below: A high proportion of stamps from the Cayman Islands highlight the fauna and flora of the Caribbean, but the leisurely way of life also features.

10

11

12

13

14

15

16

17

18

1

2

3

4

5

6

7

8

9

BRITISH WEST INDIES

The islands generally grouped under this heading are scattered around the Caribbean and fall geographically into two main archipelagos known as the Leeward and Windward Islands. The Leeward Islands at one time formed a political union, consisting of Antigua and Barbuda, the British Virgin Islands, Dominica, Montserrat and St Christopher Nevis Anguilla. It was formed in 1871, putting into constitutional effect an informal federation dating from the 1670s. The Windward Islands, however, were always separate colonies. The West Indies, a major source of sugar for Britain, also assumed an important strategic role after the loss of its American colonies.

Left: Admiral Lord Nelson was commander of the West Indies station in the late 18th century and is commemorated to this day by the naval dockyard. It was from here that he set sail for his final decisive battle at Trafalgar in 1805.

LEEWARD ISLANDS

While each colony of the Leewards originally had distinctive stamps, a general issue was released in 1890 in the prevailing keyplate design. Stamps of this type, differing solely in the profile of the reigning monarch [1], continued until the federal union was dissolved on 1 July 1956. In 1903 the various islands, objecting to the loss of philatelic revenue, had resumed the issue of their own stamps, which were used in conjunction with the general series.

Antigua had its own stamps from 1862. Until 1982 they were thus inscribed [3], but since then they have also borne the name of its dependency Barbuda [4]. Stamps of the Leeward Islands overprinted "Barbuda" were briefly introduced in 1922 but Barbuda did not resume stamps of its own until 1968. A long series (1968–71) portrayed every British monarch since William the Conqueror [2], while stamps inscribed "Antigua & Barbuda" are now overprinted "Barbuda Mail" for specific use there. From 1979 to 1991 the uninhabited island of Redonda, forming part of this group, had prolific issues in its name that pandered to the most popular themes [5].

Dominica introduced stamps in 1874 and these continued in the usual colonial style until 1968, when the island was granted associated statehood and became more prolific and innovative in its issues, notably with the D-framed definitives of 1969 [6]. It became independent in November 1978, assuming the name of the Commonwealth of Dominica [7].

Montserrat's stamps date from 1876. At one time its sole claim to fame was the lime juice supplied to the Royal Navy to prevent scurvy (hence the American term "limey", originally applied to British seamen), but since 1971 it has acquired a reputation for prolific stamp issues, although these have been considerably moderated in recent years. Most issues are generally thematic [8] with a strong element of royal pomp and circumstance [9].

St Christopher [10] and Nevis [11] issued their own stamps from 1870 and 1868 respectively until 1890, then used the stamps of the Leeward Islands. When distinctive stamps were resumed in 1903 they chose the title "St Kitts-Nevis" for a joint series. After the island of Anguilla celebrated its tercentenary in 1950 its name was added to the title, which is now "St Christopher Nevis Anguilla" [12].

Following the grant of associated statehood in 1967, Anguilla agitated for independence and seceded that September, overprinting its stamps accordingly. Its secession was contested at first, but the dispute was resolved by placing Anguilla under a British Commissioner, hence the curious inscription [13]. Since June 1980 the other islands have had separate postal administrations, with stamps inscribed "Nevis" [14] and "St Kitts" [15].

WINDWARD ISLANDS

The Virgin Islands adopted distinctive stamps in 1866 and these continued to be thus inscribed until 1968 [16], when the epithet "British" was added to avoid confusion with the American Virgin Islands. Ironically, the US dollar (discreetly indicated on stamps by the abbreviation "U.S.Cy") has been the currency of the British Virgin Islands since 1962. Unusually for the West Indies, the islands' stamps continue to focus on local customs, marine life and flora, with a strong emphasis on the British royal family. A set of 1969 commemorated Robert Louis Stevenson, whose adventure story *Treasure Island* was set in the islands.

Grenada had a conventional philatelic history from 1861 to 1967, when it was granted associate statehood, but since then it has become one of the world's most prolific issuing countries, producing about 5,000 stamps by 2004. Many sets are produced in sheetlets of from 6 to 20 *se-tenant*, devoted to many subjects that have little relevance to the country, ranging from dinosaurs to American entertainers. The Grenadines of Grenada are almost as prolific, with separate issues

Below: The Virgin Islands paid tribute to the Princess of Wales (left), while Grenada honoured President Reagan's visit with an overprint (right).

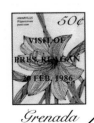

Stamps for All Occasions

The smaller the Caribbean island, the more prolific the stamp issues. The Grenadines of Grenada and St Vincent rival each other in their bid to produce stamps for every conceivable occasion and celebrity. The islands that first put Michael Jackson and Madonna on stamps have even produced images of every team that reached the finals of the World Cup football championships in recent years.

for Carriacou and Petite Martinique that often cover the same topics as Grenada itself.

St Lucia began issuing stamps in 1860 and followed the prevailing colonial policy until it was granted associate statehood in 1967, followed by complete independence in 1979. Since 1983 it has liberalized its stamp policy, although there has been some attempt to maintain the integrity of stamps by a relative adherence to subjects of indigenous interest [17].

It pales into insignificance alongside St Vincent. Here, stamps in the colonial style were issued from 1861 to 1963, when the island was granted ministerial government and the stamp contract passed out of the hands of the Crown Agents to an American company. Complete independence was gained in 1979. Since then new issues have risen to several hundred each year. Equally prolific were the issues of the Grenadines of St Vincent (1973–94) [18], followed by the numerous stamps from individual islands Bequia, Canouan, Mustique, Union Island, Palm Island and the Cayes of Tobago.

10

11

12

13

14

15

16

17

18

MEXICO

The United States of Mexico lie south of the USA, geographically part of North America but culturally and linguistically part of Latin America. The area was the home of a highly developed civilization long before Hernando Cortés and his conquistadors toppled the empire of Montezuma early in the 16th century. Under Spanish rule, New Spain extended from Guatemala to Wyoming, but the secession of Texas in 1836 and war with the USA (1846–7) resulted in the loss of territory now forming the states of California, Arizona, New Mexico and parts of Utah, Idaho, Washington and Oregon, leaving Mexico's boundaries more or less where they are today, along the Rio Grande del Norte. Until the 1920s Mexico suffered frequent

revolutions, breakaway regimes and changes of government, followed by a period of anti-clericalism and extreme socialism before the country emerged from anarchy.

Left: A map of Mexico appeared in the series of 1915 signifying the re-unification of the country after a period of civil war.

DICTATORS AND FOREIGN INTERVENTION

All the stamps issued from 1856 [1] until 1879, with one notable exception, portrayed Miguel Hidalgo, who had proclaimed Mexico's independence from Spain in 1810. The inherent instability of the country for much of the 19th century encouraged the intervention of the United States in the 1840s and European nations during the 1860s. When Mexico suspended its payment of foreign debts in 1861 it was occupied by British, Spanish and French troops. The French stayed on and, taking advantage of the American Civil War, installed the Austrian Archduke Maximilian as emperor [2]. In 1867 the USA invoked the Monroe Doctrine, forcing Napoleon III to withdraw his troops. Maximilian surrendered to the republicans, led by Benito Juarez [4], and was executed at Queretaro on 19 June.

Stamps in the 1870s were printed by the American Bank Note Company and share the characteristically florid frames found on US stamps of the same period [3]. A curious feature of many Mexican stamps from 1868 to 1883 was the overprinting of district names and numbers.

REVOLUTIONS AND CIVIL WARS

The dictator Porfirio Díaz held power in Mexico from 1876 to 1911, but was ousted by a popular revolt that began in 1910. He was succeeded by the liberal Francisco Madero [5], who was overthrown and murdered by his general Victoriano Huerta in February 1913. This outrage provoked a civil war that lasted until 1915 and involved various factions, led by Pancho Villa, Emiliano Zapata, Venustiano Carranza and Alvaro Obregon, who eventually joined forces as the Constitutionalists.

Numerous overprints and local issues appeared all over Mexico during this period, followed by a general series [6] in 1914. In October that year, however, Villa and Zapata broke with Carranza and proclaimed a provisional government by the Convention of Aguascalientes. Mexican stamps were overprinted by the Conventionists [7].

The Constitutionalists retook Mexico City in August 1915. Zapata and Villa were murdered in 1919 and 1923 respectively, and Carranza introduced a new constitution in 1917 that laid the foundation of the modern state. However, it fell to Obregon to realize the aims of the revolution.

MODERN MEXICO

Although the Revolution Monument graced the definitive series of 1934–6 [8], the vast majority of stamps from that time forward avoided contentious political issues. Old enmities with Mexico's powerful northern neighbour were forgotten by the time of the New York World's Fair in 1939 [9]. A traditional view of the country was deliberately fostered, even in the series of 1956 celebrating the stamp centenary [10], but by that time Mexico was tending to look back to its ancient roots for inspiration [11].

Mexico was the first country to portray President Kennedy, in connection with his state visit in June 1962 [12]. As a result of this visit, the Chamizal Treaty was signed in 1963, whereby the USA returned some land along the Rio Grande. A stamp of 1964 showed Kennedy and President Lopez-Mateos shaking hands on the deal [13]. A long-running series, introduced in 1973, highlighted Mexican exports [14]. More recent stamps resemble mini-posters, not only for Christmas [15] but for many anniversaries, though the quality of offset lithography has improved in recent years [16]. A series of 1993 portrayed Mexican film stars, although Dolores del Rio [17] was the only one to make it big in Hollywood.

A more subtle, delicate style of design emerged in the 1990s. Mexican patriotism was stronger than ever but colours were generally much lighter and more restrained than previously [18]. An interesting stamp of 1997 commemorated the St Patrick's

Below: A stamp issued in 1994 to publicize National Week of Patriotic Symbols features the Mexican flag.

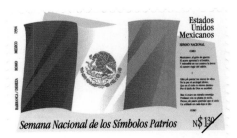

Semana Nacional de los Símbolos Patrios N$1.30

One Small Step for Man

Many countries celebrated the achievement of the Apollo 11 mission to the Moon in 1969, and most depicted the astronauts Armstrong and Aldrin on the lunar surface. Mexico was alone in adopting a more symbolic approach, using Neil Armstrong's footprint in moon dust to create a very powerful image.

Battalion – Irishmen who volunteered to fight for Mexico in the war against the United States [19].

Like the USA, Mexico favours single stamps for commemorative purposes, and these are mostly denominated at the domestic letter rate, with the intention of informing and motivating the Mexican people rather than promoting a national image to the world at large. Stamps are released at frequent intervals and cover all manner of subjects and events. A relatively high proportion pay tribute to Mexican personalities, very few of whom are known outside their own country (or, in fact, all that well known within it either).

A spate of 50th-anniversary stamps since the 1990s testifies to the enormous social and economic progress of Mexico in the years following World War II. By contrast, a recurring series in recent years has featured the glories of Mexico's architecture from the Spanish colonial era, although this is exceptional: the vogue for thematic sets, so prevalent elsewhere, has never really caught on in Mexico.

12

13

14

15

16

17

18

19

1

2

3

4

5

6

7

8

9

10

CENTRAL AMERICA

With a long and unenviable reputation for revolution, the countries of Central America were the original banana republics, with one-product economies largely in the hands of foreign (mainly US) investors. They share a common profile, characterized by a mainly impoverished population ruled by a handful of landowners with US business interests paramount, most notably over the development and operation of the Panama Canal. Not surprisingly, the character and subjects of their stamps often reflect their status as client states of the USA.

Left: President Jimmy Carter and President Torrijos of Panama signing the treaty that ceded the Canal Zone back to Panama in 1977.

COSTA RICA

The "rich coast" facing the Pacific began issuing stamps in 1863, and early issues tended to portray dead politicians [1]. Stamps overprinted for the remote province of Guanacaste were in use in the 1880s due to local currency differences [2]. Pictorial themes appeared in the 1930s, sport being a very early topic. Institutions such as Rotary [3] reflected the Americanization of the country. From 1947, when Roosevelt was honoured, the great and good of the USA were often portrayed, ranging from Father Flanagan, founder of Boys Town, on a children's charity set of 1959, to John Kennedy and John Kennedy Junior [4].

EL SALVADOR

The volcano of San Miguel appeared in 1867 on the first stamps of the country named in tribute to the Saviour [5]. The early stamps were often overprinted or surcharged for re-issue but more pictorial designs appeared in the 1930s. Some very attractive sets engraved by American and British firms appeared in the 1940s, notably the Roosevelt memorial issue of 1948, which comprised 12 stamps and two miniature sheets [6]. Stamps of more recent times have been lithographed in full colour and cover a wide range of topics, from sport to wildlife and scenery [7].

GUATEMALA

Another smoking volcano graced the arms stamps of Guatemala [8], adopted in 1871, but its most enduring image is the long-tailed quetzal. First appearing on stamps of 1881 [9], as a national icon it has been reprised on many issues down to the present time, usually in repose but sometimes in flight [10]. Philatelically one of the more conservative countries, Guatemala tends to stick closely to subjects of domestic interest. Such issues include several propaganda stamps laying claim to British Honduras (later Belize).

HONDURAS

The triangular seal of Honduras, with its sun rising over a volcano, formed the motif of the first stamps, issued in 1866 [11], but by 1878 the country had become infected with the craze for dead presidents [12], which continued until the 1930s. From 1946 onwards Honduras discovered a lucrative market in long sets honouring American heroes, starting with Roosevelt. The series of 1959 for the 150th birthday of Abraham Lincoln ran to 24 stamps and included his log cabin birthplace [13] and the Gettysburg address.

NICARAGUA

In the stamps of Nicaragua, from their inception in 1862, the smoking volcanoes really came into their own [14].

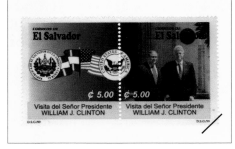
Unfortunately, the series of 1901 showing Momotombo issuing smoke [15] deterred the US Congress from its original plan to drive the canal across Nicaragua, and thereafter the Panama lobby triumphed. Among the non-political US celebrities honoured was the humorist Will Rogers, with a piece of subliminal advertising for Pan-American Airways for good measure [16]. Because of currency fluctuations, stamps were overprinted "B" (Bluefields) in the province of Zelayo [17] and in Cabo Gracias a Dios.

PANAMA

The most southerly of the republics was originally a province of Colombia and from 1887 it issued stamps thus inscribed but showing the isthmus of Panama. In 1903, when Colombia refused to lease territory to the USA for the construction of the canal, Panama declared its independence. The US Navy prevented Colombia from taking action and stamps were overprinted to blot out the Colombian inscriptions. Panamanian stamps grew lavish in their coverage of US subjects. This has been less noticeable since the fall of the Noriega regime and emphasis is now on modernization and social reform.

The canal was not opened until 1915 but from 1904 onwards stamps were overprinted or inscribed with the words "Canal Zone" [18]. Many of them portrayed the engineers who built the canal [19] or depicted its landmarks [20]. The US lease expired in 1999 and ordinary Panamanian stamps have been used since then.

BELIZE

The only British colony in Central America, British Honduras had its own stamps from 1865. Bicoloured pictorials showing local products and Mayan ruins appeared from 1938 until 1962, when a series featuring local birds was printed by multicolour photogravure. In 1964 the colony was granted self-government and was renamed Belize in 1973, the series then current being overprinted accordingly. Continual friction with neighbouring Guatemala (which laid claim to the colony) delayed the grant of full independence until September 1981.

Belize continues to pursue a conservative policy regarding new issues and the vast majority of them concentrate on subjects of indigenous interest. Its stamps are firmly rooted in the colonial past, with numerous issues featuring the British royal family. Among other themes, primary products such as logwood rank highly, but Belize is also proud of its status as the originator of chewing gum [21]. The Cayes of Belize, a chain of islands off the coast, had a typewritten local stamp in the 1890s and this seems to have inspired the "regional" stamps that appeared briefly in 1984–5.

Below: Oliver Stanley was one of the few British politicians to achieve philatelic recognition. The airport of British Honduras was named after him when he was Colonial Secretary.

11

12

13

14

15

16

17

18

19

20

21

COLOMBIA, ECUADOR AND VENEZUELA

Occupying the north-west corner of South America, these countries cover the area from the Atlantic coast to the equatorial region of the Pacific. Once part of the Spanish Empire under the name of New Granada, the region declared independence in 1813 and was united by Simon Bolivar to form the Republic of Greater Colombia, named in honour of the man who discovered it. However, it disintegrated in 1829–30 and the component states have been separate ever since.

Left: This Colombian stamp marked the 150th anniversary of the Spanish rout at Caribobo, which freed New Granada and led to the Republic of Greater Colombia.

COLOMBIA

Following the break-up of the short-lived republic, Colombia reverted to its old Spanish colonial name and by 1859, when its first stamps appeared [1], the country was a loose union of states known as the Granadine Confederation. Two years later it changed its name to the United States of New Granada and in 1862 adopted the name of the United States of Colombia [2]. It changed its name for the fourth and last time in 1886 to become the Republic of Colombia [3].

Relatively crude stamps were lithographed locally but from time to time Colombia went to the great American or British printers. The earliest attempt at a multicolour treatment was in 1947, when Waterlow of London printed a series featuring local orchids, combining intaglio with lithography [4]. Colombia was noted for stamps produced for specific services, such as the "Extra Rapido" service [5]. The vast majority of stamps pertain strictly to Colombia, with only the occasional nod at an international figure [6].

States Issues

The constitution of 1832 divided the country into 18 autonomous provinces, reduced in 1858 to nine. The federal government encouraged the provinces to establish their own postal services and all produced their own stamps at various times from 1865, but after 1886 this was gradually curbed and the last stamps were abolished in 1906.

Antioquia began issuing stamps in 1868 and although not the first to do so it was by far the most prolific, producing almost as many stamps as the other eight states combined. In the first decade the stamps concentrated on the state arms, followed by the head of Liberty in the 1870s and 1880s and finally a portrait of local hero, General Cordoba [7]. Bolivar was the first to adopt distinctive stamps, beginning in 1863 with a stamp showing the national seal that is arguably the smallest stamp ever issued. Later stamps bore a profile of Simon Bolivar, after whom the province was named [8].

Boyaca issued stamps only between 1899 and 1904 but in that short time produced the most varied of all the states issues: a medley of portraiture [9], heraldry and the monument to the Battle of Boyaca during the War of Independence. Cauca issued only two typeset stamps in 1902 [10] while Cundinamarca's stamps, issued from 1870 to 1904, concentrated on the national arms [11]. Heraldry was the principal feature of the stamps produced by Santander between 1884 and

1903 [12] and by Tolima from 1870 to 1904. Stamps were also issued by Panama from 1878 until it seceded from Colombia in 1903.

ECUADOR

At one time the Inca kingdom of Quito and later part of New Granada, Ecuador was liberated in 1822 but left Greater Colombia in May 1830 and was established as a republic, taking its name from the Equator, which runs through it. Stamps were introduced in 1865 [13], national arms being followed by presidential portraits [14].

The 1920s and 1930s were a period dominated by frequent overprints and surcharges. Design improved in the late 1930s and culminated in a set of 14 celebrating the 150th anniversary of the American constitution, recess-printed in New York in four colours – a tour de force for the time [15]. The American connection was reinforced a year later with a long set for the New York World's Fair and since then stamps have included the only one to show Vice President Nixon and one of the few to show little John Kennedy Junior saluting his father's coffin [16]. Nowadays, tourism is the most important industry, reflected in numerous stamps publicizing the Galapagos Islands and other attractions [17–18].

VENEZUELA

Columbus reached the north coast of South America in 1498 during his third voyage and named the region

Below: A stamp of Venezuela was issued in 1969 to mark the 150th anniversary of the Battle of Boyaca.

Cartographic Conflict

At various times since 1894 Venezuela has issued stamps laying claim to extensive tracts of neighbouring Guyana. A series of 1965–6 backed this claim by reproducing various maps published from 1775 onwards showing the disputed territory.

Venezuela (Little Venice) because of the numerous lagoons in the delta of the Orinoco. The first stamps were introduced in 1859 and showed the arms of the Venezuelan Federation.

The country changed its name to the United States of Venezuela in 1866 and stamps thus inscribed were released [19]. From 1871 to 1903 all but a handful of stamps portrayed Simon Bolivar [20]. Apart from a series of stamps issued in 1951–3, which featured the arms of the 24 provinces and ran to several hundreds, Venezuela has pursued a fairly modest policy, with a penchant for patriotic themes. It is interesting to contrast the restrained monochrome engraving of the stamps celebrating the centenary of independence in 1921 [21] with the multicolour lithography of recent years.

In November 1863 a Scottish entrepreneur, Captain Robert Todd, was awarded the contract to convey mail from Venezuela to St Thomas in the Danish West Indies (now the American Virgin Islands). Stamps depicting the SS *Robert Todd* and inscribed with all the names of the ports served were issued between 1864 and 1873. During the Civil War of 1899–1903 many local provisional stamps appeared.

13   14

15

17

18

19   20

21

16

1

2

3

4

5

6

7

8

9

BRAZIL AND GUYANA

Brazil occupies approximately half the continent of South America and is the only country in the Western Hemisphere to derive its language and culture from Portugal. It was discovered in 1500 by Pedro Cabral and settled in 1532. During the Napoleonic Wars, when João VI was driven from Portugal, he established his court in Brazil in 1808. In 1822, after his return to Portugal, his son Pedro I declared Brazil to be an independent empire, which continued until 1889 when Pedro II abdicated and a republic was proclaimed.

Left: One of several stamps issued in 1932 to celebrate the quatercentenary of the colonization of Brazil shows a map of South America with the Brazilian territory shaded.

BRAZIL: EMPIRE

Dom Pedro II succeeded his father as emperor in 1831, at the tender age of six, and reigned until 1889. When he was barely 17, Brazil became the first country in the world to follow Britain's example by introducing adhesive postage stamps, popularly known to collectors as Bull's Eyes on account of their circular shape. In 1943 stamps identical but for the inscription marked their centenary [1]. Dom Pedro appeared on stamps printed in New York [2], his beard becoming whiter as he advanced in years. Ousted by a military coup, he was exiled to Europe and died in Paris in 1891.

REVOLUTION AND REVOLT

Although its subsequent history was not as turbulent as that of many of its neighbours, Brazil had its share of rebellions in remote provinces, as well as occasional revolutions. A series of 14 stamps issued in April 1931 celebrated the revolution of 3 October 1930, with portraits of politicians and quotations from their speeches. Obscure at the time, they are well-nigh baffling today. Few now recall why Vargas said: "Rio Grande stands by Brazil", to which Pessoa responded, "I say No!" [3].

A revolt broke out in São Paulo in July 1932 and a provisional government was established. It was suppressed by federal troops on 2 October, but not before revolutionary stamps [4] had been issued. The United States of Brazil became a Federative Republic in 1946, but following a military coup in 1964 the country was a dictatorship until March 1985, when democratic government was restored. None of the later upheavals had any impact on stamps.

REPUBLIC

The vast majority of Brazilian special issues have been single stamps covering a wide range of topics and personalities. A strong feature is the issue of stamps marking visits by other heads of state, a tradition dating from 1920 when Albert, King of the Belgians, paid a visit. In addition to small-format definitives, Brazil has issued very tiny stamps for compulsory use to raise money for child welfare [5].

Most stamps are produced at the Brazilian Mint and the quality of production has improved considerably since the 1950s [6]. Symbolic motifs are frequently used and often demand a second glance [7–8], although the ban on drinking and driving could not be clearer [9]. At the same time there is considerable nostalgia for the past, as exemplified by the bilingual stamp recalling the age of steam [10] and the many stamps harking back to imperial glory [11].

GUYANA

The vast tract of territory on the north-west coast of Brazil, bordering with Venezuela, was colonized by the British, French and Dutch. The first stamps of British Guiana were the extremely rare Cottonreels of 1850. In 1898 the colony belatedly celebrated Queen Victoria's diamond jubilee with a set featuring local scenery [12]. A pictorial definitive series of 1934 included a portrait of Sir Walter Raleigh and his son [13]. British Guiana gained independence in May 1966 and adopted the ancient indigenous name, Guyana. Between 1981 and 1994 Guyana overprinted earlier stamps, yielding almost 3,000 different varieties. Since 1994 sanity has returned, although it still ranks among the most prolific stamp-issuing countries, with a predilection for popular themes [14–15].

The only French colony in South America, French Guiana lies between Brazil and Surinam. It formerly included the notorious penal settlement of Devil's Island, but nowadays the territory is better known as a base for European experiments with the Ariane space rockets. French Guiana began issuing distinctive stamps in 1886, when several of the French colonial general series were surcharged with new values and overprinted "Guy. Franc". By 1892 the general colonial stamps were being diagonally overprinted "Guyane", and these were shortly followed by the colonial keytypes inscribed with the name at the foot.

Below: Surinam was the first country to celebrate Commander Alan Shepard's sub-orbital flight of 5 May 1961.

A pictorial series, introduced in 1904, featured a giant anteater, a gold-miner and palm trees in the capital Cayenne; the series was followed by rather garish bicoloured stamps in 1929 and more attractive intaglio pictorials in the 1940s. A definitive series featuring the tricolour was printed in London for the Free French [16], followed by a series showing scenes of native life [17]. French Guiana became an overseas department of France in 1946 and ordinary French stamps have been in use there since 1948. The inland territory of Inini was separately administered and had its own stamps from 1930 to 1946 [18], when it was re-incorporated with French Guiana.

The Dutch colonized Surinam, which issued colonial keytypes from 1873 and later distinctive designs, especially after 1954 when it became an autonomous state. Since then stamps have honoured America's first astronaut, Alan Shepard, and the 30th anniversary of Amelia Earhart's flight to South America [19]. Surinam became an independent country in 1975 but the stamps have continued in the same style.

11

12

13

14

15

16

17

18

19

BOLIVIA, CHILE AND PERU

Much of the area occupied by these three republics once formed the mighty Inca empire, overthrown by the conquistadors led by Francisco Pizarro in 1531–3. Because of its immense mineral wealth the region became the most prosperous of all Spain's possessions in South America, and it was here that the struggle for independence was fiercest and most prolonged. War at sea eventually gained the countries' independence but it was another naval campaign, the Pacific War of 1879–85, that lost Peru her southern nitrate districts and Bolivia her access to the ocean.

Left: Victories on land by Simon Bolivar and José de San Martín were clinched by the defeat of the Spanish navy by the British naval commander Thomas Cochrane, 10th Earl of Dundonald. Unjustly convicted of fraud, imprisoned, disgraced and dismissed from the Royal Navy, he went to South America and used his considerable talents to secure the liberation of Chile, Peru, Brazil and later Greece. His exploits won him a pardon and reinstatement. Dying an admiral, he was buried in Westminster Abbey.

BOLIVIA

Released in 1867, Bolivia's first stamps featured a condor, symbolic of the Andes [1]. They were soon followed by allegorical and armorial designs recess-printed in New York [2]. In 1901 Bolivia switched to portraits of historical figures [3] but adopted pictorialism in 1916, with scenes of Mount Ilimani and Lake Titicaca [5]. Having lost its Pacific seaboard to Chile, it waged a stamp war with neighbouring Paraguay over the Gran Chaco [4]. Its claims to the Chaco Boliviano eventually led to the war of 1932–5, which left both countries on the verge of bankruptcy.

Many later stamps featured designs depicting the scenery, wildlife and culture of the Quechua Indians of the Altiplano [6]. Commemorative issues harked back to the battles of the War of Independence [7] but the Pacific War was best forgotten in Bolivia.

Like the other countries of UPAEP (the postal union of the Americas) Bolivia now issues stamps each year in the prevailing topic [8]. In 1986 the boliviano collapsed, resulting in hyperinflation. Since the currency reform of 1987 and the introduction of the new boliviano, the country's economy has been relatively stable.

CHILE

The longest of the Latin American countries, extending from the tropics to the sub-Antarctic, Chile is hemmed in between the Andes and the Pacific. Virtually all of its stamps portrayed Columbus from 1853 [9] until 1910. In that year the centenary of independence was celebrated by a long set [11] of which the highest denomination portrayed Admiral Cochrane. The admiral also appeared in ensuing definitive sets [10].

The Pacific War had been fought by Chile to gain access to the nitrate deposits jointly owned by Peru and Bolivia, and this valuable asset was the subject of many stamps in the 1930s and 1940s [12]. Commemoratives tended to concentrate on the struggle for independence, often tastefully recess-printed at the Chilean Mint [14]. More strident offset lithography tends to be favoured increasingly [15]. In the postwar period, Chile became embroiled with Argentina over rival claims to a slice of Antarctica, and this was a frequent subject for stamps.

Chile produced a set of four stamps in 1910 for use in the offshore islands of Juan Fernandez [13] and in more recent years has issued "regional"

Antarctic Rivalry and Co-operation

Both Chile and Peru followed Argentina's example and developed an interest in Antarctica in the years after World War II. While the stamps of Chile and Argentina became increasingly strident, with maps claiming the same territory, Peru's involvement was much more low key. Eventually the Antarctic Treaty of 1988, to which they all subscribed, took the heat out of the situation. They have since tended to co-operate in scientific research.

stamps for Easter Island, which is now a major tourist attraction.

The overthrow of the democratically elected Marxist President Salvador Allende in 1973 ushered in an era of military dictatorship under General Augusto Pinochet, but stamps of this period studiously avoided political controversy. After Pinochet was ousted in 1989, a more liberal policy ensued and a number of stamps portrayed the writer Pablo Neruda (who had been exiled) as well as Allende himself.

Although Chile pursues a relatively moderate policy with regard to new issues, in 1996 it released a set of 60 stamps each warning against a specific

accident – in the home, on the roads, at school and in the workplace, as well as warnings on alcohol and drug abuse and hints on safety in leisure activities.

PERU

Pending the introduction of its own stamps [18] in 1858, Peru made use of freight labels supplied by the Pacific Steam Navigation Company. From 1866 most Peruvian stamps were recess-printed by rival New York firms. After the Chilean occupation in 1881 stamps were overprinted with the Chilean arms [16]. When President Morales Bermudez died suddenly in 1894, shortly before his term of office expired, stamps were overprinted with his portrait as a mark of respect [17]. These are arguably the first mourning stamps to be produced by a government postal administration (as opposed to the German private posts in 1888).

Peru was one of the first countries to adopt photogravure, in 1924, and throughout the 1930s many fine examples from England were released, notably the long series celebrating the quatercentenary of Lima in 1935 [20]. Since World War II, however, most stamps have been lithographed locally. Co-operation with other Latin American countries is a recurring theme [21], along with frequent references to the region's pre-Columbian civilizations. Boundary disputes with Chile and Bolivia [19] still fester and have several times brought Peru to the brink of war with her neighbours.

Below: This se-tenant *pair of stamps was issued in 1992 mainly for tourists' postcards from Easter Island, but is also valid on mail from mainland Chile.*

12

13

14

15

16

17

18

19

20

21

1

2

3

4

5

6

7

8

9

10

ARGENTINA, PARAGUAY AND URUGUAY

These three countries, lying south of Brazil, were first visited by Spaniards in 1512–20 but were not colonized until the late 16th century and were still relatively undeveloped when they threw off the Spanish yoke in 1810–11. Argentina and Uruguay lie on opposite sides of the River Plate, while Paraguay is one of South America's two landlocked countries, lying north-west of its neighbours.

Left: The Battle of Maipu in 1818 marked the turning point in the struggle for independence from Spain. Having liberated Argentina, José de San Martín crossed the Andes to free Chile and Peru.

ARGENTINA

Three of the Argentine states had their own stamps in the 1850s, those of Buenos Aires featuring a steamship. Cordoba [1] had an armorial design but Corrientes blatantly plagiarized the Ceres stamps of France. General issues for the Argentine Confederation [2] were issued in 1858–60, followed by stamps of the Republic [3]. Argentina stuck to dead heroes and presidents until the 1930s, San Martín predominating, but had the distinction of producing the first commemorative stamps in the Western Hemisphere in October 1892 to celebrate the quatercentenary of the first voyage made by Columbus [5]. Between 1913 and 1938, stamps were overprinted for the use of eight separate government departments [4].

A set of 25 marked the revolution of 1930 [6], the first of many issues that reflected the turbulent politics of Argentina in later years. Other stamps looked back to the heroic struggle for independence [7] or pursued the government's long-running battle with Britain over the Falkland Islands and territory in Antarctica [8].

PARAGUAY

This landlocked country had the misfortune to be ruled by a series of tyrannical dictators, the last of whom

declared war on Argentina, Uruguay and Brazil (1864), almost destroying Paraguay as a result. The first stamps appeared in 1870, the year this disastrous war ended [9]. History repeated itself when Paraguay became involved in a dispute with Bolivia over the Gran Chaco. A war fought in the stamp album with rival map stamps [10] escalated into bloodshed in 1932–5; this time Paraguay won a Pyrrhic victory.

In the 1930s and 1940s many stamps were printed in England [11] but after World War II American printers predominated [12]. Relations with Argentina improved in the 1950s and stamps portraying the two dictators, Stroessner of Paraguay and Peron of Argentina, set the seal on this [13].

Since 1962 Paraguay has issued a prodigal number of stamps, from space research [14] to nude paintings [15], of little relevance to the country itself.

Below: Stamps issued by Buenos Aires in the 1850s bore a steamship, hence their nickname of Barquitos ("little ships").

URUGUAY

In the 17th century this region on the east bank of the River Plate was fought over by Spain and Portugal, and when Spanish supremacy was smashed in 1810 local hero José Artigas tried to create a separate state, known as the Banda Oriental. To maintain independence Artigas had to fight Spain, Buenos Aires and the Portuguese. In 1825 Brazil and Argentina went to war over the disputed territory, and the matter was resolved only when Britain intervened to force the belligerents to recognize Uruguay's independence in 1830. Uruguay, which won Olympic soccer gold medals in 1924 and 1928, hosted the first World Cup in 1930 and celebrated the centenary of independence by winning the trophy.

Uruguay's first stamps, introduced in 1856, are popularly known as the Montevideo Suns. They were followed in 1866 by a series in which the numerals were the dominant feature [16]. The full title República Oriental del Uruguay means "republic on the east bank of the River Uruguay", and it appeared on many later stamps. Unlike most Latin American countries,

Below: One of a series showing historic engravings of Montevideo (top) contrasts with the poster style of the 1990 stamp honouring the Engineer Corps (bottom).

Land of Fire and Gold Dust

The island of Tierra del Fuego at the southern tip of Latin America was discovered by Magellan in 1520 as he rounded Cape Horn, and named "Land of Fire" by him from the bonfires of the natives. Argentina and Chile partitioned the island in 1881 and six years later Julius Popper established gold-mines in both parts. Mail taken to Punta Arenas in Chile bore a 10c stamp – representing neither Chilean nor Argentinian currency but centigrams of gold dust.

which followed the US fashion for presidential portraiture, Uruguay preferred allegorical subjects [17] and historical vignettes, either lithographed locally or recess-printed in England. In recent years a more symbolic approach has been adopted, with designs rendered in a semi-abstract poster style. Visits from heads of state of many countries, from France and Italy to Israel [18], have been a fertile source of stamp designs, bolstering Uruguay's sense of its global importance.

Occasionally Uruguay has issued stamps and miniature sheets whose validity has been cast into doubt because they were not on general release in post offices. These include the sets marking the Montreal Olympics, the 30th anniversary of the United Nations and the Apollo-Soyuz joint space mission (1975), and the Nobel laureates, World Cup football championship, Lindbergh, Rubens and Zeppelin sets (1977). Apart from these lapses a fairly modest policy has been pursued, confined mostly to single stamps.

11

12

13

14

15

16

17

18

1

2

3

4

5

6

7

SOUTH ATLANTIC ISLANDS

Dotted around the South Atlantic are several remote island groups, the last remnants of the British Empire, consisting of the Falkland Islands and St Helena, with the dependencies of South Georgia and the South Sandwich Islands (to which is appended British Antarctic Territory) on the one hand, and Ascension and Tristan da Cunha on the other. The Falklands, which have been in British hands since 1833, have relied on sheep-farming, and St Helena has been a coaling-station. Only Ascension, with its communications and NASA installations of recent years, has real importance today. The Falklands and South Georgia were invaded and occupied by Argentina in 1981, precipitating war with Britain.

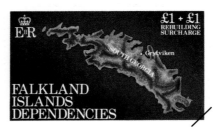

Left: Following the liberation of the Falklands and South Georgia, £1 stamps featuring maps of the islands were sold at a premium of 100 per cent in aid of the reconstruction of the islands. Such a high premium was contrary to UPU guidelines.

FALKLAND ISLANDS

The stamps of the Falkland Islands departed from the usual British colonial pattern in having distinctive designs, even though they stuck rigidly to the tradition of royal portraits. In 1929 a definitive series was introduced with a profile of George V over a tiny vignette of a fin whale and gentoo penguins, but it was not until 1933, with a long series celebrating the centenary of the British colony, that bicoloured intaglio pictorials were adopted. This remained the norm until 1968, when multicolour photogravure became fashionable. The stamps of recent years have sometimes referred to the war with Argentina [1], but birds and seals continue to be the dominant subjects [2], with occasional scenes of island life [3] and visiting ships.

FALKLAND DEPENDENCIES

Although a small undated stamp inscribed "South Georgia" (intended to be marked on letters below the postage stamp) was occasionally used to cancel mail to these territories, it was not an overprint in the true sense. The first stamps of South Georgia, with similar sets for the South Orkneys [4], South Shetland and Graham Land, were issued in 1944, followed by a general series in 1946. In 1954 a pictorial definitive series featured scientific ships that had been associated with the area.

Stamps of the Falkland Islands Dependencies were replaced in 1963 by separate issues for British Antarctic Territory and South Georgia [5]. Stamps inscribed for the former remain in use, but from 1980 to 1985 South Georgia reverted to stamps of the Falkland Islands Dependencies. In 1985 it and the South Sandwich Islands ceased to be dependencies of the Falkland Islands and began issuing stamps bearing their joint names [6].

British Antarctic Territory has issued stamps continuously since 1963. The Silver Jubilee stamps of 1977 alluded to the time spent in the region by the Duke of Edinburgh, unusually portraying him bearded [7]. Other stamps allude to the area's wildlife [8] and the work of the scientific research stations.

ST HELENA

Blue stamps denominated 6d were introduced in St Helena in 1856, but between 1864 and 1880 they were printed in different colours and surcharged accordingly for use as various values from 1d to 5s. In later years the colonial keytypes were used, although some pictorial designs appeared from

1903 onwards. As in the Falklands, the centenary of the crown colony in 1934 was celebrated by a long set of bicoloured intaglio pictorial stamps, establishing a precedent for later issues. Multicolour photogravure was adopted in 1961 [9]. Apart from some stamps alluding to Napoleon's exile, most recent issues have been preoccupied with island scenery and flowers [10]. Stamps in support of the Hong Kong stamp show of 1994 featured islanders' pets, and a wide range of other topics includes sea slugs and medical scientists. The stamps celebrating Elizabeth II's silver jubilee in 1977 showed the royal family visiting the island [11].

ASCENSION

This remote island was an outpost of the Royal Navy and used ordinary British stamps until 1922, when overprinted St Helena stamps were adopted, followed by a pictorial series in 1934. It has since followed the same

Above: The garden on Green Mountain featured on a 1975 stamp marking the 160th anniversary of British settlement.

Below: Base B and the postmark of Deception Island appear on a British Antarctic stamp.

Ducal Connections
The "capital" of Tristan da Cunha is called Edinburgh, named in honour of Prince Alfred, the first Duke, who visited the island aboard HMS *Galatea* in 1867.

pattern, issuing more colourful stamps since the 1960s. Many issues refer to its importance as a communications centre, the 1986 Christmas stamps appropriately including an image of George V making the first royal Christmas broadcast for the BBC [12]. Scenery, bird life and landmarks [13] provide the staple fare for its stamps.

TRISTAN DA CUNHA
Named after the Portuguese navigator who discovered it in 1502, Tristan da Cunha remained a desert isle until Napoleon was exiled to St Helena. Its garrison was evacuated in 1816 leaving behind Corporal Glass, who became the patriarch of the little community.

Stamps of St Helena with an overprint were introduced in 1952, followed by pictorial issues that reflect the scenery and wildlife [14] or mark the few historic events, such as the evacuation in 1961 following the eruption of the volcano, or the visits of scientific expeditions [15]. While its first stamps were overprints on those of St Helena, the position was briefly reversed on 12 October 1961, when a quantity of Tristan stamps held in St Helena was overprinted "St. Helena Tristan Relief" and surcharged in sterling (although the stamps were denominated in South African cents). Only 434 complete sets were sold (mostly to passengers of a visiting liner) before the issue was suppressed.

1

2

3

4

5

DANMARK

1972 - 1997

6

7

8

9

10

EUROPE

The European contribution to philately is immense: it includes the first adhesive (1840), bicoloured (1843) and pictorial stamps (1845), as well as many technological advances, from intaglio in the 1840s and photogravure in 1914 to holographic stamps (1988) and heat-sensitive inks (2001).

WESTERN SCANDINAVIA

As a collective name for the countries of north-western Europe, Scandinavia is often used to include not only Denmark, Norway and Sweden but also Finland and the North Atlantic islands colonized by the Vikings in the Middle Ages: the Faroes, Iceland and Greenland. The Vikings were hardy seafarers who penetrated even North America around AD 1000; in the early 11th century Cnut (Canute), king of Denmark and Norway, also ruled England. In 1397 Queen Margrethe I united Norway, Sweden, Iceland, Greenland and Finland under the Danish crown, a union that lasted until 1523, when Gustavus Vasa drove the Danes out of Sweden. In the 17th century Sweden was the greatest power in the Baltic, but its expansion into

Russia was checked in 1709 and a century later it was forced to cede Finland to the tsar. Norway remained part of Denmark until 1814, when it was transferred to Sweden, but in 1905 the Norwegian parliament voted for independence, electing a Danish prince as Haakon VII. Iceland became a republic in 1944.

Left: The eruption of Hekla in Iceland in 1948 was marked by a set of seven stamps showing different views of the volcano.

DENMARK
The first of the Scandinavian countries to adopt stamps, Denmark's first issue consisted of the 2rbs and 4rbs (rigsbank skilling) stamps – small, square with a security underprint [1]. A feature common to the main Scandinavian countries is the use of a numeral motif for the low-value stamps that is retained in use for many years. The Danish waves design [2] has been in use, with modifications, since 1905. The first commemoratives appeared in 1920 to celebrate the recovery of Northern Slesvig from Germany [3]. The Nordic countries preferred a small format for special issues, such as the set marking the 400th anniversary of the Reformation in 1936 [4].

From 1953 to 1956 Denmark celebrated its millennium as a kingdom with ten stamps, one for each century.

The top value [5] showed the memorial to the war of 1864, in which Denmark was defeated and lost Slesvig to Prussia. Stamps honouring the Red Cross in 1966 bore the titles of international Red Cross organizations in 32 languages, plus a Latin motto – the largest number of different languages on a single stamp up to that time [7]. The postal printing works has continued to use intaglio to this day, but in recent years multicolour lithography has also been employed effectively, as in the stamps celebrating the silver jubilee of Margrethe II [6] and the Youth series, which included a close-up of a tongue with a stud in it [8].

NORWAY
Both Norway and Sweden introduced stamps in 1855 but while Norway portrayed King Oscar of Sweden [9]

Sweden preferred armorial designs. Both countries would later follow the same pattern as Denmark, using a numeral motif for the lowest values and heraldic design for the middle denominations and a portrait of the monarch on the high values. This meant that the only stamps that needed to be changed at the outset of each new reign were the relatively little-used high values.

For the most part Norway preferred the cheap letterpress process, reserving intaglio for the occasional high-value commemorative, but in 1928 the contract passed to Emil Mostue, who used lithography for a short period before introducing photogravure. This was used most effectively in the tourist propaganda series of 1938 [11] and the Queen Maud charity set of 1939 [12].

Both Denmark and Norway were overrun by Nazi Germany in 1940. While Christian X remained in Copenhagen to raise the morale of his people, Haakon VII went to Scotland to regroup his forces there. In Norway the Germans installed Vidkun Quisling [13], whose name has become a byword for treachery; the date on the stamp was that on which he was asked to form a government. The definitives were overprinted with a large letter V for Victory [14], but this boomeranged when the Resistance painted the slogan "Vi Vil Vinne" (We will win) on roads, a scene depicted on one of the stamps issued by the Norwegian government in exile [15].

Increasing use of multicolour lithography has brightened the appearance of Norwegian stamps in recent years [16]. The inauguration of the National Junior Stamp Club in 1997 was marked by two stamps crammed with different thematic subjects [10].

DANISH POSSESSIONS

Iceland had been a Danish colony since Viking times and its earliest stamps [17] were closely modelled on those of the mother country. In December 1918 it was declared an independent kingdom under Christian X but it became a republic in 1944. Since 1938 many of its stamps have featured geysers and glaciers [19], the volcanic destruction of Heimaey and the birth of the island of Surtsey.

Greenland had free postage until 1938, though parcels had to bear special stamps [18]. During World War II, when stamps were unavailable from Denmark, a series was recess-printed by the American Bank Note Company. Since 1950 Greenland's stamps have followed the Danish style but reflect the culture and traditions of the Inuit population. Bilingual inscriptions have been in use since 1963.

The Faroes had the unusual distinction of their own provisional stamps during World War II but did not get a permanent series until 1975 [20]. Since then the stamps have continued to depict the extraordinary scenery of these islands.

Record Longevity

The posthorn design of Norway's low values was introduced in 1871 – and is still in use. Over the years it has changed currency (1877), lettering (1893) and printer several times, and switched from letterpress to photogravure (1934), then intaglio (1962) and multicolour lithography (1997). Norway even celebrated its centenary with a pair showing the 3sk of 1871.

11

12

13

14

15

16

17

18

19

20

1

2

3

4

5

6

7

8

9

10

EASTERN SCANDINAVIA

Sweden was the dominant Baltic power from the Middle Ages to the end of the 17th century. Sverker I (*c.* 1134–56) united the Swedes and the Goths, and his crusade to Christianize the pagan Finns marked the beginning of the Swedish conquest of Finland. The Union of Kalmar (1397) united Denmark, Norway and Sweden under one ruler, but in 1520 the Swedish noble Gustavus Vasa raised a revolt against the Danish king that restored Swedish independence. Under his successors Sweden extended its rule over the whole of Finland and south of the Baltic. Sweden's power was checked when Poland, Denmark and Russia combined against Charles XII in a long war (1700–20), as a result of which it lost Estonia, Livonia and Ingermanland. Finland and the Aland Islands were ceded to Russia in 1809.

Left: Since 1956 the Nordic countries have issued stamps in uniform designs to symbolize their close postal co-operation. In 1967 the subject of these stamps was the Nordic House in Reykjavik, Iceland.

FINLAND

Until 1917 Finland was a Russian grand duchy and its early stamps were inscribed in both Cyrillic and Roman alphabets [1]; later issues were trilingual, with the name of the country in Russian, Finnish and Swedish [2]. When russification was at its height at the turn of the 20th century the stamps were identical to the Russian series [3], apart from the currency (the markka, divided into 100 penniä). Finland's first independent stamps were designed by its leading architect, Eliel Saarinen [4].

Most stamps were recess-printed in single colours [5] until 1966, when multicolour lithography was adopted [6]. Annual issues for the Red Cross and anti-TB campaign followed the same trend, with themes reflecting Finnish scenery and wildlife [7].

Most definitive issues since 1917 are in a small upright format and depict the lion rampant, a device seen on the tombs of the Vasa kings of Sweden. These have varied from time to time and designs featuring scenery and landmarks have been favoured for the high values [8]. Stamps portraying Marshal Gustav Mannerheim were overprinted for Eastern Karelia, occupied by the Finns from 1941 to 1944 [9].

ALAND ISLANDS

The Aland Islands in the Baltic were ceded to Russia in 1809. Of immense strategic importance, their great fortress at Bomarsund was destroyed by an Anglo-French fleet in 1854 and the islands were demilitarized and declared neutral. The mainly Swedish inhabitants were granted autonomy in 1922.

Regional stamps were introduced in 1984 [10] but since January 1993 the Aland postal service has been completely independent. Its stamps concentrate on the islands' scenery and distinctive culture, with a popular annual issue featuring island churches [11]. Their endearingly homespun character is reflected in genre scenes of island life. A beauty contest for cats in 2003 to elect "Missy Aland" resulted in the winners, Tovis [12] and Randi, being portrayed on a couple of stamps.

SWEDEN

Adhesive stamps were introduced in July 1855 and showed arms or numerals [13], a tradition continued in the low-value definitives to this day. No portrait of the king appeared until 1885, when Oscar II was shown on the higher denominations [14]. In 1920 stamp production passed from private firms to the Stamp Printing Office and Swedish stamps were subsequently recess-printed [15] in booklets or coils, distinguished by the lack of perforation on one or more adjoining sides, or two opposite sides [16] respectively.

Sweden was the home of Alfred Nobel, the armaments millionaire who created the prizes named in his memory. He himself appeared on stamps of 1946 to mark the 50th anniversary of his death, and in 1961 Sweden began issuing a set each year portraying the Nobel laureates since 1901 [17].

A joint issue with Finland in 1967 publicized Finnish settlers in Sweden and Swedish settlers in Finland. Each country issued two stamps symbolizing solidarity, designed by Pentti Rahikainen and lithographed at the State Bank Note Printing Works in Helsinki [18]. Since this major turning point Swedish stamps have been much more colourful, increasingly employing offset lithography. At the same time their scope has widened considerably, from rock 'n' roll [19] to the endearing charm of Carl Larsson's paintings [20].

11

12

13

14

15

16

The Greatest Master of Line Engraving

In 1960 a young Polish engraver named Czeslaw Slania began work at the Swedish Stamp Printing Office. Over the ensuing 45 years he engraved more than 1,000 stamps for his adopted land and many other countries (including the UK and USA). Universally recognized as the maestro of portrait engraving, in 1991 he was accorded the singular honour of a souvenir sheet as a 70th birthday tribute – which he engraved himself. Although at the time that was his greatest masterpiece, he surpassed it in March 2000 with this magnificent work, his 1,000th stamp engraving. Appropriately, he reproduced the painting *Great Deeds of Swedish Kings* by the 17th-century artist David Klöcker Ehrenstrahl.

17 mars 2000
CZESLAW SLANIAS 1000:e FRIMÄRKE

Mittpartiet ur
David Klöcker Ehrenstrahls målning från 1695
"Svenska konungars berömliga bedrifter"
i Drottningholms slott.

17

18

19

20

VIKINGS IN STAMPS

The word "Viking" came to be synonymous with "warrior", but it originally meant "bay people" and alluded to those who came from the inlets and fiords of western Norway and terrorized all of Europe between 780 and 1050. The image purveyed by the monastic chronicles – of bloodthirsty murderers and ruthless pillagers of Christendom – dies hard, but Viking history has now been substantially revised. Their influence in Britain is evident in place names from Ipswich and Harwich in the south to Lerwick and Haroldswick in Shetland.

Today, the Vikings are depicted in a more positive light, with a highly developed civilization and a strict code of honour. They were not all looters and rapists but accomplished craftsmen in wood, stone and metal, and skilled builders of ocean-going vessels far ahead of their time.

The Vikings had a distinctive religion based on a rich mythology with its own pantheon of gods and lesser deities. Above all, it was their daring seamanship that has proved their lasting legacy. Not so long ago Christopher Columbus got all the credit for finding the New World; now the prior claim of the Vikings has been proven by archaeological discoveries.

Below: The Scandinavian countries issued miniature sheets in 2004 showing characters from Norse mythology, such as Thor and Ran on this sheet from the Faroes.

While Scandinavian philately has been much enriched by Viking subjects, their impact elsewhere has provided material for stamps from many countries. Significantly the longship is the most important symbol of that era, for it was this craft that made possible the extraordinary expansion of the Vikings between 900 and 1100.

Norsemen raided Brittany and Gaul, laid siege to Paris and were bought off by grants of land in what came to be known as Normandy. Although they acquired a veneer of civilization from the Franks, it was the same tough fighting men who invaded and conquered England in 1066. Half a century earlier King Cnut had also conquered England and briefly created a vast Norse empire that stretched from Arctic Norway and Sweden to western Scotland and much of Ireland as well as the Faroes, Iceland, Greenland and the north-eastern seaboard of America.

Above: Viking ship on an early stamp of Estonia (top) and an Arctic Viking stamp from Greenland, showing an Indian arrowhead from a Viking grave and a Viking coin found in Maine.

Below: Floki and his raven on an Iceland miniature sheet, 2003.

Right: Miniature sheet from the Faroes showing the Vikings' Atlantic voyages.

Below: Tynwald, named from the Norse for "assembly field", celebrated its 1,000th anniversary in 1979.

Above: The name Viking remains a byword for exploration: the space mission to Mars, honoured by this American stamp, recalls the intrepid Atlantic voyages of 1,000 years ago.

Right: In 2000 Iceland issued two stamps featuring Viking architecture, including this reconstruction.

Above: Dragon figurehead of a Viking ship on a Danish stamp (left); Leif Erikson's statue in Reykjavik, Iceland, featured on an American stamp in 1968 celebrating his arrival in and exploration of Vinland, believed to be Maine (centre); Viking warriors and longships arriving on the Isle of Man on a stamp of 1973 (right).

While Hrolf the Ganger (later Duke Rollo of Normandy) was carving a large fief in the lower Seine basin, others penetrated the Mediterranean, colonized Sicily and Malta and got as far as Constantinople, which they knew as Miklagard (big garden). The followers of Rurik sailed north into the Black Sea and penetrated the valleys of the rivers Don, Dnieper and Volga, laying the foundations of Russia and the Ukraine. The indigenous peoples invited the strangers, whom they called Rus (red-haired) to bring law and order. Rurik answered the call and founded Novgorod (new town), the first of many cities that included Kiev and Smolensk. Viking ships can be found on the first stamps of Estonia as

well as on more recent issues from Poland, Ukraine and Lithuania.

Of all the lands the Vikings settled, Iceland has remained most faithful to Norse culture. They first arrived in 874, driving out or enslaving the Irish hermits they found there. Icelandic stamps recall their arrival at Reykjavik and the establishment in 930 of the Althing, the world's oldest democratic assembly.

Banished from Iceland in 980, Erik the Red and his followers sailed to the far west, where he discovered southern Greenland. Three sets and matching miniature sheets from Greenland in 1999–2000 tell the story of the rise and fall of the Arctic Vikings. Though Greenland was treeless, the abundant driftwood in its bays encouraged Erik's

son Leif the Lucky to look for land farther west. Around 1000 he discovered three territories, Helluland (Baffin Land), Markland (Newfoundland) and Vinland (wine country, believed to be Maine). Stamps from many countries, including Canada and the USA, acknowledge Leif Erikson's discoveries.

Many stamps of the Isle of Man, under Norse rule until 1266, allude to its Viking heritage. Stamps of Ireland also reflect Viking history, from the founding of Dublin to the Battle of Clontarf in 1014. Numerous stamps with a Viking theme have been issued by Denmark, Norway and Sweden, illustrating Viking craftsmanship from the carved stones of Gotland to the Jellinge style of curvilinear ornament.

1

2

3

4

5

6

7

8

9

10

11

BRITISH ISLES

Eighty years ago there was a single stamp-issuing authority for the whole of the British Isles. Today, there are five, and of these Royal Mail (which is responsible for the stamps of the United Kingdom) also produces country or regional stamps for England, Scotland, Wales and Northern Ireland. The first division came in 1922, when the 26 counties of southern Ireland became the Irish Free State. Wartime provisional issues in the Channel Islands were followed by the regional issues of 1958, and postal autonomy in 1969 for Guernsey and Jersey was followed by that for the Isle of Man in 1973. At first, regional stamps, apart from those of the offshore islands, were confined to Scotland, Wales and Northern Ireland, but England has also had its own stamps since 2001. In 1840, when Rowland Hill introduced adhesive postage stamps, no country name was necessary, and in deference to Britain's premier position, the Universal Postal Union decreed in 1874 that Britain alone would be exempt from the rule requiring the country name to appear on stamps. Ever since then, the head of the reigning monarch has been sufficient identification.

Left: In 1995 Royal Mail issued two stamps to celebrate the bicentenary of the birth of Sir Rowland Hill, portraying him as a young man and in old age. The latter also incorporated the Penny Black.

CONSERVATIVE POLICY

The design of the Penny Black (1840) was regarded as so perfect that it remained in use for 40 years, changing colour in 1841, adopting perforations in 1848 and acquiring check letters in all four corners in 1858 [1]. When the rate for postcards and printed matter was halved in 1870 the solution was to issue a stamp half the size of the Penny [2]. Separate stamps for revenue purposes were introduced in 1853, but postage and revenue duties were combined from 1881 onwards. As a result, the Penny Lilac [3] is arguably the world's greatest stamp, at least in terms of its being produced in quite astronomical quantities up to 1902.

Attempts to improve the appearance of the Victorian stamps led to the mainly bicoloured Jubilee series of 1887. Most of the designs were retained in the reign of Edward VII, with his profile substituted [4]. The stamps from 1880 onwards were mainly printed by letterpress; the George V series [5] was adapted to

photogravure in 1934 [6]. George V, a keen philatelist, requested that the intaglio process, which had been used from 1840 to 1879, should be revived for the high values, popularly known as the Seahorses [7].

FIRST COMMEMORATIVES

Although commemorative postal stationery had been produced in 1890 for the jubilee of penny postage, no adhesive commemorative stamps were issued until 1924, when new stamps were produced for the British Empire Exhibition [8], though sales were confined to the showgrounds. Britain produced very few commemoratives until the 1950s; those that were issued were confined to events of national, international or royal significance [9].

PHOTOGRAVURE

The definitives for the brief reign of Edward VIII broke new ground, using a design that was ideally suited to the photogravure process [10]. The clock turned back again a year later, when the definitives of Edward's brother George VI added the heraldic flowers of the United Kingdom [11]. For the Coronation stamp of 1937 the king and queen were portrayed side by side [12] whereas the Silver Wedding stamps of 1948 featured conjoined busts [13]. Special issues in the immediate postwar years were heavily symbolic in character [14].

EARLY ELIZABETHAN STAMPS

The first definitives of the reign of Elizabeth II, introduced in 1952, were based on a facing portrait of the queen by the photographer Dorothy Wilding [15]. One of the four designs for the Coronation stamps, issued in 1953, showed a full-face portrait with the coronation regalia [17]. The first definitives were superseded in 1967 by a series that returned to the style set in 1936 by the Edward VIII series, using an effigy of the queen sculpted in plaster by Arnold Machin [16].

The tempo of special issues increased in the 1960s; at the same time the first bicoloured stamps since 1910 appeared [18]. Symbolism gave way to pictorialism [19] and the first stamps to commemorate a historic personality

Below: Four stamps issued in 1964 depicted characters from Shakespeare's plays to mark his quatercentenary, and in 1966 Robert Burns was belatedly commemorated (bottom).

The World's Most Prolific Series

No one could have foreseen that the British definitives first issued in 1967, known as the Machins after the sculptor who modelled the queen's head, would become not only one of the world's longest-running series but also the most prolific of all time. Even on a simplified reckoning there have been well over 200 different denominations and colours since 1967.

The design was retained when Britain introduced decimal currency in 1971. It has been produced by several printers, using photogravure, lithography, intaglio and even letterpress and embossing, in gummed sheets and self-adhesive booklets. But taking into account all the variations in paper, perforation and phosphor bands, the number of collectable varieties runs into thousands.

appeared in 1964, although the Post Office argued that these marked the Shakespeare Quatercentenary Festival (a major national event) rather than honouring William Shakespeare himself. Nevertheless, protests in Scotland that the bicentenary of the birth of Robert Burns in 1959 had been ignored led to the issue of two commemorative stamps in 1966. That year, in which Post Office policy on special issues broke free, also witnessed stamps in honour of the football World Cup, including a last-minute "special" to celebrate England's victory [20], and the first British Christmas stamps, featuring two designs by young children – another novelty [21].

12

13

14

15   16

17

18

19

20   21

1

2

3

4

5

6

7

8

9

10

11

12

BRITISH REGIONAL ISSUES

Historically the British Isles consisted of three kingdoms (England, Scotland and Ireland), a principality (Wales) and three crown dependencies (Guernsey, Jersey and the Isle of Man). For more than 80 years after the first issue in 1940 the stamps produced by the British Post Office were used in all of these areas. Today, however, separate issues appear for use throughout the United Kingdom, in England, Scotland, Wales and Northern Ireland, and Guernsey, Alderney, Jersey, the Isle of Man and the Irish Republic, reflecting the different history, culture and outlook of each territory, yet often revealing subjects common to all. Many events and personalities that might not be considered to merit the issue of British stamps are celebrated by the offshore islands.

Left: The first of an Irish series issued in 1969 devoted to Irish Art reproduced The Last Supper and Crucifixion, *a stained glass window in the chapel of Eton College in England, designed by the Dublin-born artist Evie Hone.*

RECENT DEVELOPMENTS IN BRITISH STAMPS

In recent years the use of intaglio combined with photogravure has resulted in stamps with much sharper outlines. Many modern British stamps have designs that bleed off into the perforations, although the motifs are often obscure, such as the series of 2002 for the centenary of J.M. Barrie's *Peter Pan* [1]. Just how far British design moved in the latter part of the 20th century can be gauged by comparing the stamps of 1981 and 1986 celebrating the marriages of Prince Charles [2] and Prince Andrew [3]: the latter showed a much more informal approach to its subject. A series issued in 2003 entitled Extreme Endeavours broke new ground by portraying a living person other than royalty on a stamp – it showed Sir Edmund Hillary approaching the summit of Everest in 1953 [4].

REGIONALISM

Although the Channel Islands and the Isle of Man had been agitating for their own stamps since the 1930s, nothing was done to implement this until 1958, when distinctive stamps appeared not only in each of the offshore islands but also in Scotland, Wales and Northern Ireland. Like the "unified" series they bore no name, and all had to bear the Wilding portrait of the queen as their dominant feature. But the stamps, designed by local artists, gained their individuality from the inclusion of heraldic devices and local symbolism: the ducal crown and lily of Guernsey [5], the arms and mace of Jersey [6], the triskeles (three-legged symbol) and ring-chain of Man [7], the crown, thistle and saltire cross of Scotland [8], the dragon and leek of Wales [9] and the red hand of Ulster and flax blossom of Northern Ireland [10].

Following the advent of decimal currency in 1971 the remaining regions received standardized designs based on the Machin portrait with their national emblems in the upper left-hand corner [11–14]. The Manx series was discontinued in 1973 following the island's postal autonomy, but the others continued until 1999–2000, when different motifs were produced for each of four stamps covering the basic postal rates [15]. England joined in 2001.

IRISH FREE STATE

Following the Easter Rising (1916) and War of Independence (1919–21), the 26 counties in the south and west of

Ireland attained dominion status as the Irish Free State, which introduced its own stamps in 1922. At first British stamps were overprinted in Gaelic, using monastic uncials to signify the Provisional Government of Ireland. This was followed by an overprinted series inscribed "Saorstat Eireann" (Irish Free State) [16].

The first of the distinctive stamps appeared on December 6, 1922, the very day the Free State came into being. The designs, rich in Celtic symbolism, included one showing a map of an undivided Ireland [17]. They continued in use until 1968, when they were replaced by a series illustrating ancient Irish art treasures.

REPUBLIC OF IRELAND
The first step to complete independence came in 1936 when Eamon de Valera used the abdication of Edward VIII to draft a new constitution formally abandoning the Free State title in favour of Eire. In 1939 two stamps celebrated the 150th anniversary of the US constitution and the installation of the first US president – they were the first of many stamps that emphasized the close ties between Ireland and the USA [19]. The Republic of Ireland was formally inaugurated in April 1949 with the only stamp ever to use this title for the country [18]. Since then the name Eire has been retained, although the penchant for inscriptions in the Irish language (spoken by only 20 per cent of the population) has

Below: Irish stamps issued in 2004 celebrated the jubilee of Pope John Paul II (left) and combined the theme of Valentine's Day with the Chinese Year of the Monkey (right).

Bogus Fenians
In 1967 Ireland issued two stamps to mark the centenary of the Fenian rebellion in Canada and reproduced the stamps allegedly issued at that time. It was only after the issue that it transpired that the "stamps" were the bogus production of a Boston stamp dealer, "Honest Allan" Taylor.

greatly diminished. Interestingly, it has been used on recent stamps that reflect Ireland's enthusiasm for the European Union [20–21].

Special issues take pride in Irish inventions such as the air pump, the tractor, the steam turbine and the submarine [22]. Major naval figures include Commodore Barry, co-founder of the US Navy, and William Brown who founded the Argentinian Navy, while the exploits of the polar explorer Sir Ernest Shackleton were the subject of an issue in 2004. The pantheon of heroes and martyrs in the long struggle for independence range from the leaders of the ill-fated Easter Rising to Wolfe Tone, Michael Collins and Eamon de Valera. Literary figures are legion on stamps and range from medieval chroniclers to modern poets and playwrights. Sporting attractions range from Gaelic football and hurling to sailing [23], while scenery and wildlife are well covered. Ireland's devotion to Catholicism is featured prominently but other faiths have also been honoured. Since 1985 Ireland has issued stamps for Valentine's Day, more recent issues linking this to the Chinese Lunar New Year.

13

14

15

16

17

18

19

20

21

22

23

1

2

3

4

5

6

7

8

BRITISH OFFSHORE ISLANDS

The Isle of Man and the Channel Islands are not, strictly speaking, part of the United Kingdom but are dependencies of the Crown with their own parliamentary systems. The Isle of Man, situated between Ireland, Scotland and England, was under Norse rule until 1266, then briefly ruled by Scotland. The Earls of Derby and later the Dukes of Atholl were the Lords of Mann (*sic*) until 1765 when the island passed to the Crown. The Channel Islands comprise the bailiwicks of Guernsey (with its dependencies Alderney and Sark) and Jersey – the last remnants of the Duchy of Normandy. The Channel Islands were under German occupation during World War II.

Left: In 2004 Jersey issued a set of stamps in se-tenant *pairs to celebrate royal connections dating from the Norman Conquest. Each pair featured an island landmark alongside a portrait of the monarch in whose reign it was constructed.*

GUERNSEY

Both Guernsey and Jersey were occupied by German forces in May 1940 and were not freed until May 1945, during which time they ran out of British stamps. In Guernsey 2d stamps were bisected – as shown on a stamp of 1990 marking the 150th anniversary of adhesive stamps [1] – pending locally printed stamps [2], which ceased to be valid after the liberation. British stamps were used from then until 1969, when both bailiwicks took over their own postal services and introduced distinctive stamps. Guernsey's first definitives showed portraits of medieval rulers based on silver pennies [4].

The stamps of the offshore islands often focused on subjects overlooked by the British Post Office. Guernsey's stamps marked the St John Ambulance centenary [5] and John Wesley's ministry to the island [6] among many other events. Connections with nearby France have resulted in many stamps, such as the series of 1992 showing the cartoon character Asterix the Gaul [7]. In 2004 a set marking the 60th anniversary of D-Day (which bypassed the islands) paid tribute to the Red Cross ship *Vega*, which brought provisions after the island was cut off by the Allied advance in Normandy [8].

Guernsey's dependency Alderney has had "regional" stamps since 1983. Though distinctive to that island, they are also postally valid in Guernsey [9]. Circular stamps marking the centenary of FIFA in 2004 showed "playground school footie" [10].

JERSEY

As well as the armorial stamps issued in 1941–3 Jersey had a set of six pictorial definitives in 1943–4, designed by the well-known local artist Edmund Blampied but printed in Paris. The artist even managed to incorporate the royal monogram GR (flanking the value) under the noses of the Nazis [3].

Scenery and royal portraiture were featured in the definitives of 1969, which were re-issued in 1970–1 with decimal currency, followed by those of the parishes (1976–80) and the arms of the island's prominent families in 1981–8. Flowers, scenery and bird life have been covered in more recent sets.

One of Jersey's first special issues marked the 25th anniversary of the liberation, a subject that has been alluded to in several subsequent sets. Loyalty to the Crown is manifest in the many stamps portraying members of the British royal family: Elizabeth II's golden jubilee was celebrated in 2002 by stamps depicting the Crown Jewels [11]. Short sets are also produced frequently, covering numerous topics from tourist attractions to the island's remarkably diverse wildlife [12]. Since 1996 a £1 miniature sheet has been released annually to mark the Chinese New Year. Designed by Victor Ambrus, these stamps feature the relevant animal of the Chinese zodiac wearing a multicoloured scarf.

ISLE OF MAN

Although it had the option of postal autonomy in 1969, at the same time as Guernsey and Jersey, the Isle of Man did not follow suit until 1973. Following the style of the regional stamps of 1958–71, the first definitives that were issued incorporated the triskeles, the three-legged emblem of the island, and a Hiberno-Norse ring-chain motif. A second series, introduced in 1978, retained the triskeles but dispensed with the curvilinear ornament in order to place greater emphasis on landmarks of the island [13]. Later sets featured island birds (1983–5), Manx railways and trams (1988–92) and ships (1993–7), including the *Waverley*, the world's last

Below: Isle of Man stamps have featured Princess Margaret in Guide uniform (1985) and Queen Alexandra as Princess of Wales in 1885.

Puzzle Pieces

Two stamps that often puzzle collectors bear the portrait of George VI. Without a country name, they must be British, but they are not to be found under Great Britain in the catalogues. They were issued by Britain, in 1948, but celebrated the third anniversary of the liberation of the Channel Islands and are thus regarded as the forerunners of the modern stamps. Both depict islanders gathering seaweed for manure, based on paintings by the Jersey artist Edmund Blampied.

sea-going paddle-steamer, which plies the route between Glasgow and the Isle of Man [14].

Special issues have explored the island's Norse heritage but also proudly show the Manx contribution to the world at large. The Lifeboat Institution was founded by Sir William Hillary, a native of the island [15] while Manx connections with the USA have yielded several sets [16]. The Isle of Man granted votes to women in 1881, before anyone else [17]. Members of the British royal family, in their official roles, have been a popular subject, and include the late Princess Margaret and Queen Alexandra, depicted as Princess of Wales for the centenary of the servicemen's charity SSAFA (Soldiers, Sailors and Air Force Association).

The island is world-famous for its Tourist Trophy (TT) motorcycle races and these have appeared on a number of sets since 1973. The most recent combines them with the comedian George Formby, who made his screen debut in *No Limit* (1936), filmed during the 1935 TT races.

9

10

11

12

13

14

15

16

17

1

2

3

4

5

6

7

8

9

BRITISH EUROPEAN TERRITORIES

British stamps have been issued in a number of territories in continental Europe that it acquired as a result of various military campaigns. The first of these was Gibraltar, which had belonged to Spain since the expulsion of the Moors in 1492. Lying on the northern side of the straits at the western end of the Mediterranean, called the Pillars of Hercules by the ancients, it derived its name from Gibel Tarik (Tarik's rock) after the Moorish chief-

tain who seized it in the 8th century. It was captured by an Anglo-Dutch expedition in 1704 and remains British despite frequent attempts by Spain to regain it.

Left: The 1960 definitive series of Gibraltar featured a map of the straits, graphically illustrating the strategic importance of the Rock. The badge of the colony is, in fact, a bunch of keys, and it would be true to say that Gibraltar itself was the key to British mastery of the Mediterranean in both world wars, particularly during anti-submarine campaigns.

GIBRALTAR

The postal service was controlled from London until 1886 and used ordinary British stamps, identified only by an obliterator with the letter G in the centre. When control was transferred to Gibraltar itself the earliest distinctive stamps were merely those of Bermuda, overprinted [8]. Pictorial definitives were introduced gradually from 1931, using two-colour recess printing from 1928 to 1953 [1]. A more stylized approach was adopted in 1960 for a series showing the fauna and flora of the Rock, including the famous Barbary ape, the only higher primate found in Europe [2]. Ships [3], insects [4] and views of Gibraltar old and new were depicted on later issues.

Of the special issues, many alluded to the Great Siege of 1779–83 and the importance of the Rock as a British garrison and coaling station, but by the 1960s issues such as the Sea Angling Championships [5] were publicizing Gibraltar as a tourist destination. The first Christmas stamp reproduced a stained glass window from a Glasgow church [6].

Although only an associate member of the EU (through the UK), Gibraltar has produced a number of stamps that relate to it [7], including a sheetlet featuring the euro coinage, despite the fact that Gibraltar uses sterling currency.

MALTA

From the 16th century until 1798 Malta was the base of the Knights of St John, who had been ousted from Rhodes by the Turks. The French under Napoleon seized the island in 1798 but were driven out by a local rebellion assisted by the British, who then took over. Like Gibraltar, the postal service was run from London, and British stamps with the obliterator M were used until 1885, but from 1860 the island had a distinctive 1/2d stamp for local mail.

Pictorial stamps appeared from 1899 and included a view of the Grand Harbour at Valletta on the 1/4d stamps [9]. The strategic importance of the island fortress was shown during World War II, when Malta was besieged by Axis forces. George VI conferred the George Cross on the island in 1942, and thereafter it appeared on many of the stamps alongside the name [12]. Malta also received a commendation scroll from President Roosevelt [10].

Malta became an independent state in 1964, and its first definitive series featured landmarks illustrating its history since the Stone Age [11]. Many later stamps highlighted the glorious architecture and art from the time of the Knights [13]. On December 13, 1974, Malta became a republic within the Commonwealth [14]. In 1989 it hosted a summit conference between Presidents Bush and Gorbachev [16]. Its importance as a holiday destination goes back to the early 19th century, when Sir Walter Scott spent some time there [15]. More recent stamps have noted major international sporting events [17].

CYPRUS
During the Napoleonic Wars Britain gained control of the Ionian Islands in the Adriatic off the Greek coast. Ordinary British stamps were used in

Below: John F. Kennedy on a Cypriot stamp of 1965 (top). Stamps of Northern Cyprus cover international anniversaries (middle) as well as the annual Europa issues (bottom).

Refugee Tax
Compulsory stamps showing a child surrounded by barbed wire have been issued with various dates since 1977, in aid of refugees from Northern Cyprus.

Cephalonia, Corfu and Zante until 1859, when a set was produced of three undenominated stamps portraying Queen Victoria, with their values determined by their colour [18]. These stamps were withdrawn in 1864 when Britain handed the three islands over to Greece.

The Treaty of Berlin (1878) assigned the administration of Cyprus to Britain, and overprinted British stamps [19] were used until 1881. The island was nominally Turkish until 1925, when it was made a British crown colony. Pictorial definitives, dwelling heavily on the Greek classical period, appeared from 1934.

Cyprus became a republic within the Commonwealth in 1960. Although stamps since then have mostly alluded to the glories of its Greek heritage, issues mourning the death of John F. Kennedy quoted his speech on self-determination for Cyprus. Sadly, Cyprus was torn apart by ethnic violence, leading to the Turkish invasion and partition of the island in 1974. A breakaway regime known as the Turkish Republic of Northern Cyprus has had its own stamps since the island was partitioned. Mail to and from Northern Cyprus is routed through Mersin in mainland Turkey.

10

11

12

13

14

15

16

17

18

19

1

2

3

4

5

6

7

8

9

10

11

THE BENELUX COUNTRIES

Belgium, the Netherlands and Luxembourg, historically known collectively as the Low Countries, were at one time ruled by the same monarch, reigning as King of the Netherlands and Grand Duke of Luxembourg, but in 1831 the Belgians seceded and elected Prince Leopold of Saxe-Coburg-Gotha as their king. When William III of the Netherlands died in 1890 the union with Luxembourg was dissolved because Salic Law forbade the succession of a female. The grand duchy passed to Duke Adolf of Nassau, the nearest male heir. When Grand Duke William IV died in 1912 the law was changed to allow his daughter Adelaide to succeed to the throne. All three countries were overrun by the Germans in 1940; when they were liberated in 1944 they decided to form a commercial union known as Benelux.

Left: Since 1964 the Benelux countries have issued stamps in a common design to celebrate important anniversaries of the union, which served as a model for the EEC and EU.

BELGIUM

Adhesive postage stamps were adopted in Belgium in 1849, followed by Luxembourg and the Netherlands in 1852. All three countries have many similarities and parallels in their stamps, reflecting their common historical, political and cultural heritage. Each country has been responsible for innovations. While Luxembourg was the first country to issue stamp booklets (1895) and miniature sheets (1921), Belgium pioneered railway parcel stamps (1879) and continues to produce them to this day [1]. Between 1893 and 1914 stamps were issued with labels attached to signify that mail was not to be delivered on Sundays [2].

In August 1914 the Germans invaded Belgium in violation of the Treaty of London (1839), which had guaranteed its neutrality. The definitive series of 1919–20 shows Albert I wearing a steel helmet, alluding to his command of the Belgian Army during World War I [3].

All three Benelux countries have frequently issued stamps with a charity premium, a recurring theme being the younger members of the royal family. Baudouin of Belgium made his philatelic debut on the Anti-tuberculosis Fund stamps of 1936 [5]. His mother, Queen Astrid, was killed in a car crash in 1935; a black mourning stamp [6] was followed by a set in different colours but with the same portrait edged in black. A stamp of 1957 for the 50th anniversary of the Edith Cavell Nursing School recalls the British nurse, shot by the Germans as a spy in World War I [7].

The Low Countries were overrun by the Germans in 1940. Belgium celebrated its liberation in 1944 with definitives showing the lion rampant and "V" for victory [4]. Since 1893 Belgian stamps have been inscribed in both French and Flemish, but two different versions of the liberation stamps were produced, with the titles rendered as "Belgie-Belgique" and "Belgique-Belgie" to satisfy Flemish and Walloon national pride. Despite deep-seated differences between the two communities, Belgium has been a model for European unity.

Brussels is the seat of the European Parliament, and the first elections were celebrated on stamps of 1979 [10]. Belgium's main artistic contribution to contemporary philately has been the extensive use of images from strip cartoons and comics [8].

NETHERLANDS

Holland remained neutral in World War I but during World War II it was under German occupation from May 14, 1940, until May 6, 1945. Dutch Nazis formed a government that collaborated closely with the invaders, reflected in the wartime definitives showing ancient Germanic symbols [12]. Charity stamps were issued in 1942 – a device to raise money for the Netherlands Legion, a unit of the Waffen SS [9]. The Dutch royal family escaped to England and thence to Canada, and stamps printed in England were used by the exiled administration. Following the liberation in 1945 they were put on sale in the Netherlands.

Since 1866 the vast majority of Dutch stamps have been printed by Johan Enschedé of Haarlem, using a wide range of processes and techniques. In the postwar period Dutch stamp design has been particularly innovative, at times verging on the avant-garde. The silver jubilee of Queen Juliana was appropriately marked by a stamp of 1973 with a silver surface. In 1970, the Netherlands broke new ground with the world's first stamps to be designed by computer [11]. Recent Dutch stamps have ranged from the minimalist [13] to the strident [14], though the design of the stamp honouring Anne Frank was restrained and dignified [15]. Since 1934 special stamps have been issued by the International Court of Justice [16].

LUXEMBOURG

The stamps of the grand duchy were introduced in 1852 (at the same time as those of the Netherlands) and the first issues portrayed William III as grand duke. Later issues paralleled those of Belgium and the Netherlands and showed the same penchant for charity stamps [17], with causes ranging from child welfare to the protection of nature and other worthy causes. In March 1945 liberation from German occupation was marked by stamps thanking the United States [18].

Birth, Marriage and Death

The Netherlands pioneered special stamps for business mail in 1997 and followed this up with a stamp for the announcement of a baby's birth. In January 1998 a stamp symbolizing light across darkness was launched for bereavement notices and condolence, while March the same year saw a distinctive self-adhesive stamp for the announcement of weddings or congratulations to the happy couple. Such stamps have since been emulated elsewhere.

Luxembourg still makes extensive use of intaglio engraving [19] in both portrait and scenic stamps. Most of its stamps are inscribed in French, but occasionally Letzeburgisch (a German dialect) is used [20]. Undenominated stamps lettered A or B indicate first or second class postage [21].

As a founder member of the European Coal and Steel Community – the forerunner of the European Community – the importance of Luxembourg as an administrative centre is reflected in many of the stamps it has issued in more recent years, while historic sets are reminders of the role of the grand duchy in the Burgundian dominions of the Middle Ages.

12

13

14

15

16

17

18

19

20

21

1

2

3

4

5

6

7

8

9

10

11

12

SWITZERLAND

The Swiss Confederation was formed in 1291, when Nidwalden, Schwyz and Uri joined forces to resist Austria. Its independence was confirmed in 1648 and today it consists of 24 cantons, each with its own laws and customs. Constitutions of 1848 and 1874 created a union modelled on that of the USA. This gives the cantons considerable autonomy except in defence, external relations and the postal service.

Left: Zurich and Geneva, had their own stamps as early as 1843, while Basle adopted a stamp in 1845. A federal postal system was not created until 1850, with stamps for the entire country.

A PROBLEM SOLVED

The problem of providing stamps for a country with four official languages (French, German, Italian and Romansch) was solved by inscribing them in Latin: the name Helvetia was derived from the Celtic tribe that inhabited the Alpine regions at the dawn of the Christian era. For the same reason, it was important to avoid heraldry or symbolism associated with any particular canton, so the Swiss cross and allegorical figures were adopted [1].

A few stamps, mainly for the Red Cross and the National Fête, were inscribed "Confoederatio Helvetica" [3] but the majority stuck to "Helvetia" [4]. Out of the National Fête issues developed the annual charity stamps inscribed "Pro patria" (For the fatherland) from 1952, usually adopting attractive themes [2]. Since 1913 Switzerland has also produced stamps each year inscribed "Pro juventute" (For youth) and often featuring subjects of interest to young people [5]. In recent years some quirky stamps have appeared, such as the 2000–1 definitives showing typical Swiss scenes in the form of snowstorm paperweights [6].

Until 1932 stamps were printed at the Federal Mint in Berne but thereafter responsibility passed to the postal service, which had its own printing works. Many stamps from that time until 2002 were also produced by the private firm of Courvoisier, which built up a global reputation for fine colour photogravure.

AN INTERNATIONAL HEADQUARTERS

Despite the fact that Switzerland had been the seat of the United Nations and its predecessor, the League of Nations, since 1922, this traditionally neutral country did not become a member of the UN until 2002 [7]. The League of Nations had its headquarters on the outskirts of Geneva and until it was dissolved in 1945 it used Swiss stamps overprinted for the purpose [8]. From 1923 until 1950 Swiss stamps were also overprinted for other international bodies located in Geneva, such as the International Labour Office [9], but distinctive stamps [10] have been provided since then. Subsequently stamps were also provided for the use of the International Education Office [13], the World Health Organization [11], the World Meteorological Organization [12], the International Refugees Organization, the Universal Postal Union in Berne [15], the International Telecommunications Union [14], the World Intellectual Property Organization and the Geneva headquarters of the United Nations itself, occupying the Palais des Nations [16], which originally housed the League. (For stamps issued by the UN from its headquarters in New York, *refer to* the stamps of the United States Possessions and Territories.)

Switzerland has been in the forefront of philatelic technology in recent years, pioneering a number of gimmicks that have hit the headlines. A sheet marking the centenary of the Swiss chocolate industry resembled a bar of chocolate, with simulated wrapping in the silver foil sheet margins. The stamps gave off the aroma of chocolate when gently rubbed. A set of five stamps in 2002 celebrating the centenary of the teddy bear was produced in different shapes for each stamp. In 2000, it broke new ground with the world's first textile stamp, a self-adhesive Fr5 stamp embroidered by a firm in St Gallen. This has since been copied by other countries. In 2004 Switzerland even produced a Fr5 stamp made from a square section of real wood, the design being the actual grain of the timber.

LIECHTENSTEIN

Associated with Switzerland is the tiny principality of Liechtenstein, founded in 1719. It achieved autonomy in 1806 and became fully independent in 1866. It originally used Austrian stamps but began issuing its own in 1912, although Austria continued to be responsible for the external postal service and its stamps could also be used in Liechtenstein until 1921.

The earliest stamps of the principality included a reference to the Austrian Post at the foot [17]. The Austrian connection ended in 1920 and thereafter stamps made no reference to Austria. Instead, Liechtenstein became aligned with Switzerland and in 1921 it adopted Swiss currency. At first its stamps continued to be printed in Vienna, but after 1924 they were usually printed in Switzerland, either by the postal printing works in Berne using the intaglio process [19], or in photogravure by Courvoisier.

Many of the stamps feature paintings and sculpture in the art collections of the Prince of Liechtenstein, regarded as some of the finest in the world [18; 20]. This tiny country, with a population of only 30,000, may be one of Europe's leading financial centres, but it also has a largely rural economy depending on traditional occupations such as cheese-making [21]. The Ruritania-like quality of Liechtenstein is also reflected in the many stamps featuring knightly escutcheons, with antique lettering to match.

Below: The garnished escutcheon of Georg Marxer, 1745, appeared in the first set devoted to the arms of the Bailiffs of Liechtenstein (1980).

13

14

15

16

17

18

19

20

21

GERMAN STATES

Germany was a large part of the Holy Roman Empire, a loose federation of about 1,800 kingdoms, principalities, duchies and free cities that endured until 1806. After 1812 Germany was reduced to a federation of 32 states, of which Prussia was the strongest. From 1849 onwards many states issued their own stamps. Under Bismarck, Prussia absorbed several states in the wars of 1864 and 1866 and after it defeated France in the war of 1870–1 the German Empire (Deutsches Reich) was proclaimed at Versailles, completing the process of unification. The Prussian postmaster General Heinrich von Stephan, used his experience of unifying the postal services of the German states to create the Universal Postal Union in 1874.

Left: The highest denomination of Germany's definitive sets of 1900 and 1902 portrayed Kaiser Wilhelm II making a speech at the celebrations marking the 25th anniversary of the German Empire in 1896.

Only half the states in existence before the unification of Germany issued their own stamps; others relied on the services provided by the Counts of Thurn and Taxis from their headquarters in Frankfurt. Separate issues were needed for each currency – which was groschen in the northern states and kreuzer in the southern states – and the designs for these areas had a rectangular or circular format respectively [1–2]. In 1867 the Thurn and Taxis network was purchased by the North German Confederation.

INDIVIDUAL STATES
The individuality of the various states was reflected in their stamps, particularly in the early period. Numeral designs were originally favoured but heraldic motifs soon came into fashion, those of the grand duchy of Baden (1862–71) being typical [3].

Bavaria's first stamps concentrated on numerals but after the accession of the mad King Ludwig II it adopted the fashion for stamps with the coat of arms embossed in colourless relief [5]. Bavaria continued to have its own postal service until 29 April 1920, the last series appearing earlier that year, a curious blend of avant-garde art and traditional Catholic values [4].

At the other extreme was the Hanseatic town of Bergedorf, which introduced stamps in 1861. Each was printed in black on different colours and in different sizes in ascending order of value [6]. From 1420 to 1867 the town belonged jointly to Lübeck and Hamburg, alluded to in the initials in the corners of the stamps.

World Firsts
The Prince Regent Luitpold finally appeared on stamps in 1911, marking his 90th birthday. These stamps have the distinction of being the first in the world to be produced by photo-lithography (left). Luitpold was succeeded as regent by his son, who ascended the throne as Ludwig III in 1913. Ludwig's stamps also broke new ground, being the world's first to be produced by the photogravure process (right).

1

2

3

4

5

6

7

8

9

10

11

12

13

14

The imperial free city of Bremen issued stamps from 1855 to 1867, showing the civic arms [7]. The duchy of Brunswick had stamps showing the white horse emblem from 1852 [9], switching to embossed stamps in 1861. Hamburg, a free city from 1510, adopted stamps in 1859, all showing its triple-towered badge [8]. Lübeck, a free city since 1226, joined Hamburg in 1241 to form the Hanseatic League. Armorial stamps were used from 1859 [11] and embossed from 1863 to 1867.

The kingdom of Hanover had armorial stamps from 1851 to 1855, then switched to a numeral design for pfennig values [12] and a profile of George V for the higher denominations. Hanover was on the losing side in the Austro-Prussian War of 1866 and its stamps were suppressed following annexation by Prussia. From 1856 the grand duchy of Mecklenburg-Schwerin issued stamps that could be divided into quarters [10]. The adjoining state of Mecklenburg-Strelitz introduced stamps only in 1864, using the embossed style then in fashion [13] and a similar pattern was followed by the grand duchy of Oldenburg [14].

Prussia adopted stamps in 1850, originally portraying Friedrich Wilhelm IV [15], but his successor Wilhelm I preferred embossed armorial stamps from 1861, setting the trend for other states whose stamps were printed at the Prussian State Printing Works in Berlin. Saxony began with numerals, progressed to royal portraiture and from 1863 used embossed stamps in the Prussian manner [16]. Schleswig and Holstein were German duchies ruled by the Danish monarch but they rebelled in 1848 and issued a stamp in 1850 [17]. In 1864 Austria and Prussia invaded and stamps were issued in each duchy [18]. Disagreement between the allies led to the war of 1866.

The kingdom of Württemberg began issuing stamps in 1851, using numerals followed by embossed arms [19] and numerals again from 1869. Although it joined the German Empire in 1871 it had its own postal service,

British Outpost
The strategic island of Heligoland was seized by Britain during the Napoleonic wars, but its postal service was operated by Hamburg. and stamps portraying Queen Victoria were printed in Berlin, with dual sterling and German values. The island was ceded to Germany on 9 August 1890.

with distinctive stamps, until 1902. When its posts were absorbed into the Reich service Württemberg continued to issue special stamps for government correspondence until 1920 and municipal service stamps until 1924 – the only states' issue to feel the effects of hyperinflation in 1923 [20]. There were even commemorative issues in each category for the jubilee of William II in 1916, featuring the royal arms and the king's portrait respectively [22]. The only states' pictorials were the official mail series of March 1920, showing views of Stuttgart, Ulm, Eilwangen or Tubingen [21].

THE MOVE TOWARDS UNIFICATION
The North German Confederation, led by Prussia, was established on 1 January 1868, and the stamps of the member states were replaced by numeral designs [23] in groschen or kreuzer currencies. A special stamp was provided for Hamburg which used its own schillings [24]. Stamps issued in French currency were produced for use in Alsace and Lorraine in 1870, absorbed into the Reich in 1871 [25]. Collectors also regard the semi-official air stamps as states' issues [26].

15   16
17   18
19   20
21
22   23
24   25

26

GERMAN REICH

The period from the unification of Germany in 1871 to the fall of Hitler in 1945 was one of immense material progress accompanied by political instability. Pulling together a ramshackle conglomeration of states with their own distinct history and culture was a superhuman feat, although it led to autocracy under Kaiser Wilhelm II. Germany's demand for "a place in the sun" and its commercial rivalry with Britain and France led inevitably to World War I. Resentment at the harsh terms of the 1919 Treaty of Versailles and mass unemployment in turn led to the rise of fascism. The collapse of the monarchies in 1918 had no impact on stamps, which were still inscribed "Deutsches Reich".

Left: Adolf Hitler, an Austrian who served in the Bavarian Army, founded the National Socialist German Workers' Party. Briefly imprisoned for an attempted coup in 1923, he gained power constitutionally in 1933, but rapidly destroyed German democratic institutions. Stamps were issued for his birthday each April, usually with exorbitant premiums for the Hitler Culture Fund. Nazi Germany often used philately for propaganda.

THE EMPIRE

The earliest stamps of the empire featured the German eagle [1], but in 1899 a series portrayed the actress Anna Führing in the role of Germania [2], epitomizing the aggressive style of the kaiser. Remarkably these stamps survived the empire by three years. Under the Weimar Republic the imperial inscription remained but definitives emphasized the working classes [3].

Germany began to suffer the effects of inflation during World War I and it escalated in the early 1920s, reaching its peak in November 1923. The 1 milliard (thousand million) mark stamp [4], released only in Bavaria, is known as the Hitler Provisional because it was issued a few hours before he staged his *putsch* in Munich on 9 November. There were few special issues in the Weimar period but significantly many had premiums in aid of the welfare fund to alleviate poverty [5].

THE THIRD REICH

By the beginning of 1933 the Nazis were the largest party in the Reichstag and President Hindenburg had no alternative but to appoint Hitler as chancellor. Once in power, the Nazis dissolved parliament, banned all political parties except themselves and imprisoned communists, socialists, trades unionists and anyone who dissented from their political philosophy. Hitler was hell-bent on reversing the terms of the Treaty of Versailles. Stamps of the 1930s became increasingly propagandistic, publicizing the annual party rallies [6] and showing the führer in belligerent mood. The stamps for the party rally of 1937 [7] formed a miniature sheet whose slogan translated as "He who will save a nation must think heroically." Other stamps charted the expansion of the Reich, from the restoration of the Saar in 1935 [8] to the union with Austria in 1938 [9].

Later in 1938 Hitler demanded the Sudetenland, the German part of Czechoslovakia; Czech stamps were overprinted "Wir sind frei!" (We are free!) with the swastika [10]. Danzig was subsequently absorbed into the Reich on 1 September 1939, its stamps being suitably overprinted [11], and the invasion of Poland the same day was the first act of World War II.

The definitives continued to portray Hindenburg until 1941, when Hitler put his own portrait on the regular

A Breakaway State

In 1923, when Germany was wracked by inflation, the French seized the opportunity to detach the Rhineland (then occupied by its troops) and create an independent buffer state known as the Rhineland Republic. German stamps were overprinted "R.R." for this purpose, but protests from Britain, the USA and Germany itself led to the plan being aborted.

series [12]. Wartime stamps continued the strident Nazi messages [13–14]. As the tide of war turned, Hitler renamed his empire Grossdeutsches Reich (Great German State) and this was expressed on the last issues of the Nazi regime [16]. Ironically the very last stamps, issued as the Russians were advancing through the ruins of Berlin, honoured stormtroopers of the SA and SS [15].

PLEBISCITES

After World War I many districts of the empire from Schleswig to Silesia held plebiscites to decide their future. Under Allied supervision plebiscites took place in Allenstein (East Prussia) and Marienwerder (West Prussia), both of which voted to remain German. Memel was placed under French administration but was seized by Lithuania in 1923. Schleswig was divided into two zones, the north voting to return to Denmark and the south voting to remain in Germany. Upper Silesia was partitioned between Germany and Poland. Distinctive stamps were issued in each district. The Saar, a special case, fell to the French, who wished to secure the rich iron and

coal industries. German and Bavarian stamps were overprinted [18] pending pictorials printed in Paris [17]. When a plebiscite was finally held in 1935 the district reverted to Germany.

FREE CITY OF DANZIG

The Baltic port of Danzig had been part of Poland for centuries though it enjoyed considerable autonomy and its population was predominantly German, the descendants of traders who had arrived in search of amber. In 1795 it came under Prussian rule, following the third partition of Poland.

By the early 20th century Danzig was the capital of West Prussia and its inhabitants 95 per cent German, but the newly reconstituted Poland demanded the return of Danzig, a vital outlet for Polish trade and commerce. Under the Treaty of Versailles, the problem of satisfying Polish demands was met by creating the Free City of Danzig, in which Poland enjoyed considerable rights. This source of friction between Germany and Poland was violently resolved when Hitler invaded Poland and Danzig once more became the capital of West Prussia. The politics of the Free City mirrored those of Germany itself, with the local Nazis in power from 1934 onwards.

German stamps were overprinted [19] pending the supply of distinctive stamps showing the crowned double cross or a Hanseatic cogge [20]. The special issues reflected the essentially German character of Danzig, including a set for the 150th birth anniversary of the philosopher Schopenhauer [21].

OCCUPATION

By 1942 Hitler had overrun most of Europe, from the Pyrenees to the Arctic, from the Atlantic to the Black Sea. German definitives were overprinted for use in many areas, from Alsace [23] and Lorraine [22], which were soon reabsorbed into the Reich, to large parts of Russia, redesignated Ostland [24]. After the capitulation of Italy, the Germans occupied territories formerly under Italian control [25].

14
15
16
17
18
19
20
21
22
23
24
25

1

2

3

4

5

6

7

8

9

10

11

12

13

POSTWAR GERMANY

In May 1945 a defeated Germany was partitioned by the Americans, British, French and Russians, and the capital Berlin was divided into four sectors. What began as a scheme to prevent a united Germany from ever again threatening the free world soon turned into the battleground on which the Cold War was mainly fought. Germany split into East and West in 1948 and the breach widened with the Soviet blockade of Berlin and later the erection of the Berlin Wall, which never deterred the truly determined from escaping to the West.

Left: In 1965 the Federal Republic commemorated 20 years of refugees fleeing westward with this 20pf stamp. Mail addressed to the Democratic Republic bearing this stamp was either returned to sender or had the offending stamp painted over.

FOUR-POWER CONTROL

For the Anglo-American zones stamps inscribed "AM" (Allied Military) with a large "M" (Military) in the centre and "Deutschland" at the foot [1] were brought over from the USA, later reprinted in Britain and ultimately in Germany itself. The French had a general series [2] followed by separate stamps for Baden, Württemberg and the Rhineland-Palatinate [3]. The six regions of the Soviet zone each released their own stamps in 1945–6 [4], and many towns also produced their own issues. From February 1946 until 1948 the Soviet zone used the stamps of the Anglo-American zones [5].

Growing disparity in the value of the mark in the East and West led to currency reform in 1948, but it also precipitated the split between East and West. Stamps were overprinted to distinguish their respective use [6–7]. The three western zones became the Federal German Republic in September 1949 and a month later the Soviets created the German Democratic Republic. The western sectors of Berlin became a Land (province) of the Federal Republic on 1 September 1950, and this issued its own stamps until 1990.

FEDERAL REPUBLIC

Stamps with the inscription "Deutsche Bundespost" (German Federal Post) were used in the West from 1950 [8].

From time to time trouble flared between the two republics when the Bundespost issued stamps showing places in the East, such as the Treptow Gate in Neubrandenburg as part of the definitive series of 1964–9, whose theme was 12 centuries of German architecture [9]. One of the first multi-coloured stamps marked the centenary of the arrival of the political refugee Carl Schurz in America [10].

After the highly propagandistic stamps of the Third Reich, West German stamps concentrated on historical events and personages. Definitives bore famous buildings or presidential portraits, accident prevention (1971–4) and industry and technology (1975–82). From 1986–7 onwards two series ran side by side, featuring famous women (sheet stamps) and tourist attractions (coil stamps).

WEST BERLIN

Stamps used in West Berlin were often identical to those in West Germany, but with the inscription "Deutsche Bundespost Berlin". However, Berlin often produced distinctive stamps, especially with a theme that was particular to the city. One of the earliest issues featured the Freedom Bell, based on the Liberty Bell and the gift of the American people [12]. Other stamps charted the rebuilding of the city and such landmarks as the Kaiser Wilhelm

Memorial Church, preserved in ruins as a reminder of the war [14]. The Brandenburg Gate, shown on many stamps of the GDR as well as West Berlin [13], served as a symbol of the divided city.

Both the Federal Republic and Berlin issued stamps mourning John F. Kennedy [15], whose impassioned speech at the Berlin Wall struck a chord with his audience. The later stamps of Berlin highlighted the cultural heritage of the former German capital [16] but also paid frequent tribute to the Allies, whose airlift of supplies broke the Soviet blockade of 1949 [17].

DEMOCRATIC REPUBLIC

The stamps of East Germany reflected the doctrinaire politics of the regime almost to the end, with stamps commemorating Communist figureheads [18] and symbolism strongly redolent of the USSR in the Stalinist era [19]. In many ways, the GDR was the conscience of Germany, tackling issues – such as Kristallnacht, when the Nazis destroyed Jewish shops and synagogues [20] – that were ignored or glossed over in the West, such as the atrocities committed in the concentration camps. At the same time, however, many reflected the totalitarian and militaristic nature of the GDR itself [21–22].

In 1973–5 a definitive series featured famous buildings. The last definitive series, introduced in 1980, consisted of the same designs but in a reduced size [23]. A long-running series consisted of stamps issued each spring and autumn to mark the world-famous Leipzig Fair. Normally a pair of stamps was released in each case but an exception was the set of four with matching miniature sheet issued in 1965 to mark the 800th anniversary of Leipzig and an international stamp exhibition held at the same time.

The Ostmark was replaced by the Deutschmark on 1 July 1990, necessitating new stamps simply inscribed "Deutsche Post" [24]. Stamps bearing the letters "DDR" remained valid for postage until 31 December 1991 [25].

History Repeats Itself

After World War II, the Saar was administered by France from May 1945 and had distinctive stamps from January 1947, French currency being introduced in November 1947. The Saar reverted to Germany in 1957 and stamps were then issued with the German inscription "Saarland", often in the same designs as those of West Germany, until July 1959, when German currency was introduced.

UNITED GERMANY

On 3 October 1990, the Democratic Republic was absorbed into the Federal Republic and thereafter only one type of stamp was used throughout Germany. One of the first sets to appear was a pair issued on 6 November that year celebrating the opening of the Berlin Wall [11]. Since 1995 stamps have been simply inscribed "Deutschland".

A casualty of reunification was the separate postal service of West Berlin, whose stamps were discontinued in September 1990. The following January, a stamp of united Germany celebrated the bicentenary of the Brandenburg Gate. Thereafter Berlin, as the restored capital of the whole country, featured prominently. Many stamps since 1991 have portrayed historic figures. In 2003 a stamp portrayed Georg Elser, the man who tried to kill Hitler at a Munich rally in 1939, and previously a stamp showing the date "20 Juli 1944" behind bars alluded to the bomb plot of that year – both rare examples of Germany coming to terms with its past. Stamps of recent years have been more overtly thematic.

14   15

16   17

18   19

20   21

22

23

24   25

1

2

3

4

5

6

7

8

9

10

11

AUSTRIA AND HUNGARY

At the height of its power, the Habsburg Empire occupied most of the basin of the Danube, from Bohemia to Transylvania, from Galicia to the Adriatic. It was a conglomeration of many races, tongues and creeds, held together on the principle of "divide and rule". Hungary had been an independent kingdom since the 10th century but in the 17th century accepted Habsburg protection against the Turks. In 1848, the year of revolutions, the Hungarians rose in a revolt that was suppressed by Austria aided by Russia. Thereafter Hungary was absorbed by Austria, a situation that was inherently unstable. So completely assimilated were these countries that they used the same stamps when they were adopted in 1850 [1]. After the *Ausgleich* (compromise) of 1867 both countries had their own stamps.

Left: The embodiment of the empire was Franz Joseph I, who succeeded in the aftermath of the 1848 revolution, at the age of 18, and ruled his ramshackle dominions for almost 70 years. His private life was marred by tragedy: the execution of his brother Maximilian, the assassination of his wife and the suicide of his son Rudolf.

AUSTRIAN REPUBLIC

The empire survived the aged kaiser by only two years, collapsing at the end of World War I. Not only did Hungary break away, but Transylvania passed to Romania and the Alpine and Adriatic provinces went to Italy, while entirely new countries such as Czechoslovakia and Yugoslavia were created and Poland was reconstituted. Austria, once the heart of a mighty empire, was reduced to the size of Scotland, with a similar population. There was a strong movement in favour of union with Germany, and in 1918–21 stamps were actually inscribed "Deutschösterreich" (German Austria). In 1920 they were overprinted "Hochwasser" to raise money for flood relief [3]. The definitive issues of 1934–8 featured provincial costumes [2].

In the 1930s Hitler, the Austrian-born dictator of Germany, had ambitions to add his native land to the Third Reich, and in 1934 the Nazis murdered the Austrian chancellor, Engelbert Dollfuss [4]. The last stamps of the republic were the first Christmas stamps, issued in 1937. People imagined they could see the baleful image of Hitler in the rose [5], an ill omen.

In April 1938, on the eve of a plebiscite, the Nazis marched into Austria without a shot being fired.

Austria was liberated by the Allies in May 1945. The Russians issued stamps showing the hammer and sickle [6] while the French, British and Americans had an innocuous posthorn design, produced in Washington [7]. The second republic was proclaimed soon afterwards. Costumes were the subject of a long-running series [8], rendered this time in photogravure. Various subjects, from scenery and architecture to myths and legends, have been used since then, the current issue being aimed at the tourist industry [9].

Austria is a land of music, and numerous stamps from 1922 onwards have honoured the great composers such as Haydn, Mozart, Beethoven and Strauss, while very recent stamps have portrayed Oscar Peterson [10], Riccardo Muti and Seiji Ozawa as well as the Rolling Stones. Nostalgia for the Habsburgs has seen the release of several stamps portraying Franz Joseph and his wife Elisabeth, assassinated in 1898. Appropriately, "Sissi", as she was affectionately known, is the subject of a new musical [11].

HUNGARY

For a few years after the creation of the dual monarchy in 1867, Hungary and Austria had identical stamps that merely portrayed the man known in one country as Kaiser Franz Joseph and in the other as Kiraly Ferenc Joszef. The only inscription was the abbreviation "kr", denoting *kreuzer* in Austria and *krajczar* in Hungary. The first specifically Hungarian stamps were intended for the imperial tax on newspapers that enabled transmission free of postage. A series portraying the monarch with the Hungarian arms below but no inscriptions appeared in 1871 and it was not until 1874 that stamps bore the country name. A new currency, based on the *korona* (crown) of 100 *filler* was adopted in 1900; stamps thus denominated showed the aged king wearing the Hungarian crown or the Turul, the mythical bird of the Magyar people.

A series depicting harvesters was introduced in 1915 and bore the inscription "Magyar Kir. Posta" (Hungarian Royal Post). The design endured until 1926 but underwent changes of inscription and various overprints reflecting the turmoil of 1919–24. At the end of World War I, Hungary went rapidly from a people's republic [12] to a soviet republic under Bela Kun [13]. A right-wing coup led by Admiral Horthy established a separate government at Szeged [14] and when the communists were driven out their overprints were blotted out by a wheatsheaf [15]. Hungary remained "a kingdom without a king, ruled by an admiral without a navy", as the continued abbreviation for *kiralyi* (royal) in the later stamps indicated [16].

History repeated itself after World War II (in which Hungary had been allied to Nazi Germany) when a provisional government [18] was followed by a republic (1946) and a people's republic (1949). In the communist era Hungary gained notoriety for its large number of stamps, including strictly limited editions of imperforate varieties. From 1949 until 1990, when communism collapsed, stamps were

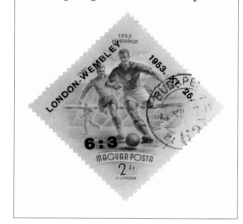
merely inscribed "Magyar Posta" [19–20] but since then "Magyarorszag" (Hungarian State) has been used. The output has been much more restrained but includes themes previously banned. Recent issues include stamps honouring Raoul Wallenberg, the Swedish diplomat who saved the lives of many Jews but died in a Soviet camp [17] and the countdown to Hungarian entry into the European Union in 2004 [21].

MISCELLANEOUS ISSUES
Stamps inscribed "K.u.K. Militärpost" were used in Bosnia and Herzegovina (*see* Yugoslavia) but stamps inscribed "K.u.K. Feldpost" were employed in World War I [22]. As well as a general issue there were separate sets for the occupation of Italy, Montenegro, Romania and Serbia, while stamps issued by the French, Romanians and Serbs marked their occupation of Hungarian territory. The Danube Steam Navigation Company had its own stamps for mail carried on its steamers along the river and in the Black Sea ports, originally denominated in kreuzer but later in the international currency of gold centimes [23].

1

2

3

4

5

6

7

8

9

10

11

CZECHOSLOVAKIA

Czechoslovakia, in the heart of Europe, was a creation of the Treaty of Versailles, uniting the Czechs of Bohemia and Moravia (formerly under Austria) with the Slovaks and Ruthenes (formerly under Hungary). The inclusion of three million Germans and 700,000 Hungarians created problems in the late 1930s. The Czechs and Slovaks spoke very similar languages, but culturally, historically and economically they were very different. They won their independence in 1918 as a reward for helping the Allies against the Central Powers.

Left: The architect of the new country was a Moravian, Thomas Masaryk, who campaigned before and during the war to secure self-determination for Czechoslovakia.

PREWAR REPUBLIC

Before the creation of the republic, the Czech legions were present at the Western Front, in Italy and in eastern Europe, fighting on the Allied side. During the Russian Civil War the Czechoslovak army in Russia controlled the Trans-Siberian Railway and issued its own stamps [1]. After independence in October 1918 the first postal service was operated by the Boy Scouts [2]. Later, stamps of Austria and Hungary were overprinted [3]. Almost from the outset the republic was beset with problems, at first concerning the Slovaks, who felt they were the junior partner, and later with the large German community in the Sudetenland. In the 1930s both factions were manipulated by Hitler for his own ends.

DISMEMBERMENT

In 1938 Czechoslovakia was forced to surrender the Sudetenland to Germany. At the same time the demands of the Slovaks led to a compromise: to give the Slovaks equal billing, stamps were briefly issued with the country name rendered as "Cesko-Slovensko". That vital hyphen, however, failed to stem the tide. In January 1939 the Slovak parliament was inaugurated [5]. In March stamps of Czechoslovakia were overprinted "Slovensky Stat", soon followed by definitive stamps portraying the Slovak leader, Father Hlinka [4].

On 15 March 1939, the Carpatho-Ukrainian parliament was inaugurated with a stamp inscribed in Cyrillic [6]. By noon the same day the Hungarians had invaded and annexed Ruthenia. It was liberated by the Red Army in 1944 and briefly functioned as an independent republic with its own stamps [7], before it was absorbed by the USSR.

In March 1939 Germany invaded the rump of Czechoslovakia, establishing a protectorate under the name of Bohemia and Moravia. Czechoslovak stamps were overprinted, pending the supply of distinctive stamps inscribed in German and Czech [8]. Following the assassination of Reinhard Heydrich by members of the Czech resistance, a stamp showing his death mask was released [9]. Special stamps were provided for Theresienstadt concentration camp [11]. Many people fled to France and Britain, where an exile government issued its own stamps, including one portraying Josef Gabcik, who assassinated Heydrich [10]. The War Heroes set was subsequently released in Czechoslovakia itself in August 1945.

POSTWAR REPUBLIC

Czechoslovakia was reconstituted in 1945 following liberation by the Red Army [12], but by 1948 the country had been totally absorbed into the communist bloc. Stamps of 1945 marked the first anniversary of the

Slovak Rising [13]. Doctrinaire communism was not reflected in stamps to the same extent as in the other Iron Curtain countries, and at least portraiture of Lenin [14] was rendered with the usual impeccable taste.

Having been an enthusiastic exponent of line-engraving and fine intaglio printing since the mid-1920s, Czechoslovakia developed a very distinctive style. Its delicate motifs are exemplified by the Shakespeare stamp in the Cultural Anniversaries set of 1964, showing Bottom from *A Midsummer Night's Dream* [16]. Several stamps remembered the destruction of the villages of Lidice and Lesaky as a reprisal for the killing of Heydrich, while others recalled the horrors of the concentration camps [15]. Latterly Czechoslovakia produced numerous sets of wide thematic appeal.

CZECH REPUBLIC

Communism collapsed in 1990 when democratic elections brought to power the poet and dissident Vaclav Havel. In April the country officially became the Czech and Slovak Federative Republic (although this was not reflected in the name printed on stamps). This reflected a sincere attempt to hold the country together on an equal basis, but the federation was amicably dissolved at the end of 1992. There was some debate about reviving the name of Bohemia and Moravia but it had too many bitter memories. Instead the term Czech Republic was adopted. A large stamp showing the lion of

Below: One of three stamps of 1997 marking the 110th anniversary of Hašek Jaroslav's satirical novel The Good Soldier Schweik.

Ill Omen

The first Czechoslovakian definitives were designed by Alfons Mucha, the outstanding exponent of Art Nouveau, and showed the Hradcany in Prague. In the original the sun, symbolizing the dawn of the republic, appeared to the right of the castle, until it was pointed out that that was where the setting sun appeared – an ill omen. The stamps were withdrawn and re-engraved without the sun.

Bohemia [17] was followed by definitives portraying President Havel [18]. Later definitives have featured landmarks, ornamental doorways [19] and the signs of the zodiac. Special issues are beautifully engraved but a refreshing element of levity creeps in occasionally [20].

SLOVAKIA

If the stamps of Slovakia appear similar, it is because they are engraved and printed in Prague. Like the Czech Republic, Slovakia began with stamps showing the national emblem [21]. Both countries issue large art stamps, a recent one celebrating the work of Andy Warhol, of Slovak origin [22].

Slovakia pursues a moderate new issue policy. The definitives of 1993–2002 are in the old Czechoslovak style, with landmarks and scenery as their subject. Recent issues have become more colourful by printing in a combination of intaglio engraving and offset lithography. The vast majority of special issues are released as single stamps, apart from a trio each January highlighting major anniversaries of the coming year. Regular issues include Europa (May), Christmas (November) and Stamp Day (December).

12

13

14

15

16

17

18

19

20

21

22

1   2

3   4

5   6

7   8

9   10

11

12   13

POLAND

This country in eastern Europe rose rapidly from a small duchy in the late Middle Ages to become an empire that stretched from the Baltic to the Black Sea, encompassing modern Lithuania, Belarus and the Ukraine. It had a very turbulent history, suffering invasion by Mongols, Turks, Hungarians, Swedes and latterly Russia, Prussia and Austria, which took large slices of territory in 1772 and 1793 and then dismembered what was left in 1795. Napoleon briefly restored much of the country but after his defeat the neighbouring powers again partitioned the country, much of which nominally became a kingdom under the personal rule of the tsar. For 120 years Poland in the historic sense ceased to exist.

Left: Poland's finest hour came in 1410 when its army soundly defeated the Teutonic Knights at Grunwald. The battle's 550th anniversary was celebrated by one of the largest stamps up to that date. Jan Matejko's vast painting was engraved by Czeslaw Slania.

Prussian, German or Austrian stamps were used in the areas controlled by these powers. The Russians allowed the Poles a stamp in 1860, which was identical to the contemporary Russian issue apart from the inscription using the Roman alphabet [1]. Following the revolt of 1863–5, however, the stamp was suppressed. During World War I German troops avenged the Teutonic Knights' defeat at Grunwald at nearby Tannenberg, defeating the Russians and occupying much of Russian Poland for the rest of the war.

POLISH REPUBLIC
A republic was proclaimed on 3 November 1918, bringing together the territories previously under German, Austrian and Russian rule. At first German [2], Austrian [3] and Austro-Hungarian military post [4] stamps were overprinted for use in their respective areas. At the same time various local "town" posts had their own stamps [5]. Even when the postal authorities of the new republic issued their own stamps, separate issues had to be made in the north and south, denominated in the currencies of Germany and Austria respectively [7].

Issues for the whole country did not appear until February 1920. The first prime minister was Ignacy Paderewski, the celebrated pianist [8]. Most stamps in the two decades of the first republic were printed in letterpress or lithography, but intaglio was used for a set of 13 in 1938 celebrating the 20th anniversary of independence with a look back at the great events in Polish history since the Middle Ages [6].

NAZI OCCUPATION
On 1 September 1939, Germany invaded Poland, and 17 days later the country was again partitioned, Stalin seizing the land east of the River Bug. While eastern Poland disappeared into the USSR, parts of the west were absorbed into the Reich, while Warsaw and the central region constituted the General Government, a German protectorate. At first, Polish stamps were overprinted, the swastika blotting out the original designs [9], but soon distinctive stamps were released, including a definitive series portraying Hitler [10]. The large Jewish population was herded into ghettoes in Warsaw and Lodz, renamed Litzmanstadt, which had its own posts [11]. From there,

Prisoners' Posts

Large numbers of Polish soldiers were held in the German camps at Grossborn, Murnau and Woldenberg, where they organized their own postal services, complete with stamps engraved and struck by hand. The issues boosted morale and celebrated many events – including, in 1942, the 450th anniversary of the discovery of America with a view of the Capitol in Washington!

Jews were despatched to the extermination camps. Many Poles escaped to other countries, notably Britain, where their forces were reconstituted and fought with great distinction in the Battle of Britain and subsequent campaigns of World War II. A government in exile set up in London issued its own stamps, including a charity stamp of 1944 commemorating the Warsaw Uprising [12], while Polish forces in Russia and Italy had similarly distinctive stamps.

REPUBLIC REGAINED

The Polish republic was proclaimed again in September 1944 at Lublin, which had been liberated by the Red Army. The first stamps portrayed Romuald Traugutt [13] and other heroes of the struggles for freedom in the 19th century. In February 1945 stamps were overprinted as each major city was liberated [14]. Later, stamps were printed in Cracow and included one remembering the horrors of the Majdanek extermination camp [15]. Although Poland was firmly in the communist bloc, its strong Catholic traditions softened the banality of Stalinism. Stamps might pay tribute to Russian space achievements [16] but they also acknowledged the humanitarianism of Eleanor Roosevelt [17]. A tricolour stamp of 1971 celebrated Polish participation in the Paris Commune [19]. The profound influence of Catholicism on this deeply religious society was only enhanced by the election of the first Polish pope. After Cardinal Karol Wojtyla became Pope John Paul II in 1978 his portrait appeared with increasing frequency on the stamps of his native land, culminating in the celebration of the 20th anniversary of his papacy [18].

The collapse of the USSR in 1991 freed Poland from the grip of communism, but under the Solidarity movement, which began in 1980 in the shipyards of Gdansk [21], the country had already begun to move in a democratic direction. As early as 1961 stamps alluding to the rulers of the former Polish kingdom were being released, while Poland's contribution to European culture was emphasized by the frequent appearances of the composer Chopin and the poet Mickeiwicz. Although prewar Poland had a bad record for anti-semitism, the postwar republic compensated with stamps honouring the heroes of the Warsaw Ghetto and individual martyrs of the Holocaust such as the children's writer Janusz Korczak. The one glaring omission was any reference to the Polish home army or the troops who fought on the Allied side in World War II, a deficiency that was not remedied until the 1980s.

In the prewar period Poland had external post offices in Odessa and Danzig (Gdansk) issuing distinctive stamps [20]. Danzig became part of Poland in 1945. The Russians took a large part of eastern Poland (now in Lithuania, Belarus and the Ukraine) but compensated Poland with most of East Prussia and Silesia.

14

15

16

17

18

19

20

21

1

2

3

4

5

6

7

8

9

10

11

BALTIC STATES

The republics of Estonia, Latvia and Lithuania are collectively known as the Baltic States. Though ethnically and linguistically distinct, they have a shared history and many cultural and political links that have been emphasized since the restoration of independence in the 1990s. All three were part of the Russian Empire until the Revolution of 1917, but by that time they had been occupied by the Germans (with whom the Baltic landowning class had close blood ties). They became independent in 1918 but were forced by Stalin to accept Soviet garrisons in 1939. Absorbed into the USSR a year later, they were "liberated" by the Germans in 1941 and re-occupied by the USSR in 1944–5. In 1990 they mounted a protest by forming the Via Baltica, a human chain from Tallinn in the north to Kaunas in the south, as a prelude to demands for independence.

Left: Since independence, the Baltic States have made a number of joint issues, such as this sheetlet of 1995 featuring a map of the three countries linked by the Via Baltica. The stamps depict scenes in the respective capitals.

ESTONIA

The first stamps released in Estonia, in November 1918, were lithographed locally [1] and actually preceded the use of tsarist stamps diagonally overprinted "Eesti Post" [2]. Stamps often had symbolic motifs or showed workers [5]. The last issue of prewar Estonia was a set of four to celebrate the centenary of adhesive stamps [3] only days before the country was swallowed up by the USSR. On 20 August 1991, it declared its independence again and began issuing stamps on 1 October. All stamps since then have been lithographed locally by Vaba Maa of Tallinn, showing scenery and landmarks [4] and including a long-running series showing lighthouses [7].

The definitives issued since 1991 have featured the three lions emblem, reviving the symbol of the prewar republic [6]. The rapid depreciation of the Soviet rouble led in 1992 to the re-introduction of the kroon (crown) tariffed at 16 old roubles and divided into 100 senti. The vast majority of Estonian stamps are issued as singles,

with occasional sets of six devoted to the Finno-Ugric peoples, the captive breeding programme at Tallinn Zoo and other somewhat esoteric subjects.

LATVIA

When it declared independence on 18 November 1918, Latvia was still under German occupation, and its first stamps were printed on the back of German military maps. The liberation of Riga was marked by stamps in 1919 showing the city skyline [10]. Stamps for the Red Cross fund (1919–20) were printed on the back of Bolshevik banknotes [8]. The 20th anniversary of independence was celebrated in 1938 and showed General Balodis and scenes from the anti-Bolshevik campaign [9].

In October 1939 the USSR acquired the right to garrison Latvia and a year later Latvia "begged" to be admitted to the Soviet Union, the last stamps showing the arms of the new soviet socialist republic [11]. Along with Estonia and Lithuania, Latvia was liberated by the Germans in 1941 and Russian stamps were overprinted accordingly [12]. The independence of Latvia was recognized by the USSR on 9 September 1991. Soviet stamps were overprinted and surcharged [13], augmenting an arms series issued shortly before [14]. Since then Latvian stamps have covered a wide range of modern themes [15].

LITHUANIA

Having proclaimed its independence in February 1918, Lithuania cast around for a German prince suitable to become king, but monarchy was on the wane and in November 1918 a republic was declared. Following some typeset stamps, Lithuania obtained stamps from Berlin [16] followed in 1921 by a series designed and printed in Kaunas [17].

A major setback was the invasion of Central Lithuania by a Polish volunteer corps under General Zeligowski. Stamps inscribed in Polish were issued in 1920–2 [18] before the area around Vilnius was annexed by Poland. When Poland was invaded and dismembered in 1939, Lithuania's share was the return to it of Vilnius, celebrated by an overprint on the stamps marking the 20th anniversary of independence [19]. In exchange, however, Lithuania had to accept a Soviet garrison and in August 1940 it was absorbed by the Soviet Union.

Independence was declared on 11 March 1990, but was not recognized by the Russians until 6 September 1991. The majority of stamps issued since then have been lithographed in Leipzig or Berlin, often emphasizing

Below: One of a series of stamps issued by North Ingermanland in 1920 shows a church burned down by Bolsheviks.

Still in Business

Many of Lithuania's prewar stamps were printed in Kaunas (the temporary capital) by the firm of Spindulys. Despite expropriation and nationalization under communist rule the company managed to survive and had the honour of printing the first stamps of the restored republic, but as it lacked a perforator the stamps had to be cut apart. In a subsequent printing, grey dots were added to simulate the perforations.

the country's long history. Annual issues have portrayed the men who signed the original declaration of independence in 1918 [20].

The overall character of the stamps since the restoration of sovereignty has been to catch up on the historic events and major figures denied philatelic recognition during the Soviet period [21]. The distinctive character of the country is also reflected in the long-running series devoted to provincial costumes, while illustrations from the Red Book of Lithuania cover the country's endangered fauna and flora.

NORTH INGERMANLAND

This territory north of Estonia briefly won its freedom from Russia in 1919–20 and issued its own stamps. The first series was closely modelled on contemporary Finnish stamps but was soon followed by a bicoloured pictorial set that alluded to outrages committed by the Bolsheviks. By the Treaty of Dorpat (Estonia), North Ingermanland reverted to Russia in October 1920.

12

13

14

15

16

17

18

19

20

21

1

2

3

4

5

6

7

8

9

10

11

12

RUSSIA

The world's largest country, Russia attained its greatest size, estimated at 22.5 million sq km/8.6 million sq miles, before the revolution of 1917. The loss of Finland, the Baltic States and eastern Poland in 1918–19 reduced it by 780,000 sq km/300,000 sq miles, but Stalin all but made that good by 1945. Even today, the Russian Federation, shorn of 14 of the republics that formerly made up the Soviet Union, still stretches from the Baltic to the Pacific, occupying the northern part of Europe and Asia. This vast, sprawling country of many different nationalities, languages and cultures, developed over two centuries. Its disastrous involvement in World War I

brought down the monarchy, and a moderate socialist republic was soon overthrown by the Bolsheviks led by Lenin, founder of the communist regime that endured for 70 years.

Left: Vladimir Ilyich Ulyanov, known as Lenin, was the Marxist revolutionary who led the Bolsheviks to power in 1917. Numerous stamps were issued from his death in 1924 onwards. This stamp of 1953, marking the 29th anniversary of his death, shows him during the October Revolution.

FALL OF THE TSARIST EMPIRE

Russia adopted adhesive stamps in 1858, having relied on pre-stamped envelopes since 1845. The format of the Russian stamps [1] was much smaller than that adopted by Britain and other countries and, indeed, has survived to this day. Variations on the theme of imperial arms continued up to the October Revolution of 1917, but in 1913 the Romanov dynasty celebrated its tercentenary with a portrait gallery of tsars from Michael I to the ill-starred Nicholas II [2], who abdicated in March 1917.

The Bolsheviks seized power in November 1917 and created the Russian Socialist Federal Soviet Republic (RSFSR). Tsarist stamps were overprinted with a hammer and sickle within a star and surcharged to cope with inflation [3]. Distinctive stamps symbolized revolution and liberty [4] and commemorated the fifth anniversary of the revolution [5]. Images of soldiers, workers and peasants [7] replaced tsarist symbols.

Civil war broke out in 1918 and dragged on until 1922. It was remembered philatelically by the ephemeral issues of breakaway governments from

the Crimea to the Far East and the armies of Denikin, Wrangel, Avalov-Bermondt and others [8].

UNION OF SOVIET SOCIALIST REPUBLICS

Before his death in 1924 Lenin had clawed back a considerable part of the former empire, which had broken away at the revolution. In July 1923 he formed the Union of Socialist Soviet Republics, joining the RSFSR to the Ukraine, Belorussia and Transcaucasia. The Uzbek and Turkmen republics were added in 1924, the Tajik in 1929 and the Kazakh and Kirghiz republic in 1936. In 1940 Stalin added the Baltic States.

Following Lenin's death in January 1924 a set of four mourning stamps [9] appeared, and was reissued annually on the anniversary of his death until 1929. Lenin also appeared in many of the subsequent definitive sets, as well as countless special issues thereafter that formed part of the massive personality cult that grew up around him. By contrast, Stalin, his successor, appeared only twice – alongside Lenin on stamps marking the 10th and 20th anniversaries of the latter's death. For much of the Soviet period stamps were extremely propagandistic and introspective, either continually exhorting the workers to do better or trumpeting Soviet achievements, such as the mass flight over the North Pole in 1937–8 [10].

After the outbreak of the Great Patriotic War (set in motion by the German invasion of the USSR in 1941), the majority of stamps extolled the feats of Soviet heroes. However, a rare example of Soviet recognition of the Anglo-American contribution to the war effort came with two stamps of 1943 marking the 26th anniversary of the revolution and the Tehran Conference [6].

The issue of small-format definitives continued unabated from 1929 [11] to the 1960s [12] and beyond. In the post-Stalinist era stamps broadened in scope, noting cultural celebrities of other lands. The USSR was the first country to honour Scotland's national poet, Robert Burns, with a stamp in 1956 on the 160th anniversary of his death [13]. By the 1960s multicolour offset lithography went hand in hand with a more thematic approach and the Soviet Union's participation in international sporting events of the era [15], combined with occasional reminders of the Cold War [16].

RUSSIAN FEDERATION

One of the last issues of the USSR appeared in October 1991 and honoured heroes who helped defeat the attempted coup by communist hardliners [14]. By that time the Baltic States had declared independence and the USSR itself was formally dissolved on 29 December. Since January 1992 stamps have been inscribed "Rossija" and its Cyrillic equivalent. A small-format horizontal definitive series featured landmarks from the tsarist era [17] while special issues ranged from the splendours of old Russian decorative art [18] to wildlife [19] and children's cartoons [20]. Space achievements continued to rank high [21] and included a stamp celebrating a joint Russian–German space flight [22]. The

Stamps As Money
During World War I there was an acute shortage of small silver coins so the government reprinted the Romanov commemoratives of 1913 on cardboard with inscriptions on the reverse signifying their validity as coins.

500th anniversary of the discovery of America by Columbus was marked by a stamp showing the Stars and Stripes and the new Russian flag – actually the old tsarist flag revived.

Under the Soviet regime more than 6,000 stamps were issued, but in the years since the collapse of communism a more moderate policy has been pursued, omitting the political propaganda of the former era. Instead, like other former communist states, Russia has been engaging on a catching-up exercise, honouring personalities and anniversaries that would have been forbidden previously. Numerous sets in the past decade have extolled the glories and achievements of the tsarist period, culminating in the 3r stamp of 1998 commemorating the 80th anniversary of the death of Tsar Nicholas II. This stamp was issued with a se-tenant label portraying the entire royal family, murdered by the Bolsheviks at Ekaterinburg in 1918. Other issues have portrayed Peter the Great, notably the series of 2003 for the tercentenary of St Petersburg.

13

14

15

16

17

18

19

20

21

22

1

2

3

4

5

6

7

8

9

10

11

ALBANIA

The Balkans were the most unstable part of Europe in the late 19th and 20th centuries. The political upheavals of the dying years of the Turkish Empire, and the struggles between the various ethnic groups that continue today, are reflected in the bewildering array of stamps marking liberation from Turkish rule and the intervention of various European powers, as well as the rivalries of the different nationalities. Nowhere was this truer than in Albania, one of the most remote and backward outposts of the Ottoman

Empire, where most of the inhabitants were Muslim and divided into two main tribes, the Ghegs and Tosks, but with large minorities of Greeks in the south and Slavs in the north and east.

Left: A pair of stamps marked the first anniversary of the death of Mikel Koliqi, the first Albanian cardinal, in 1998.

INDEPENDENCE, INVASION AND ISOLATION

During the First Balkan War, Albania declared its independence of Turkey. Its first stamps, issued in June 1913, were contemporary Turkish stamps overprinted "Shqipenia" (Albania) with the double-headed eagle. When these ran out, the Albanians resorted to makeshifts produced by typewriting and various rubber handstamps [1].

In February 1914 the provisional government invited a German prince, William of Wied, to be king. Stamps bearing his portrait were printed in Austria but never issued as such [2], and William returned to Germany when war broke out in August. Albania was a battleground between opposing forces in World War I, but for a time (1914–16) Essad Pasha ruled Central Albania until he was driven out by the Austrians [3]. In December 1916 French troops invaded from Salonika and established the autonomous province of Koritsa, which lasted until the French withdrew in 1920 [4].

A provisional government under Turhan Bey was established at Shkoder (Scutari) in December 1918, backed by an inter-allied commission to protect Albania from the Serbs. Austrian revenue stamps were overprinted and used until 1920 [5]. A regency was created

at Shkoder in February 1920, continuing until January 1925. Ironically its first stamps were those of Prince William with the portrait obscured [6].

In December 1924 the national assembly voted for a republic and Ahmed Zogu Bey was elected president. The overprint signifies the return of the government to Tirana [7]. In 1928 the assembly voted for a return to a hereditary monarchy and elected the president, who took the title of King Zog I, the last republican series being appropriately overprinted [8].

On 7 April 1939, Italian troops invaded Albania and ousted Zog. Soon afterwards Victor Emmanuel III of Italy was proclaimed king of Albania [9]. The surrender of Italy in 1943 created a vacuum in the Balkans that was soon filled by the Germans. Stamps overprinted "14 Shtator 1943" (14 September) marked the German occupation [10]. Albanian partisans led by Enver Hoxha drove out the Germans and declared the Democratic State of Albania on 22 October 1944 [11]. The constituent assembly declared Albania a people's republic on 11 January 1946, effecting the country's 12th change of status in 35 years [12].

The doctrinaire communism of the Hoxha era was reflected in stamps portraying Marx, Lenin and Stalin [13] or showing wartime partisans and the triumph of socialism. Stereotyped motifs were not enhanced by the poor quality of the printing. From 1961, however, a more thematic approach was adopted in a bid to earn hard currency, and numerous sets featured birds, flowers, wild animals, cattle, dogs and other popular subjects. At the same time, Albania's gradual emergence from self-imposed isolation as the last bastion of Stalinism in Europe was reflected in stamps marking participation in the Olympic Games and other sporting contests. As the quality of printing improved, numerous sets reproduced paintings, mosaics and sculpture.

On 29 April 1991, Albania cast off communism and became a democratic republic. This change has been reflected in stamps honouring personalities and events banned in the communist era. Another sign of the times is the production of stamps in recent years by Alex Matsoukis, the leading Greek stamp printer.

ITALIAN POST OFFICES

In the closing years of Turkish rule Italy operated post offices in Albania, using Italian stamps overprinted "Albania" [14] or the names of the principal towns of Durazzo [15], Janina [16], Scutari [17] and Valona [18], but surcharged in Turkish currency. The last of them, in Scutari and Valona, were closed in 1918 but the Italians maintained a toehold in Albania, having occupied the island of Sazan (Saseno)

Below: A number of stamps were printed locally during the Greek occupation of southern Albania during World War II. This issue from the town of Erseka was based on the Greek flag.

Handstruck Stamps

The oddest of the Epirus provisionals was the set of four produced by Greek insurgents at Chimara in February 1914, with the skull and crossbones and the countermark of the area commander.

in the Gulf of Valona in October 1914 and remained there until 1943. Stamps were issued in 1923 [19].

GREEK OCCUPATIONS

In 1913 the European powers decided that Epirus should form part of Albania, but the mainly Greek population thought otherwise and rose in revolt. A provisional government was established in 1914 and stamps showing a rifleman were printed in Corfu [20] followed by stamps showing the double-headed eagle and Greek cross flag, overprinted at Koritsa [21]. Other issues were produced at Moschopolis [22] and other towns, including a set showing the Greek flag. In December 1914 the powers agreed that Greece should occupy the territory that had declared its independence, which was now renamed Northern Epirus. Greek stamps thus overprinted were in use from then until June 1916, when the region was occupied by Italian troops and returned to Albania in 1919.

In 1939 Italy seized Albania and from here the invasion of Greece was mounted in October 1940. However, the Greeks counterattacked and not only drove the invaders out but pursued them into southern Albania. Greek stamps overprinted to signify "Greek Occupation" were in use in Epirus until April 1941 [23].

12

13

14

15

16

17

18

19

20

21

22

23

BULGARIA AND ROMANIA

The countries bordering the Black Sea's west coast were important powers in the Middle Ages, but succumbed to Turkish rule until the 19th century. Moldavia and Wallachia united to form the kingdom of Romania in 1881. The principality of Bulgaria, created by the Congress of Berlin in 1878, remained under Turkish suzerainty until independence in 1908.

Left: After 1878 Bulgaria south of the Balkan Mountains remained under the Turks, who produced stamps for use in Eastern Roumelia, as this area was called. In 1885 the people rebelled and declared the state of South Bulgaria, overprinting stamps before uniting with the north.

KINGDOM AND PRINCIPALITY

The Danubian principalities of Moldavia and Wallachia [1] gained autonomy in 1858, later uniting to form Romania under local hero Prince Alexander Cuza. In 1866 he was forced to abdicate in favour of a German aristocrat, Prince Karl of Hohenzollern-Sigmaringen [2], who proclaimed himself King Carol I in 1881. In 1906 Romania celebrated Carol's 40 years on the throne by issuing no fewer than 43 stamps, including one of the earliest charity (semi-postal) sets showing Queen Elisabeth – better known as the poet Carmen Sylva – spinning, weaving and tending a wounded soldier [3].

The principality of Bulgaria, though nominally under Turkish suzerainty, was politically and economically dependent on Russia and France, as reflected in the centime currency of the first stamps [4]. Prince Ferdinand of Saxe-Coburg was chosen by the European powers to rule the principality, shown on the stamps of 1901. He assumed the title of tsar in 1909, reviving Bulgaria's ambitions to dominate the Balkans [5].

BALKAN WARS AND WORLD WAR I

Bulgaria achieved its greatest extent as a result of the First Balkan War of 1912–13, adding Western Thrace, which gave it access to the Aegean.

Stamps overprinted at the time [7] referred to it as a war of liberation, but it triggered off a second war in which Bulgaria faced its erstwhile allies Greece and Serbia and was shorn of Thrace, which went to Greece. Resentment at this led to Bulgaria's alignment with Germany and its old enemy Turkey in World War I. A set of stamps was projected in 1915, when Bulgaria again briefly occupied Macedonia and the Dobrudja, but was not actually issued until 1921 [6].

Romania entered World War I on the Allied side in 1916 but suffered heavy losses in 1917–18. Its reward, however, was the cession by Hungary of Transylvania, for which Romania overprinted Hungarian stamps at Cluj and Oradea in 1919 [8]. During the war Romania was largely overrun by troops of the Central Powers, and stamps were issued or overprinted by Austria, Bulgaria and Germany for those areas under their control [9–11].

THE SHADOW OF FASCISM

Both Bulgaria and Romania embraced fascism in the 1930s and were allied to Germany in World War II. In 1930 Boris III married Princess Giovanna of Italy, a political marriage that drew Bulgaria into Mussolini's orbit [12].

In Romania six-year-old King Michael succeeded his grandfather Ferdinand in July 1927. He was shown

1

2

3

4

5

6

7

8

9

10

11

on the definitive series of 1928 [13], but abdicated in favour of his father Carol II, who had been passed over on account of his turbulent private life. He gained the throne in 1930 as a result of a coup but was forced to abdicate in 1940 [14]. Michael became king a second time and played a major role in the overthrow of the fascist dictatorship of Antonescu in 1944. Although Romania was occupied by the Red Army Michael held on to his throne until the end of 1947, when Romania became a people's republic [15].

Bulgaria changed sides when it was occupied by the Red Army in 1944 but remained a kingdom under the boy king Simeon [19] until September 15, 1946.

RISE OF COMMUNISM

For a brief period Bulgarian stamps were simply inscribed "Republic" [16] but soon it was officially styled a people's republic, denoted by the inscription "Narodna Republika", later shortened to "N.R." The communist propaganda of the early issues soon gave way to a revival of national pride in Bulgaria's long history [17]. Communism never supplanted the Orthodox faith, which was reflected in numerous stamps featuring monasteries and religious art [18].

As everywhere else in the communist bloc, early issues in both countries were dominated by propaganda, but by

Below: For the Europa Tales and Legends theme (1997), Romania depicted Dracula and Vlad the Impaler.

The Times Correspondent
In 1921 the first Englishman to appear on a foreign stamp was James D. Bourchier, the Balkans correspondent of *The Times*, whose despatches in 1877 helped to influence public opinion in favour of the Bulgars.

the 1960s a more liberal policy was in force. Romania played a prominent part in publicizing international cultural figures such as Shakespeare [20]. This policy has continued to the present day, especially since the overthrow of the Ceausescus in 1989 and the restoration of democracy. Stamps of 1999 portrayed Charlie Chaplin as well as Laurel and Hardy [21].

In the wake of the collapse of communism in eastern Europe, Bulgaria became a democratic republic on 15 November 1990. There was no change in the stamps, which had long since shed the "N.R." inscription and adopted bilingual captions.

12

13

14

15

16

17

18

19

20

21

1

2

3

4

5

6

7

8

9

10

FORMER YUGOSLAVIA

The kingdom of Yugoslavia was an artificial creation of the Allied Powers at the end of World War I. At its core was the kingdom of Serbia, a Turkish province from 1458 until 1804, then an autonomous principality under Turkish suzerainty until its independence was proclaimed by the Treaty of Berlin in 1878. It was closely allied to the tiny principality of Montenegro, which, alone of the Christian areas in the Balkans, retained its independence after the collapse of the Byzantine Empire in 1453.

Left: The first special issue of the new kingdom in 1921 was a set of three charity stamps for the disabled soldiers' fund. This stamp reproduced Uros Predic's painting of the Kosovo Maiden tending a wounded man on the battlefield in 1389.

SERBIA

While Montenegro had been ruled by a prince-bishop, Serbia was headed by one or other of two rival clans. In 1866, when stamps were introduced, the nation was ruled by Prince Michael Obrenovich [1], whose father Milosh had ousted Kara Georg (Black George). Michael was murdered in 1868 and succeeded by his nephew Milan, who proclaimed himself king in 1882 and abdicated in 1889. His son, Alexander I, succeeded him and reigned until 1903, when he and his consort were brutally murdered by a group of officers. This atrocity brought to the throne Peter, grandson of Kara Georg, whose first stamps were those portraying his luckless predecessor with the portrait blotted out by the royal arms [2]. Peter commanded the Serbian army in the Balkan Wars and the opening campaign of World War I [3].

Although Serbia was overrun by the Central Powers, the Serbian army managed to escape to Corfu, where it used French stamps overprinted [4] – the first instance of a postal service in exile. The Serbs shared this misfortune with their Montenegrin allies.

MONTENEGRO

In contrast with the bloody history of Serbia, Montenegro was ruled for 60 years by Prince Nikita and fought in the Russo-Turkish War (1877–8) and

the Balkan Wars. Stamps were introduced in 1874 but to Montenegro goes the credit for issuing the first commemorative stamps by a European government, celebrating the 400th anniversary of printing, in January 1893 [5]. These overprints on the definitive series were followed in 1896 by a long set marking the bicentenary of the Petrovich dynasty [7]. Nikita proclaimed himself king in 1910 [8] but in 1919 he fled to the French Riviera where he died in 1921.

KINGDOM OF THE SERBS, CROATS AND SLOVENES

Nikita's kingdom merged with the new state that was known originally as the Kingdom of the Serbs, Croats and Slovenes. These peoples had been ruled by Hungary and Austria respectively. The kingdom also included part of Macedonia, a melting-pot that had been fought over by Serbia, Greece and Bulgaria in the second Balkan War (and which remains a bone of contention with Greece to this day).

They were joined by Bosnia and Herzegovina, Turkish provinces that had been occupied by Austria-Hungary in 1878. Their early stamps did not even bear a name, the Habsburg arms being sufficient identification [6]. The names (in German) briefly appeared in a pictorial series of 1906 [10] but during World War I an inscription

The Death Mask Stamps
A few months after the murder of Alexander I in 1903, Peter I celebrated his coronation and the centenary of the Karageorgevich dynasty with a set of stamps engraved and printed in France. They showed the conjoined profiles of Kara Georg and Peter but when they were turned upside down people imagined they could see the death mask of the murdered king. The stamps were hastily withdrawn from use as a result.

signifying the Royal and Imperial Military Post was substituted. To this period belongs the set of three stamps issued in 1917 in memory of Archduke Franz Ferdinand and his wife Sophie Chotek, whose assassination by Serb terrorists in June 1914 triggered off World War I [11].

At the end of that war the stamps of Bosnia and Herzegovina were overprinted "Država S.H.S." in Roman or Cyrillic lettering [12] to denote the union of Serbs, Croats and Slovenes. Hungarian stamps overprinted "Hrvatska S.H.S." were used in Croatia [9], pending the introduction of an Art Nouveau series [13]. Slovenia had a series of stamps popularly known as the Chainbreakers [14], as well as long vertical stamps with allegorical themes [15] or a portrait of King Peter [16]. A general issue for the whole kingdom, recess-printed by the American Banknote Company, appeared in 1921, portraying Peter or his son Alexander, who succeeded him that August [17]. A definitive series of 1926–7 portraying King Alexander [18] was printed in Belgrade from plates made in Austria.

YUGOSLAVIA
The name of the kingdom was changed to Yugoslavia ("land of the southern Slavs") in October 1929, in a desperate bid to hold together this ramshackle conglomeration of different religious, linguistic and ethnic groups. King Alexander realized that attempts at democratic institutions had failed and that the only solution was to impose a dictatorship based on fascist models. At the same time, strenuous attempts were made to give the different nationalities parity at all levels and this is reflected in the stamps.

The first issue of the new regime, in fact, celebrated the millennium of the ancient kingdom of Croatia; on two of the stamps King Tomislav, the first ruler of the kingdom in the 10th century, was portrayed alongside Alexander (who named his younger son after the medieval Croat hero). The stamps were released on 1 November 1929, and had obviously been designed and engraved before the political change; it was not until April 1931 that stamps inscribed "Kraljevina Yugoslavija" appeared. Commemoratives of the early 1930s highlighted events or anniversaries in Serbia and Croatia in equal measure. A new definitive series appeared in 1931 showing a facing portrait of Alexander in military uniform.

Alexander's policies, however, failed to appease growing demands from Croat separatists. Just after the fifth anniversary of the united kingdom Alexander was assassinated during a state visit to Marseilles. The entire definitive series was re-issued a few days later with a heavy black border [19] in mourning for the murdered king.

Alexander was succeeded by his 11-year-old elder son Peter. Peter had made his philatelic debut the previous year in the uniform of Sokol, a physical training and sports organization, to mark its meeting in Ljubljana [21]. A definitive series portraying the boy king appeared in 1935 [20], while a grown-up portrait of him appeared on the last definitives of prewar Yugoslavia, in 1939–40 [22].

 11
 13
 14
 15
 16
 17
 18
 19
 20
 21
 22

1

2

3

4

5

6

7

8

9

10

YUGOSLAVIA: DIVISION, RECONSTRUCTION AND CIVIL WAR

As a country of peoples of widely differing linguistic, cultural, historic, religious and ethnic backgrounds, Yugoslavia was ruthlessly held together by strong men – King Alexander before World War II and Marshal Tito after it. Without such figures, it was bound to fall apart, first due to external threat and latterly due to implosion. As ancient rivalries between Serbia and Croatia surfaced, religious or racial tensions involving the Slovenes, Macedonians and Kosovar Albanians erupted into violent warfare, bringing a new expression – "ethnic cleansing", a euphemism for genocide – into common parlance.

Left: After being occupied by the Germans, the Yugoslavs freed themselves thanks to the partisans led by Josip Broz Tito, who formed the communist government that ruled the country until the 1990s.

WARTIME OCCUPATION

On 6 April 1941, Yugoslavia was invaded by German, Italian, Hungarian and Bulgarian forces. The Yugoslavs surrendered 11 days later and their country was dismembered by the invading powers. Germany annexed Lower Styria and Italy grabbed the rest of Slovenia, while also adding to the territory it had previously gained from the invasion of Albania. Hungary acquired territory north of the Sava and Bulgaria acquired those parts of Macedonia that Serbia had seized in 1914. Yugoslav stamps were overprinted by the Italians for use in Lubiana [1], but when Italy changed sides the Germans seized this area and overprinted Italian stamps with the German name of Laibach [2].

The rest of Yugoslavia was partitioned into three states. Croatia was nominally a kingdom but was ruled by the *poglavnik* (dictator) Ante Pavelich. Yugoslav stamps were overprinted with the Croat arms [3] followed by definitives portraying Pavelich [4]. The Croat Legion fought on the Eastern Front [5]. Montenegro used Yugoslav stamps overprinted by the Italians and later the Germans, while Serbia became a puppet state [6].

As in World War I, a government in exile was formed abroad, and distinctive stamps keeping alive the name of Yugoslavia were produced in England for the use of the Yugoslav Merchant Navy working with the Allies [7].

YUGOSLAVIA RECONSTITUTED

Resistance to the enemy was split between two movements: the royalist Chetniks under Draza Mihailovic and the communist Partisans led by Josip Broz, known as Tito. The latter triumphed in 1943; the Chetniks (often accused of collaborating with the Nazis) were discredited, and the communists seized power. Stamps of wartime Serbia and Montenegro were overprinted in December 1944 to signify the Democratic Federation of Yugoslavia [8], composed of the six republics of Serbia, Croatia, Slovenia, Montenegro, Bosnia–Herzegovina and Macedonia, with the federal territory of Kosovo, whose inhabitants were predominantly Albanian.

As everywhere else in the communist bloc, the early stamps were heavily politicized, a notable exception being those of 1948 marking the 80th anniversary of the death of Laurenz

Kosir, the "ideological creator" of the postage stamp. He had proposed the use of adhesive stamps some years before Rowland Hill but his recommendation was merely filed away. By the 1960s, however, a more thematic approach, with stamps featuring wildlife, flowers and Adriatic resorts, reflected an appreciation of the global stamp market and tourism as major sources of hard currency [9].

Obligatory tax stamps (with corresponding postage due labels for mail not bearing these stamps) were a recurring feature of the post-war years. Popular annual issues included stamps for Children's Week, while Yugoslavia was the first communist country to introduce Christmas stamps, in 1966.

A set of stamps marking Tito's 75th birthday in 1967 was retained and expanded as a definitive series, followed in 1971–3 by a long series featuring landmarks and scenery.

COLLAPSE OF COMMUNISM

The collapse of communism in 1991 led to the fragmentation of the Federation, and Croatia and Slovenia seceded in May and June respectively. Both were invaded by Serbia and for a time separate issues of stamps appeared in Kraina [10] and the Baranjska Oblast. Most of the early stamps of Croatia were obligatory tax stamps to raise money for national defence, but by 1993 stamps reflected global events and personalities [11]. This pattern was also followed by Slovenia, beginning with definitives featuring the national emblem [14] but soon paying tribute to UNICEF [13] and the United Nations for its support, or providing colourful images of international appeal.

Bosnia and Herzegovina declared independence in April 1992 and armorial stamps were issued by the Sarajevo government [12]. The country was soon embroiled in war, being fought over by Croats and Serbs, each issuing their own stamps. Recent issues from the Sarajevo government include a stamp for the AIDS appeal.

Diana Remembered

Following the tragic death of Diana, Princess of Wales, in 1997, Bosnia and Herzegovina issued a stamp in her memory. It was a reminder of her work for the eradication of landmines and of the visit she made to the war-torn country shortly before her death. The design featured an informal photograph of the princess in Sarajevo, with red roses and a map of Bosnia in the background.

Following a referendum, Macedonia declared its independence in September 1991. A high proportion of its stamps were for compulsory use, to raise funds for the Red Cross, or emphasizing the cultural identity of this ancient country [15] – a matter that has caused a major rift with neighbouring Greece.

SERBIA AND MONTENEGRO

Stamps inscribed "Yugoslavia" continued to be issued in Serbia and Montenegro, generally carrying on the colourful but bland policy of catering to the international market, but occasionally making a political point, such as the Destroyed Bridges series and Bombed Buildings pair of 1999, lashing out at NATO [16–17]. During this period, however, obligatory stamps were regularly produced for Serbia alone and thus inscribed [18].

The fiction of Yugoslavia ended in 2003 when stamps inscribed "Serbia and Montenegro" were introduced. Designs for these combine the image of a country striving to fit in with the international community [20] with a constant harking back to the glories of medieval times [19].

11

12

13

14

15

16

17

18

19

20

1

2

3

4

5

6

7

8

9

10

11

12

GREECE

The Greeks had been part of the Ottoman Empire since the fall of the Byzantine Empire in 1453, but in 1821 they rebelled and began a ten-year War of Independence in which Britain, France and Russia allied to defeat

the Turks. In 1833 the European Powers selected Prince Otto of Bavaria to be King of the Hellenes, but he was deposed in 1862 and Prince William of Schleswig-Holstein-Sonderburg-Glucksburg replaced him, taking the title of George I.

Left: In 2004 the modern Olympic Games returned to Athens, where they had first been held in 1896. Numerous sets of Greek stamps publicized the Games ahead of the event and several others were issued during and after the Olympics.

CLASSICAL TRADITIONS

Stamps were introduced in Greece in 1861 [1]. Until 1911 all definitives portrayed Hermes, messenger of the gods, in various forms, and even thereafter a high proportion of stamps have drawn on the rich store of classical mythology and art. From 1927 onwards different motifs were used for the various definitive issues, and the vast majority were devoted to the glories of Ancient Greece. The 1935–9 airmails focused on mythological characters, while the airmails of 1942–3 drew on the spirits of the various winds. This tradition continues, as can be seen in the sets illustrating the labours of Hercules [3] or the 1988 definitives portraying the Olympian gods [4]. Even modern events and institutions are commemorated by designs that seek a parallel from the classical period.

BALKAN WARS

In the first hundred years of independence Greece doubled its territory. Britain ceded the Ionian Islands in 1864 and Crete (after a period of autonomy within the Turkish Empire but under Anglo-Russian administration) gradually passed into Greek hands after 1906 [2]. The largest accretion came in the Balkan Wars of 1912–13, which not only confirmed possession of Crete but also gave Greece western Thrace [5] and many Aegean islands,

such as Lemnos [6] and Samos [7]. In the second Balkan War Greece took Dedeagatz from Bulgaria [8].

Several compulsory tax stamps were issued in this period to raise money for war wounded and widows and orphans [9]. After World War I Greece seized eastern Thrace [10] but had to cede it to Turkey in 1922. This crushing defeat toppled the monarchy, marked by the overprint "Epanastasis" (Revolution), applied ironically to the remaining Victory stamps of 1913 [11]. Attempts to take over the Dodecanese Islands from Turkey in 1912 were foiled by the Italians, who held them until 1944.

MONARCHY RESTORED

The monarchy was restored in November 1935, signalled by the date and crown overprinted on all stamps then current [12]. During the period of the first republic Greece celebrated its centenary of independence with a long set portraying the heroes of that struggle [13]. Previously, two stamps of 1924 had marked the centenary of the death of Lord Byron at Missolonghi [14], and a 1927 set honoured the centenary of the naval battle at Navarino when the combined fleets of Britain, France and Russia defeated the Turks.

Preparing to invade Greece in October 1940, Mussolini issued an ultimatum, to which the Greeks replied with a resounding "Oxi!"(No!); this was

Eating His Words

In 1907 Winston Churchill, then Under-Secretary of State for the Colonies, visited Cyprus and said: "I think it is only natural that the Cypriot people who are of Greek descent should regard their incorporation with what may be called their mother country as an ideal to be earnestly, devoutly and fervently cherished…" When Britain refused the Greek Cypriot demands for *enosis* (unification with Greece) in 1954 his speech was quoted by Mrs Lena Jeger in a House of Commons debate on July 28. The relevant page from *Hansard* (the report of parliamentary proceedings) was reproduced on a set of Greek stamps, with a symbolic black blot across the middle.

the subject of two stamps on its fifth anniversary [15]. When the Italians invaded, the Greeks chased them all the way back to the Adriatic.

Coming to the aid of their allies, the Germans invaded Greece in April 1941. The royal family fled to Cairo, and Greece endured four years of occupation and privation that shattered the economy and reduced the population to starvation level. The currency collapsed and Greece suffered inflation, which was reflected in stamps that ran up to 5 million drachmae in 1944 [17]. A regency headed by Archbishop Damaskinos continued to September 1946, when a plebiscite voted to restore the monarchy.

POSTWAR PERIOD

Greece was one of the few countries to mourn the death of Franklin D. Roosevelt with an issue of stamps [16]. Although the royalist government was pro-western, a powerful communist movement arose out of the wartime partisans, which led to a long-running civil war that was reflected in several issues. A stamp of 1949 showing a column of women and children alluded to the abduction of Greek children to the neighbouring communist countries of Albania and Bulgaria [18].

From 1968 onwards Greek stamps were inscribed "Hellas", the Roman version of the country name, to conform to Universal Postal Union regulations insisting that countries should be identified in the universally recognized alphabet. In 1967 a military junta seized power, but apart from a set of 1972 marking the fifth anniversary of the revolution, the regime made little impact on stamps. In 1973 King Constantine II attempted a counter-coup and when this failed he fled to Italy. The monarchy was abolished in his absence on June 1, 1973.

These political upheavals had remarkably little effect on the stamps, which continued to lean heavily on classical subjects. If anything, references to the glories of Ancient Greece have tended to increase in recent years, as suitable motifs derived from Hellenistic civilization are found for many subjects, from the Greek presidency of the EU (the allegorical figure of Hellas driving her chariot) to the second Pan-European Transport Conference (Hermes leading Selene's chariot). In addition to a wider use of the most popular themes [19] many very recent stamps have given prominence to the Macedon of Philip II and Alexander the Great [20] as a counter to the independent republic of Macedonia. Icons are a popular subject for Christmas stamps in general but especially for the Millennium series of 2000 [21], showing the birth of Christ. Greece issues Europa stamps each year in the prevailing theme [22].

1

2

3

4

5

6

7

8

9

10

TURKEY

Although most of Turkey is geographically in western Asia, it was formerly a great European power and in 1683 the Turks even laid siege to Vienna. At the height of their power, the Sultans ruled an empire that stretched along the north coast of Africa and included the whole of the Balkans. By the 1850s, however, Turkey was "the sick man of Europe", and it lost most of its European territory in a series of wars from the 1820s to 1914. Siding with Germany and Austria in World War I, it suffered humiliating defeats and lost its Asiatic dominions: Palestine, Syria, Iraq and the Lebanon. When the Greeks attempted to seize the coast of Asia Minor in 1922, the Young Turks rose in revolt. Led by Kemal Pasha, they abolished the sultanate and declared a republic. Kemal Pasha transferred the capital from Istanbul (Constantinople) to Ankara and embarked on a process of rapid westernization, abolishing Turkish dress and compelling everyone to adopt western-style surnames. He himself took the name of Ataturk, "Father of the Turks".

Left: One of Kemal's most important reforms was the replacement of Arabic by a modified form of the Roman alphabet. Stamps of 1938 show him teaching the new alphabet.

TURKISH ISSUES

Turkey introduced postage stamps in 1863 [1], the chief motif being the *toughra* (a combination of seal and signature) of Sultan Abdul-Aziz. Stamps showing the ruler's mark or the Moslem crescent continued for some years [2]. Stamps of 1908 were overprinted "*Behie*" (discount) to compete with the foreign post offices operating in Turkey. In 1914 a new series, recess-printed by Bradbury Wilkinson in England, featured scenery and landmarks [3]. Several World War I issues showed life at the battlefront [4].

Kemal raised the standard of revolt at Ankara in April 1920. Stamps showing the first parliament house of the republic [5] were issued in 1922. By November 1923 Kemal had driven out the Greeks and extended his nationalist regime to the whole country. Since then, Kemal has appeared on more Turkish stamps than Washington has on American issues. The two men appeared on the same stamp following the 150th anniversary of the American constitution in 1939, celebrated with a large Turkish commemorative. [6]

Until 1951 stamps were inscribed "Türkiye Postalari" (Turkish Posts) and then "Türkiye Cumhuriyeti Postalari" (Turkish Republic Posts). From 1956 "Türkiye" alone was used but since 1966 "Türkiye Cumhuriyeti" has been preferred [7]. Modern stamps are lithographed in Ankara or Istanbul. While many special issues highlight the technological progress of the modern state [8], others cover historical events [9] and even foster the colourful regional costumes [10] that Kemal tried to stamp out. Tradition mixes easily with modernization [11]. Above all, Kemal himself is a constant thread running through Turkish philately; he is portrayed here on one of the stamps of 2003 celebrating the 80th anniversary of the republic [12].

ASSOCIATED TERRITORIES

Although numerous stamps reflect the invasion and occupation of Turkish territory that now forms part of Greece, Albania, Romania, Bulgaria and Russia, the process was reversed in 1898 when the Turks invaded Thessaly, a Greek province. Five octagonal stamps showing the railway bridge at Vardar were used by Turkish troops before they evacuated most of the area, which reverted to Greece [14].

In 1919 the French occupied Cilicia, formerly the *vilayet* (province) of Adana, and overprinted Turkish stamps [13] with the name and initials "T.E.O." for *Territoires Ennemis Occupés* (Occupied Enemy Territories). The territory reverted to Turkey in October 1921. In 1923 the French granted autonomy to the *sanjak* of Alexandretta and overprinted Syrian stamps for the purpose. When they planned to hand this Turkish enclave to Syria in 1938, the inhabitants rose in revolt. Following a plebiscite it became the autonomous republic of Hatay. Turkish stamps were overprinted in 1939 [15] before its re-incorporation into Turkey in June 1939.

FOREIGN POST OFFICES

For many years up to the outbreak of World War I the external posts of the Ottoman Empire were run by various foreign powers. Stamps surcharged in Turkish currency or inscribed "Levant" or the name of a town were used at the various foreign post offices.

Austria-Hungary maintained a number of offices in Constantinople, Smyrna and those parts of the Balkans that were under Turkish rule. Stamps of Lombardy and Venetia were introduced in 1867, but from 1880 Austrian stamps surcharged in paras or piastres were used [16]. The British offices used ordinary British stamps, identifiable by their cancellations, but

Below: This Syrian stamp was overprinted by the French for use in the sanjak *(region) of Alexandretta.*

Typewritten Stamps

Probably the oddest stamps to emerge during World War I were those produced by Lieut. Commander Harry Pirie-Gordon DSC, RNVR, who commanded a detachment of the Royal Navy that occupied the island of Cheustan, or Makronisi, in the Gulf of Smyrna for a few weeks in 1916. During that period the commander produced his own stamps on the office typewriter, inscribed "Long Island" (a translation of the Turkish and Greek names), with the royal monogram "G.R.I." at the top and denominated in sterling.

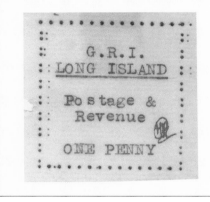

from 1885 to 1914 stamps were surcharged in Turkish currency [17]. France not only had a general issue, similar to contemporary French stamps but engraved with the name "Levant" [18], but also overprints for use at individual offices. German stamps surcharged in Turkish currency were adopted in 1870 [19].

The Italian post offices began with a general issue inscribed "Estero" (foreign) but from 1902 Italian stamps were overprinted with the name of the individual office and surcharged in Turkish currency [20]. Russia also favoured individual stamps for each of its 13 offices as well as a general series for the Russian Company for Steam Shipping and Trade, known by the abbreviation ROPiT. The British post offices were reopened in 1919–21, while Poland and Romania also operated post offices in this period.

11

12

13

14

15

16

17

18

19

20

1

2

3

4

5

6

7

8

9

10

11

12

ITALY

Like Germany, 19th-century Italy was divided into a number of separate kingdoms and duchies, while Lombardy and Venetia, the South Tirol and Italian-speaking districts north of the Adriatic were in Austrian hands. From the 1830s Giuseppe Mazzini's Young Italy movement encouraged the idea of unification. After defeat against Austria in 1848–9, Mazzini's followers

started the second War of Independence in 1859, aided by Giuseppe Garibaldi. By the end of 1860 southern Italy was unified under Victor Emmanuel II of Sardinia, though Lombardy and Venetia remained in Austrian hands until 1866 and Rome was garrisoned by the French until 1870.

Left: The battles of Magenta (appropriately depicted on a magenta-coloured stamp of 1959) and Solferino (whose carnage inspired Henri Dunant to found the Red Cross) were two of the great conflicts in the war that unified Italy.

ITALIAN STATES

Before 1860 the various states issued their own stamps. Modena and Parma [1] were duchies under Austrian rule, while Naples [2] and Sicily [3] formed the Kingdom of the Two Sicilies, ruled by Ferdinand II, nicknamed "King Bomba" from his habit of bombarding his unruly subjects from time to time. Since 754 the Pope had ruled Rome and the surrounding territory, known variously as the States of the Church or the Papal States [4]; it included the Romagna extending to the Adriatic coast [5]. The grand duchy of Tuscany [6] fell to the liberators in August 1859 and latterly had stamps featuring the arms of Savoy as a prelude to unification with Sardinia [7], whose ruler eventually became king of Italy. Stamps with his embossed profile were issued in the Neapolitan Provinces [8] following the unification of Italy, pending the introduction of lire currency there.

THE RISE OF FASCISM

Italy made further territorial gains, siding with Prussia against Austria in 1866 and winning Lombardy and Venetia, taking advantage of the Franco-German War of 1870 to drive the French garrison out of Rome, and also acquiring the South Tirol, Trieste and other Austro-Hungarian areas [9] at the

end of World War I. However, widespread discontent in the aftermath of the war led to the rise of fascism led by Benito Mussolini.

Mussolini's Blackshirts marched on Rome [10] in October 1922, and he became prime minister and subsequently dictator under the title of Il Duce ("the leader"). He was the role model for Hitler, although by World War II he was the junior partner in the Axis alliance [11]. In 1943 Victor Emmanuel III dismissed him and had him imprisoned when Italy changed sides. The Germans rapidly overran northern Italy, freed Mussolini and installed him as head of a puppet state known as the Italian Social Republic [13], which was overthrown by partisans in 1945.

POST-WAR REPUBLIC

Allied troops landed in Sicily in July 1943 and on the Italian mainland in September. In the occupied areas stamps produced in Washington [14] were issued by the Allied military government. Control was handed over to the king but in June 1946 Italy became a republic. The last of the royalist stamps [15] symbolized freedom, enlightenment, peace and justice and continued in use till 1948. A later series, known as *la Sircusa* because it

Commercial Advertising

Stamps of the 1901–22 series portraying Victor Emmanuel III were released in 1924 with commercial advertisements printed on labels. There were no perforations between the stamps and the labels, so that the public were encouraged to advertise various products every time they posted a letter.

was based on an ancient Greek coin of Syracuse, was adopted in 1953 and continued until 1980. On two occasions it was incorporated in stamps urging Italians to pay their taxes [12]. It was followed by a series featuring some of the many castles of Italy [16].

More recent special issues have been produced by intaglio or photogravure at the Mint in Rome [17]. Many Italian stamps are inspired by the sculpture of the Roman Empire, a legacy from the fascist period, rather than the influence of the Church, and religious themes are usually restricted to Old Master paintings, such as the stamps celebrating the 450th anniversary of the death of Raphael [18].

SAN MARINO AND THE VATICAN

The tiny landlocked republic in northeastern Italy, independent since the fourth century, began issuing its own stamps in 1877. By the 1900s they were its principal source of revenue and became immensely popular worldwide because of their wide-ranging topics. They included a set of 20 in memory of Franklin D. Roosevelt in 1947 [19]. Numerous sets since the 1950s have catered to the thematic market.

San Marino was very much in the forefront of developments in philately, pioneering long sets devoted to popular themes such as sports, flowers, birds, veteran cars, vintage aircraft [20] and ancient ships, as well as more esoteric subjects ranging from medieval tournaments to dinosaurs. It was also one of the first countries to issue stamps in support of the Olympic Games (1955–6) and led the way in illustrating Disney characters. More recently it has produced sheetlets for Italian operas, comic strips and science fiction. Joint issues with other countries are now common, but San Marino and Italy scored another first in 1994 with a miniature sheet containing a pair of L750 stamps (one from each country) showing St Mark's Basilica in Venice. The stamps were arranged in the sheet upside down in relation to each other, giving the impression of a reflection in the water. An inscription on the back limited the validity of each stamp to the appropriate country.

The Vatican City State was created in 1929, giving the Pope temporal powers including the right to issue stamps [21]. Not surprisingly, the vast majority of these have had a religious theme, celebrating popes, saints and the achievements of the Catholic Church down through the ages. In recent times, however, they have also addressed social and political issues of global concern, such as aid for the refugees of the world's trouble spots.

Below: In 1999 the Vatican issued this stamp to raise money for refugees from Kosovo in war-torn former Yugoslavia.

13

14

15

16

17

18

19

20

21

1

2

3

4

5

6

7

8

9

10

11

FRANCE

A thousand-year kingdom, two empires and five republics, not to mention long periods in the 20th century when governments rapidly came and went, might suggest a lack of stability in France, but against this stands a record of affluence and material progress, of martial skills and technological superiority, centuries as the acknowledged centre of the fine and applied arts, and world leadership in literature, philosophy, music and the sciences. All have been explored thoroughly in stamps whose recurring theme is the glory of France, past and present. France rightly regards itself as the cradle of

modern democracy, with the fall of the Bastille in 1789 signalling the downfall of the *ancien régime*.

Left: The assault on the Bastille, the grim fortress that symbolized the autocratic rule of the Bourbons, marked the beginning of the French Revolution.

THE SECOND REPUBLIC

Revolutions in 1830 and 1848 toppled the last of the Bourbons and Louis Philippe respectively, ushering in the Second Republic, and France adopted adhesive stamps a few months later. Without a crowned head to adorn the French "Penny Black", a profile of Ceres, the Roman goddess of agriculture, was chosen instead [1]. Shortly afterwards Louis Bonaparte, president of the republic, staged a coup and proclaimed himself emperor, taking the title of Napoleon III. For twenty years his portrait graced the stamps [2] but, after the downfall of the empire in the Franco-German War of 1870–1, Ceres was restored. Thereafter France has opted for various allegorical females, brandishing *The Rights of Man* [3] or sowing seed [4], and Marianne, the epitome of France, has appeared in many guises to the present day.

Edmund Dulac, French-born but a naturalized Briton, engraved the set printed by De La Rue at the end of World War II – some of the few French stamps produced outside France [5]. This issue was briefly preceded by a series showing the Arc de Triomphe, brought over from America by the liberators in 1944 [6]. In the same period France embarked on a long series of stamps, originally showing the arms

of Nice, Corsica, Alsace and Lorraine (lost to the Italians and Germans in 1940) but eventually covering every part of France [14].

ARTISTIC EXPRESSION

Art is a recurring theme of French stamps, from Art Nouveau motifs at the beginning of the 20th century, to the geometric style for the stamps publicizing the Paris International Exposition of the Decorative Arts in 1925 (from which came the term "Art Deco") [7]. Several stamps from 1927 onwards show the Statue of Liberty, in one instance to raise money for refugees from the Spanish Civil War [8]. Who but the French would regularly issue charity stamps on behalf of Unemployed Intellectuals [9], providing an opportunity to portray eminent figures from the world of the arts?

France was (and still is) a leading exponent of intaglio printing. By the late 1950s two-colour recess-printing was possible [10], although monochrome was often preferred, as in the stamp portraying Auguste Bartholdi, sculptor of the Statue of Liberty [11], but by 1961 multicolour intaglio was spectacularly launched with the first of the extremely popular large-format paintings sets [12], which triggered a craze for fine art stamps all over the

To the Glory of France

Napoleon Bonaparte and Charles de Gaulle, the two towering figures who gave France back its pride in itself, have been the subject of numerous stamps. This strip, released in 1971, marked the first anniversary of de Gaulle's death. The images flanking the Cross of Lorraine chart his career from brigadier-general in June 1940 to president. In 2004 France issued a set for the bicentenary of Napoleon's coronation, reviving imperial glory.

12

13   14

15

16

world. In more recent years photogravure and offset lithography have made serious inroads, often accompanied by a surreal or whimsical approach [13].

The French Post Office also provides distinctive stamps for use at the Paris headquarters of UNESCO and the Council of Europe in Strasbourg [15]. France has joint suzerainty (with Spain) over Andorra and produces distinctive stamps for it, many of which reflect the impact of France on the tiny Pyrenean principality [16].

MONACO

A possession of the Grimaldi family since the 13th century, Monaco is a medieval relic that has managed to retain its independence and move with the times. Distinctive stamps [17] were introduced in 1885; before that stamps

Below: A Delahaye motor car of 1901 was one of 14 veteran automobiles depicted in a set issued in 1961.

of Sardinia or France were employed. Prince Rainier III [18], a keen philatelist, wed the actress Grace Kelly in a fairytale romance in 1956 [19].

The home of the Monte Carlo Rally, Monaco has issued many stamps depicting cars, as well as a sought-after series showing the starting points for the rally – though why Eilean Donan Castle in the Scottish Highlands should represent Glasgow is a mystery. Although Monaco prefers fine intaglio, some recent issues have been printed in multicolour photogravure or lithography, but always at the French Government Printing Works [20].

The astonishing diversity of landscape and buildings in the tiny principality is reflected in many of the stamps, including several sets reproducing engravings or paintings of bygone Monaco. Monte Carlo is an increasingly popular venue for international conferences and exhibitions, all of which are well publicized by stamps. The tragic death of Princess Grace in a motoring accident resulted in a steady stream of stamps in her memory, latterly giving prominence to the various charities and foundations of which she was the patron. The 700th anniversary of the Grimaldi dynasty was celebrated by a long set in 1997 portraying all the seigneurs since Rainier I in 1297.

17   18

19

20

1

2

3

4

5

6

7

8

9

10

11

IBERIAN PENINSULA

The Iberian peninsula in south-western Europe is flanked by the Mediterranean and the Atlantic. In ancient times Europeans believed that the Pillars of Hercules (now the Straits of Gibraltar) marked the edge of the world and that there was nothing beyond. The Portuguese, under the guidance of Prince Henry the Navigator, were among the first to disprove this in the 14th and 15th centuries. Intrepid mariners explored the coasts of Africa, rounded the Cape of Good Hope and found the sea route to India and beyond, travelling to China and Japan. Others crossed the Atlantic and colonized Brazil. Spain, the larger partner in Iberia, would not be outdone.

Hiring a Genoese mariner, Christopher Columbus, Spain reached the New World and secured the untold wealth of the gold and silver deposits in Mexico, Peru and Bolivia. In both cases, imperial power and wealth proved to be short-lived.

Left: Many stamps of Portugal portray the navigators who gave it control of half the transoceanic world, the greatest (and most frequently depicted) being Vasco da Gama, who found the sea route to the Indies in 1497.

PORTUGAL

The stamps of Portugal from 1853 to 1880 bore albino embossed profiles of rulers [1]. After the collapse of the monarchy in 1910 the republic issued a definitive set depicting Ceres, goddess of agriculture [2]. Introduced in 1912, it continued until the 1930s: though not the longest-lived it was one of the most prolific series of all time, with numerous changes of colour and value.

In the 1920s Portugal favoured very long historical sets dwelling on past glories [3]. The centenary of adhesive stamps was celebrated in 1940 by a set portraying Rowland Hill [4]. A reminder that Portugal was England's oldest ally came in the set of 1949, which portrayed Henry the Navigator and his mother Philippa of Lancaster [5]. More recent stamps have been produced in multicolour lithography and range from the military sets of the 1980s [6] to the armorial issues of the 1990s [7]. Traditional crafts and vocations are also recurring themes [8].

SPAIN

The first stamps of Spain appeared in 1850 and bore the very homely features of Isabella II [9]. Corruption and

misrule led to the abolition of the monarchy in 1873–4, but the House of Bourbon was restored by King Alfonso XII. He died without a male heir but his wife gave birth to a son several months later. The stamps of Alfonso XIII portrayed him from babyhood to adolescence [10] and into middle age.

In 1930 the centenary of the death of Francisco Goya was marked by a set of 32 stamps portraying the artist and reproducing some of his works. Three stamps featured *The Naked Maja*, which shocked the ultra-conservative Spaniards, and were effectively used as republican propaganda, insinuating that the image symbolized the decadent lifestyle of the monarchy. The furore eventually forced Alfonso XIII to leave the country, and a republic was proclaimed in April 1931.

Royalist stamps were overprinted [11], pending the introduction of republican issues [12]. Right-wing reaction led to a military coup led by General Franco [13]. This triggered the Civil War, which lasted for three years (1936–9), yielding a large number of local stamps issued by both sides. While fascist Italy and Germany gave

Forlorn Hope

Ever since the British captured the Rock of Gibraltar in 1704 the Spaniards have tried unsuccessfully to take it back. Having failed on several occasions, notably during the siege of 1779–83, in more recent times Spain has applied economic sanctions and even issued stamps in 1969, ostensibly in aid of Spanish workers unable to cross the line to their jobs in Gibraltar, although it was the Spanish government that prevented this traffic.

considerable support to the Nationalists, the Soviet Union and communists from many parts of the world flocked to the Republican colours in what amounted to a dress-rehearsal for World War II.

Under Franco Spain was theoretically a kingdom again but in effect it was a fascist dictatorship. Bypassing Alfonso's son and heir, Franco groomed his grandson for the throne and in 1975 Juan Carlos I succeeded on the death of Franco. These political upheavals were studiously ignored in the stamps, which have tended to draw heavily on the Spanish way of life and such sports as bullfighting [14]. Many have reproduced works of art, from cave paintings [15] to the avant-garde. Other very popular and long-running series were devoted to the castles [16] and provincial costumes [17] of Spain. A high proportion reflect its Catholic conservatism, though social problems such as domestic violence [18] have also been publicized in recent years.

Apart from the Civil War, Spain has had to contend with long-running unrest in the Basque provinces and

Catalonia, which, in addition to separatist aspirations, formerly supported the claims to the throne of Don Carlos and his grandson. Carlist stamps were issued in 1873–4 [19].

ANDORRA

Spain had joint suzerainty (with France) over the Pyrenean principality of Andorra and opened post offices there in 1928. Ordinary Spanish stamps were used at first but since 1929 distinctive issues have been made. Originally inscribed in Spanish [20], they have been rendered in Catalan since 1979. Catalogues invariably describe the 1997 Christmas stamp as showing a Catalan crib figure [21]. The stamp itself is discreetly captioned "El Caganer" (the defecator), apparently a good-luck symbol in the Pyrenees.

Most Christmas stamps have concentrated on Old Master paintings of religious subjects or the decorative art of Andorran churches. Andorra is conspicuous for its new issue policy, one of the most conservative in the world, averaging only four or five stamps a year and invariably confined to subjects directly relevant to the principality. The only other regular annual issues are Europa stamps and one promoting the protection of nature. Andorra's main acknowledgment of the outside world is the occasional stamp for the Olympic Games or the football World Cup. Although it now has a single currency, the euro, separate issues of stamps are still made by France and Spain.

Below: Goya's The Naked Maja *was the first nude to appear on a stamp, and was hijacked by republicans eager to condemn the decadence of the monarchy.*

12   13

14

15   16

17   18

19   20

21

1

2

3

4

5

6

7

8

9

AFRICA

Africa was the last inhabited continent to adopt adhesive stamps, beginning with the celebrated Cape of Good Hope triangulars in 1853. Natal introduced stamps in 1857 but other states did not follow suit until the 1860s. By 1870 distinctive stamps were appearing in some Spanish colonies.

SPANISH AFRICA

As well as the Spanish-protected zone of Morocco, Spain acquired a considerable amount of territory in north-west Africa. However, most of this was in parts that were of little or no interest to the other European powers, mainly in the Sahara desert regions but also around the Gulf of Guinea.

Left: A general issue of stamps inscribed "Spanish West Africa", for use in Ifni and Spanish Sahara, was in use from 1949 to 1951. A portrait of General Franco was inset in designs featuring the scenery of the area.

GULF COLONIES

Spain's oldest colony was the offshore island of Fernando Poo in the Gulf, which it acquired from Portugal in 1778. From 1827 to 1834 Spain leased it to Britain as a naval base for the suppression of the slave trade. A British consulate was opened there in 1849 and a postal agency in 1858, using ordinary British stamps identifiable by the postmarks. This closed in 1877. Fernando Poo opened a Spanish post office in 1868 and issued a stamp portraying Isabella II (reproduced on a centenary stamp [1]) but it was soon withdrawn and from then until 1879 the stamps of Cuba were used instead.

From 1879 to 1960 the stamps of Fernando Poo consisted of contemporary Spanish stamps overprinted or inscribed thus. It was not until the creation of two Spanish overseas provinces in July 1959, one of which consisted of Fernando Poo and the island of Annobon, that distinctive stamps first appeared. The stamps were inscribed with the provincial name in letters smaller than those of the country name [2]. In October 1968 Fernando Poo joined Rio Muni to form the Republic of Equatorial Guinea.

Spain acquired the three islands of Elobey, Annobon and Corisco [3] from Portugal in 1778. Annobon is in the Atlantic south of the then Portuguese colony of St Thomas and Prince Islands; the other two are off the coast of Gabon. Spain established a protectorate over a part of the mainland of Guinea, also known as Rio Muni, in 1885, and from 1909 to 1960 the islands were joined with Fernando Poo and Spanish Guinea. Keytype stamps were used in "Spanish Continental Guinea" from 1902 to 1909 [4].

In that year both continental territory and offshore islands were combined as the Spanish Territories of the Gulf of Guinea, and stamps thus inscribed were then introduced [5]. Royal portraiture was superseded by pictorial designs from 1924 onwards [6]. The much shorter title of "Spanish Guinea" was adopted in 1949 [7] and continued until 30 July 1959, when the territory was divided into the overseas provinces of Fernando Poo and Rio Muni, covering the offshore islands and the continental portion respectively. Rio Muni issued stamps from 1960 to 1968, most issues being for Stamp Day [8] or Child Welfare [9].

Movie Stars

Typical of modern issues from the Republic of Equatorial Guinea are the stamps of 1996 honouring Marilyn Monroe, Elvis Presley and James Dean.

SAHARAN TERRITORIES

In 1885 Spain established a protectorate over the basin of the Rio de Oro (river of gold) in north-west Africa, just south of Morocco. The territory was administered from the Canary Islands and used ordinary Spanish stamps until 1905, when the keytypes were introduced [10]. The Rio de Oro region was renamed Spanish Sahara in 1924. In 1920 Spanish troops had occupied La Aguera on Cape Blanco with the intention of building an airfield for a projected route to Latin America, and for this stamps of Rio de Oro were overprinted accordingly [11]. The district was incorporated in Spanish Sahara in 1924.

In 1916 Spanish troops occupied Cape Juby at the southern end of Morocco. Stamps of Rio de Oro, Spain or Spanish Morocco were overprinted at various times [12]. Cape Juby was incorporated in Spanish Sahara in 1950 but ceded to Morocco in 1958.

Ifni was a Spanish enclave on the Moroccan coast from 1860 onwards. Before stamps were introduced in 1941, mail was franked by rubber stamp. Spanish stamps overprinted "Territorio de Ifni" [13] were used until 1950, when distinctive stamps were adopted. As in Rio Muni, most later stamps were issued for Child Welfare [14] or Stamp Day [15]. On 30 June 1969, Ifni was returned to Morocco.

Spanish Sahara started off with a distinctive series in 1924 [16] but thereafter relied on overprinted Spanish stamps until 1943, when attractive pictorials were resumed [18]. In 1975 Spain decided to relinquish the territory and it was divided between Morocco and Mauritania, but this was resisted by the Polisario movement, which proclaimed an independent Arab republic and has since issued stamps in areas under its control.

EQUATORIAL GUINEA

The Spanish colonies became the independent Republic of Equatorial Guinea in October 1968 and distinctive stamps were introduced the following year [17]. At first stamps with designs relevant to the country were issued [19] but since the early 1970s they have been frankly thematic and international in scope.

Below: In 1994 Equatorial Guinea issued this stamp portraying Neil Armstrong, Buzz Aldrin and Michael Collins to commemorate the first landing of men on the Moon.

10   11

12

13

14

15

16   17

18

19

1　　　　　2

3　　　　　4

5

6

7　　　　　8

9　　　　　10

11

NORTH AFRICA

The four countries of North Africa represented the furthest extent of Turkish rule from 1518 until the early 20th century, by which time they had become semi-independent and wholly lawless. They were the haunt of the Barbary pirates who preyed on Mediterranean shipping. European inroads began with the French invasion of Algiers in 1830 to extirpate piracy, leading to the direct annexation of Algeria in 1848 after a protracted and costly colonial war. The suppression of piracy led to the French protectorate over Tunis in 1881, although the Bey of Tunis remained as nominal ruler. As a result of the Italo-Turkish War of 1911 Libya fell to the Italians, and the following year France and Spain partitioned Morocco into protected zones, with Tangier as an international free port. Both powers had considerable difficulties with rebellious tribes. All but Morocco suffered the ravages of World War II and long, bitter conflict to attain independence in the 1950s.

Left: The North African campaign of 1942–3 was largely fought on Tunisian soil. Its liberation from German occupation was celebrated by a stamp of 1943 showing British, Free French and American soldiers.

ALGERIA
Ordinary French stamps were used until 1924 when Algeria was granted a measure of autonomy, and stamps were overprinted "Algerie" [1] pending a distinctive issue [2]. Administered by the Vichy French regime, the country was invaded by Allied forces in 1942; after the liberation stamps including the name of the French Republic were issued in 1944 [3]. Algeria continued to have its own stamps [4] until 1958, when it was again incorporated in France following the outbreak of rebellion in 1954. When the Algerians won their independence in 1962 French stamps were locally overprinted before distinctive stamps were resumed. Many stamps since then have referred to the struggles of that period [5], alternating with issues featuring landmarks [6] and the wide variety of scenery.

MOROCCO
By the late 19th century the Sherif of Morocco was virtually independent, but the strategic importance of his country led to it falling prey to rival European powers. The Agadir incident in 1911, involving the gunboat *Panzer*, almost triggered off a full-scale war between Germany and France. Britain [7], France, Spain and Germany all had their own postal services handing overseas mail, while internal services were operated by the Sherifian Posts [8].

After Morocco was partitioned between France and Spain in 1912 Tangier had its own postal services run by Britain [9], France and Spain [10]. The stamps used in the French and Spanish zones followed the styles of these countries but featured local scenes [11–12]. In 1956 both powers relinquished their protectorates and Morocco became a wholly independent kingdom [13]. Since then stamps have portrayed Muhammad V or his son Hassan II, interspersed with landmarks [14], scenery and wildlife [15].

LIBYA
Under Italian rule overprinted stamps were followed by distinctive designs that tended to highlight Libya's Roman history [16]. During World War II British stamps were overprinted "M.E.F." (Middle East Forces) for use in North Africa [17]. Later, similar overprints were produced for use in

Tripolitania. The French invaded Libya from the south and occupied Fezzan and Ghadames [19]. In 1949 Britain recognized the leader of the Senussi tribe as Amir of Cyrenaica and stamps thus inscribed appeared in 1950. In December 1951 Cyrenaica united with the states of Tripolitania, Fezzan and Ghadames to form the kingdom of Libya. It was the first country to achieve independence through the United Nations.

Stamps of Cyrenaica were over-printed, with the denominations in military administration lire [18]. Libya's stamps continued in the Italian tradition but increasingly espoused Islamic solidarity. In 1969 the monarchy was overthrown by a military coup that brought Colonel Gaddafi to power. Stamps of the Libyan Arab Republic (LAR) have boasted of its military preparedness to withstand western attempts to subvert the regime.

Below: Libya celebrated the centenary of the Universal Postal Union in 1974 with this stamp (top) showing a post-rider and Concorde to contrast mail communications old and new. A stamp (bottom) from Tunisia marked the fifth annual week promoting the health of schoolchildren in the Maghreb (Arab region of North Africa).

Surreal Stamps

A characteristic of Tunisian stamps in the early years of the republic was their surreal quality, largely as a result of the work of one designer, Hatem Elmekki. Contrasting with the dour portraits of President Bourguiba, Elmekki's designs ranged from the whimsical to the bizarre and continued to flourish for almost 40 years.

TUNISIA

The French took over this Turkish province in 1881, recognizing the Bey of Tunis but establishing a regency because the region was on the verge of economic collapse as a result of the suppression of piracy, its main source of revenue. Stamps gave an outward semblance of independence [20] but it was not until 1955 that France bowed to nationalist agitation and granted it [21]. The following year the monarchy was abolished and Tunisia became a republic, one of the more moderate and westernized of the Arab states.

Tunisia pursues a moderate new issue policy, averaging about 30 stamps a year. Most are singles focusing on matters of national and international importance; their symbolic or allegorical motifs show the pervasive influence of Hatem Elmekki. Occasional stamps portray famous Tunisians, including women (such as the singer Saliha) which is relatively unusual in Muslim countries. Since 1997 short sets have reproduced paintings by indigenous artists, while a few sets of three or four stamps have adopted a thematic line, featuring horses, reptiles, shells, musical instruments and ancient ruins.

12

13   14

15

16

17   18

19

20   21

1

2

3

4

5

6

7

8

9

10

11

EGYPT AND SUDAN

The present-day Arab Republic of Egypt day is a world removed from the great pharaonic civilization of the Nile that was flourishing by 4000 BC when the upper and lower kingdoms of Egypt were united. After 525 BC Egypt was dominated by foreign powers from the Persians to the Turks, but was running its own affairs when the British became involved in the Suez Canal in 1869 and seized control in 1882. Although still nominally under the Ottoman Empire, Egypt became a British protectorate in 1914 following the outbreak of World War I. This arrangement continued until 1922, when it was declared an independent kingdom. The monarchy was abolished in 1952 and Egypt became a republic.

To the south, and three times the size of Egypt, lay Sudan, which Mohamed Ali, Pasha of Egypt, conquered in 1822. The Egyptians were driven out of Sudan by the Mahdist revolt of 1881, but the country was reconquered in 1899 and declared an Anglo-Egyptian condominium.

Left: A set of three stamps marked the signing of the Anglo-Egyptian Treaty of 1936. Ramsay Macdonald, British Prime Minister in 1924 and 1929–35, chaired the conference and is depicted at the top of the table; the future prime minister Anthony Eden sits beside him.

FROM KHEDIVE TO KING

When Egypt adopted stamps in 1866, they were totally oriental in appearance with Arabic inscriptions [1], but the Great Pyramid became the motif of all stamps from 1867 to 1914 [2]. Egypt was then ruled by a khedive (viceroy) for the sultan in Constantinople, but when it became a British protectorate in 1914, the khedive became a sultan in his own right. As well as the obligatory pyramids, stamps of this period showed other ancient monuments [3]. Sultan Ahmed Fuad became king on 15 March 1922, and stamps portraying him were produced by Harrison and Sons of London in 1923, using photogravure for the first time [4].

KINGDOM OF EGYPT

The kingdom lasted three decades, during which various special issues drew inspiration from the pharaonic period [5]. A stamp of January 1938 celebrated King Farouk's wedding to Princess Farida of Iran [6] while a similar stamp, with a wedding group substituted, celebrated the king's 18th birthday a month later. Farouk had ambitions to throw off British influence. He ejected their troops from the Nile delta in 1947 and confined them to the Canal Zone, then abrogated the treaty regarding Sudan in 1951, signalled by overprinting the stamps in Arabic to signify that he was king of both Egypt and Sudan [7]. From 1932 to 1941 special stamps were used by the British forces in Egypt [8–9].

ARAB REPUBLIC

Farouk was forced to abdicate in 1952 and a military junta proclaimed a regency for the infant Ahmed Fuad II, then declared a republic. The Farouk stamps were overprinted with bars to blot out his face [10]. After the Anglo-French Suez venture of 1956 the spelling of Egyptian stamps was changed from French [11] to English, although the Egyptians maintained that it was American [12]. Colonel Nasser merged Egypt with Syria in 1958 to form the United Arab Republic. It was shortlived but Egypt retained the title of UAR until 1971, when "Egypt Arab

Hollow Victory

Nasser nationalized the Suez Canal in September 1956, prompting the British and French to invade Egypt. Although the brief campaign was a military success, the Allies were forced to evacuate the country when the USA and USSR (in a rare Cold War truce) joined in condemning the action and threatening sanctions. Egypt celebrated its "victory" with a stamp showing soldiers and civilians, shoulder to shoulder, resisting the enemy invasion.

Republic" [14] was chosen. Modern Egyptian stamps continue to draw heavily on pharaonic images, contrasting them with modern buildings and logos reflecting the importance of Cairo as a global conference centre [15].

SUDAN

The reconquest of Sudan by an Anglo-Expedition army commanded by General Kitchener (Later Field Marshal Lord Kitchener of Khartoum) began in 1896 and was completed in 1899. The first stamps, issued in 1897, were Egyptian stamps overprinted [16], followed by a series depicting a camel postman [13]. This design was produced by E.A. Stanton, then a *bimbashi* (captain) in the khedive's army but later a colonel in the British Army and one of Britain's foremost philatelists. He persuaded the sheik of the Howawir tribe to pose with straw-filled sacks to represent mailbags. The bags were optimistically inscribed "Khartoum" and "Berbera", although these towns were still in enemy hands at the time. So popular did the image become that it remained on stamps until the 1950s and then became the

national emblem on Sudanese coins. An interlude in 1941 used a palm tree design [17] but the camel postman was restored in 1948 for the entire definitive series. Even when pictorial motifs were adopted in 1951 the camel postman was retained for the 50p top value.

The statue of General Gordon, murdered by the Mahdists in 1885, was the subject of the airmail series of 1931 [18], while a set of nine, released in 1935, marked the 50th anniversary of his death [19]. Self-government in 1954 was celebrated by three stamps showing the camel postman. Two years later Sudan became an independent republic, with stamps showing the wings of hope over a map [20].

In 1969 a pro-communist democratic republic was proclaimed [21]. Although this totalitarian regime was overthrown in April 1985 and an ordinary republic established [22], the country has been torn apart by ethnic and religious trouble in recent years.

SUEZ CANAL

During the late 19th century, France, Britain, Greece, Italy and Russia operated post offices in Egypt, but only the first of these issued stamps specifically inscribed or overprinted for use in Alexandria and Port Said. French involvement was largely concerned with the construction of the Suez Canal, begun in 1859 and completed ten years later. Stamps printed in Paris were used in connection with a mail service operated by the Suez Canal Company between July and the end of August 1868 [23].

Below: This French stamp of 1899 was overprinted for use at Port Said (left), and in 1902 French stamps were engraved for use at Alexandria (right).

12   13

14

15

16   17

18

19   20

21   22

23

ART AND ARCHITECTURE OF THE PHARAOHS IN STAMPS

The art and architecture of ancient Egypt is extraordinary and without parallel anywhere in the world. The tombs of the pharaohs are masterpieces of engineering that defy rational explanation and we still marvel at the methods used to raise such gigantic blocks of stone with such precision. The pyramids were one of the seven wonders of the ancient world, and it is small wonder that they have appeared on numerous Egyptian stamps since 1867.

Ranking in iconic stature with the pyramids is the colossal statue of the Sphinx nearby, which is often depicted in the foreground of stamps featuring the tombs. Although these famous structures are among the largest and oldest in the world, Egypt boasts many other architectural masterpieces, such as the great temple at Karnak, built by Seti I and Rameses II.

When the temples of Abu Simbel were threatened with inundation following the construction of the Aswan Dam in the 1960s, UNESCO mounted a worldwide appeal to raise the funds to have the temples dismantled and moved to higher ground. This provoked a flood of stamps from all over the world in its support. Egypt returned the compliment with stamps showing aspects of the temples with the UNESCO emblem alongside.

The Sphinx and the gigantic seated figures of Abu Simbel are prime examples of architectonic sculpture that have never been surpassed, but dynastic Egypt also produced countless life-sized statues, heads and busts, from the exquisite head of Nefertiti, painted to re-create her fabled beauty, to the gold mask of Tutankhamun, the boy pharaoh. The discovery of his spectacular tomb in 1922 was one of the most important landmarks in archaeology

Below: A British stamp of 1972, marking the 50th anniversary of the discovery of Tutankhamun's tomb.

and it has been the subject of many definitive and special issues. The 50th anniversary of the find was celebrated by issues from Britain to Bhutan.

Not as spectacular, perhaps, but of immense importance to the emerging science of Egyptology, was the Rosetta Stone, whose parallel inscriptions in Greek and Aramaic enabled Jean-François Champollion to decipher hieroglyphics. This remarkable stone document was discovered during Napoleon's expedition to Egypt in 1798. When the French were defeated in 1801 the stone was handed over to Britain and is now in the British Museum, whose collection of Egyptian antiquities is second only to that of the Cairo Museum. The 150th anniversary

Left (clockwise from top): Egyptian stamps issued to mark the centenary of the opera Aida *in 1971, the International Conference on Population and Development, 1994, and the Cairo Statistical Congress, 1927, showing a statue of Amenhotep.*

Right (clockwise from top): Egyptian stamps featuring a gold chair back from Tutankhamun's tomb, 1972, Imhotep, god of medicine, 1928, and the World Under-17s football mascot, 1997.

AR EGYPT جمهورية مصر العربية

Above: Queen Nefertiti (1953) and Rameses II (1957) flanking a stamp of 1985 showing a slave kneeling with a tray of fruit, taken from a fresco.

Left: The souvenir sheet released by Egypt in 1972 to celebrate the 50th anniversary of the discovery of Tutankhamun's tomb shows his richly gilded second mummiform coffin.

Right: The elaborate court dress of a pharaonic messenger depicted on one of the annual issues for Post Day (1969).

مرور خمسين عاما على اكتشاف مقبرة توت عنخ آمون
50TH ANNIVERSARY OF DISCOVERY OF TOUT ANKH AMON'S TOMB

Above: Champollion and the Rosetta Stone on a stamp of 1972 marking the 150th anniversary of his translation of Egyptian hieroglyphics.

Above: Edfu Temple, depicted on an airmail stamp of 1985. Others in this series featured the pyramids of Giza and the colossal statue of Akhenaton.

Above: The Eye of Horus, flanked by the goddesses Nekhbet and Wadjet, on stamps for the 15th Ophthalmological Congress, held at Cairo in 1937.

of Champollion's breakthrough was celebrated by both Egypt and France in 1972. His discovery, and the booty brought back to Europe, triggered off a craze for all things Egyptian. It influenced everything from furniture to jewellery design in early 19th-century Europe. In the 1920s and 1930s, following the discovery of the boy pharaoh's tomb, there was an astonishing revival of Egytian style, which greatly influenced Art Deco.

The art of the pharaohs also exerted a tremendous influence on the development of Egyptian nationalism in the 19th century. Khedive Ismail commissioned Giuseppe Verdi to write the opera *Aida*, set in ancient Egypt, for

the opening of the Cairo Opera House in 1871; stamps marking its centenary depicted the opera's victory parade.

Egypt has been adept at harnessing pharaonic imagery to all manner of modern subjects. This fashion began when the statue of Amenhotep was used for the Statistical Congress stamps of 1927, while Imhotep graced stamps the following year for the Medical Congress in Cairo. The sacred Eye of Horus was an appropriate motif for the stamps of 1937 for the 15th World Ophthalmological Congress in Cairo.

These stamps set the trend for numerous more recent issues. In particular, wall paintings of the 18th dynasty from the tombs at Thebes have

provided a virtually inexhaustible source of pictures for the annual Post Day stamps. In one case, using a theme within a theme, pharaonic costumes were set within a frame derived from the great temple at Karnak.

Even events such as the Olympic Games have been given the pharaonic treatment. No matter what the topic or occasion, Egypt can invariably find a motif from pharaonic figurative or decorative art that is appropriate. The ceremonial headdress of the pharaohs has become almost a national symbol and has even lent itself to cartoon treatment, as in the mascot devised for the World Football Championships for Under-17s, held in Egypt in 1997.

FRENCH WEST AFRICA

The French colonies and protectorates in Africa were grouped into two large administrative units from 1944 until the various components became independent republics in the 1950s. They formed a vast area south of the Sahara that comprised Dahomey, French Guinea, French Sudan, the Ivory Coast, Mauritania, Niger, Senegal and Upper Volta. There was also a certain amount of adjustment territory. French Sudan was abolished in 1899

and its land was parcelled out among Senegal, Guinea, Ivory Coast, Dahomey, Senegambia and Niger, but it was reconstituted in 1921 and eventually merged with Senegal to form Mali.

Left: A stamp from the republic of Guinea shows a map of Africa with the four countries of the OERS (an organization of states bordering on the River Senegal) highlighted. This reflects the solidarity of the former colonies in French West Africa.

UNDER FRENCH RULE

Separate issues for the French colonies were replaced in 1944 by a single series inscribed "Afrique Occidentale Française" (French West Africa). They continued until 1958–9 [1] when they were superseded as the various colonies achieved independence. Before 1944 the various territories had their own stamps, mainly using one or other of the French colonial keyplate designs [2; 4–5] with the West African name as part of the permanent motif and the individual name added to the inscription. Later issues were distinctive to each territory. They were originally printed typographically in rather garish two-colour combinations [6], but intaglio was later used with the overall name reduced to the initials "AOF" [3; 7–8]. In general, these stamps provided a good insight into the scenery, landmarks, fauna and flora, tribal customs and culture of the region, yet had a distinctly French character.

INDEPENDENCE

The transition from colony to independent republic was achieved smoothly after the advent of the Fifth Republic under de Gaulle in 1958. At first the various colonies and protectorates became republics within the French Community and this was reflected in the stamps of the period, which, for the most part, continued to be engraved and recess-printed at the Institut de Gravure in Paris.

The concept of a community of independent republics, modelled on the British Commonwealth, gradually disappeared, and the various countries went their separate ways. The political changes of the 1960s are charted by the switch to multicolour photogravure or lithography, as well as a number of name changes. Dahomey [9] became a popular republic in November 1975 and changed its name to Benin but a political change in 1990 led to the "popular" being dropped [10]. At the beginning of the 20th century Benin had been the name of a coastal strip that briefly had its own stamps before being absorbed by Dahomey.

The Ivory Coast [11] retained its colonial name after the attainment of independence in 1960, astonishingly as the name reflected the traditional trade in ivory, now highly illegal. The federation of Mali was formed in April 1959 by a merger of the former French Sudan and Senegal [12]. It had become independent within the French Community on 20 June 1950, but broke up when Senegal seceded two months later and resumed its own stamps [13]. Sudan, retaining the name

Trust Territory

Following the independence of the French trust territory of Cameroun in January 1960, the United Nations ordered a plebiscite to be held in the British Cameroons, which used the stamps of Nigeria. The northern district voted to join Nigeria but the south opted to ally itself to France. Nigerian stamps overprinted "Cameroons U.K.T.T." (United Kingdom Trust Territory) were in use from October 1960 until 30 September 1961, when the Southern Cameroons became part of the Republic of Cameroon.

Mali, left the French Community. While its ties with France remain strong and are reflected in many of its stamps since 1960, Mali has increasingly pursued an independent line, paying tribute to world personalities [14] and events.

The Islamic Republic of Mauritania [15] was created as an autonomous state within the French Community in

Below: A white-collared kingfisher appeared on one of Burkino Faso's stamps devoted to aquatic birds, 1988.

November 1958 but became fully independent and left the Community two years later. The Republic of the Niger was granted autonomy within the French Community in December 1958, but became a wholly independent republic in August 1960 [16]. Its stamps followed the same pattern as other former French West African colonies. Upper Volta [17] changed its name in August 1984 to Burkino Faso.

FORMER GERMAN COLONIES

Germany joined in the scramble for Africa in 1884 and annexed territories in West Africa under the names of Kamerun (Cameroon) and Togogebiet (Togo). Overprinted German stamps were followed by the Yacht keytype stamps. Following the outbreak of World War I both territories were rapidly overrun by Anglo-French forces.

The French overprinted stamps of Gabon and Dahomey for use in the respective territories, while Britain overprinted stamps of Kamerun with "C.E.F." (Cameroon Expeditionary Force) with values surcharged in sterling. The British zones of Cameroon and Togo were incorporated in Nigeria and the Gold Coast, using the stamps of those countries, whereas the French made separate issues for Cameroon and Togo. Togo subsequently became an independent republic. Following a plebiscite under UN supervision the French and British parts of Cameroon combined to form a federal republic, with stamps inscribed bilingually.

Below: Andrea del Sarto's Virgin and Child *is one of many religious paintings on Christmas stamps from Cameroon.*

 10
 11
 12
 13
 14
 15
 16
 17

1

2

3

4

5

6

7

8

9

10

FRENCH EQUATORIAL AFRICA

Located on the western side of central Africa, French Equatorial Africa consisted of four self-governing dependencies, Middle Congo, Ubangi-Shari, Chad and Gabon, covering an area of almost 2.6 million sq km/1 million sq miles but with a population of only about two million. France's initial intention was to establish a few coastal trading posts to combat the slave trade, but in the "scramble for Africa" it acquired Gabon and the Middle Congo between 1885 and 1891, and between 1894 and 1897 Chad and the Ubangi basin were annexed. The four colonies, united in 1910, became overseas departments in 1946. In 1956 they became autonomous republics within the French Community and attained total independence in 1960.

Left: In 1952 this stamp celebrated the centenary of the birth of Pierre Savorgnan de Brazza, a Brazilian who became a French citizen in 1874, joined the navy and served in Gabon, whence he explored the hinterland north of the Congo and founded the trading post Brazzaville, now the capital of the Congo Republic.

UNDER FRENCH RULE

The frequent permutations and combinations of colonial administration under the French are reflected in the complex stamps of this region. General issues for use throughout Equatorial Africa appeared from 1937 [1] to 1961 [2], with a series printed for the Free French in London during World War II [3]. At other times the various territories had distinctive stamps. Stamps inscribed for French Congo were in use from 1891 until 1906. At first the French Colonies general issues were overprinted, then the colonial keytype series was engraved with the name [4], followed in 1900 by a pictorial set showing a stalking leopard [5]. Gabon issued its own stamps (1886–9) then formed part of French Congo (1889–1904) until it became a separate colony with its own stamps again [6].

After the break-up of French Congo in 1906, distinctive stamps were adopted by Middle Congo showing an enlarged version of the leopard design [8]. Stamps of this series, in different colours, were overprinted for use in Chad [9]. In 1915 Chad was joined to Ubangi-Shari and stamps were accordingly overprinted [10]. In 1922 they became separate colonies again and resumed distinctive stamps [11]. The stamps of Ubangi-Shari were reissued in 1924 with an additional overprint "Afrique Equatoriale Française" and these continued until 1937, when the general issues for the whole of Equatorial Africa were introduced.

INDEPENDENT STATES

All four territories opted to become republics in 1958. Their history since then has been turbulent, with revolutions and military coups or uprisings often suppressed with the aid of French troops. By the 1990s, however, greater stability gradually developed.

The restrained intaglio of the 1960s gradually gave way to exuberantly coloured stamps, usually printed by photogravure or, more recently, offset lithography. There is no common thread running through them, certainly not one that reflects the character or cultural heritage of the upper Congo basin. Rather they have succumbed to the desire to use their stamps as a means of raising hard currency overseas, hence their apparent penchant for stamps portraying American presidents or the British royal family.

Chad became a republic within the French Community on 28 November 1958. Although it is now a fully independent sovereign state it retains close ties with France, reflected in the many stamps that are not only printed there [12] but feature French personalities, notably a lengthy series of 1971–3 portraying the kings and queens of France from the Middle Ages onwards. Other series have reproduced French works of art [13], contrasting with the issues of local interest such as those featuring wildlife [14].

As a sovereign state Gabon has also retained its colonial name. Its progress from autonomy within the French Community to full independence is reflected in its stamps, which have successively portrayed Leon Mba as prime minister [7] and then as president.

Middle Congo became the Republic of Congo [15], often referred to as Congo (Brazzaville) to distinguish it from the former Belgian Congo, which was known as Congo (Leopoldville) and later Congo (Kinshasa). In 1970 it adopted the title of Popular Republic of the Congo [16], when its former Belgian counterpart assumed the title of the Democratic Republic, but since 1991 it has been simply Congo.

An interesting feature of many of these former French colonies was their preference for triangular stamps to denote postage due. Unlike postage dues in most other parts of the world, noted for their monotonous uniformity, the former French territories

Below: Typical of the flamboyant stamps issued by the short-lived Central African Empire in the 1970s is this stamp commemorating the Graf Zeppelin *flight to Chicago of 1933.*

Renaissance Man
Albert Schweitzer (1875–1965), theologian, philosopher and musician, and one of the greatest exponents of Bach's organ works, took up medicine at the age of 30 and in 1913 left Europe to establish a hospital to combat leprosy and sleeping sickness at Lambarene in Gabon. This stamp, originally released in 1960, was overprinted in 1963 to celebrate his golden jubilee in Africa. Note the view of Lambarene (left) and the organ with Bach's music, an important secondary motif for collectors of the musical theme.

favoured pictorials for this purpose with distinctive themes, such as different modes of mail transportation.

The biggest change of all came when Ubangi-Shari chose the name of the Central African Republic on attaining independence [17]. Its early stamps were recess-printed in Paris and clung to traditional art and handicrafts or distinctive fauna and flora, but by 1970 many issues had become highly politicized under the tyrannical rule of Jean Bedel Bokassa. A former French sergeant, he had become commander-in-chief in 1963 and overthrew President David Dacko in 1965, making himself life-president and then proclaiming himself emperor in December 1976. For two years the poorest country in Africa was an empire, but reverted to its republican title [18] when Bokassa was overthrown in 1979. One of the more prolific stamp-issuing countries of Africa, it produced numerous stamps with little or no relevance to Africa, far less to the republic itself.

1

2

3

4

5

6

7

8

9

THE HORN OF AFRICA

This vast region in the north-east corner of Africa includes Ethiopia, a country whose civilization dates from biblical times and which extended its sway over many neighbouring tribes until the late 19th century, when the British, French and Italians began nibbling at the edges of its territory. Today, the region consists of Ethiopia, Eritrea, Djibouti and Somalia.

Left: Haile Selassie, Conquering Lion of Judah and Emperor of Ethiopia, was driven out by the Italians in 1936 but was restored in 1941 following the British liberation. Stamps portraying the emperor in ceremonial robes were issued in March 1942. The basic stamps were printed in India and the values added in Khartoum, Sudan – a unique example of stamps produced in two countries for use in a third.

FRENCH TERRITORIES

The French were the first European power to establish a toehold in the Horn of Africa, by acquiring the port of Obock on the Red Sea coast in 1892. French colonial keytypes were used until in 1894 Obock got stamps of its own – some of the strangest of all time [1]. In 1893 the French acquired the much more important seaport of Djibouti, whose stamps were modelled on those of Obock, printed on lined paper, imperforate but with simulated perforations surrounding the designs [2]. These issues were replaced in 1902 by a series for the French Somali Coast [3]. A Free French series during World War II had the name "Djibouti" larger than the country name, on a locomotive symbolizing the railway line that linked Ethiopia to the coast [5].

In the 1960s, Somali agitation for the inclusion of the French territory in the republic led to a plebiscite in 1966 by which the people voted to remain French, but the country name was then changed to French Territory of Afars and Issas [6] to distance it from Somalia. In 1977 it became the independent republic of Djibouti [7].

ITALIAN TERRITORIES

In 1893 the Italians seized territory in the Horn of Africa and named it Eritrea, derived from the ancient name for the Red Sea. Overprinted Italian stamps [8] were followed by distinctive designs [10]. From Eritrea the Italians mounted an invasion of Ethiopia but were decisively defeated at Adowa in 1894. Nine years later, however, Italy gained a port on the Somali coast. Stamps inscribed "Benadir" (Arabic for port) were issued in 1903 [9]. Stamps inscribed "Somalia" were introduced in 1916 [11]. In 1925 Britain ceded a tract of Kenya west of the Juba River. Italian stamps overprinted "Oltre Giuba" (beyond the Juba) were issued pending a distinctive series featuring a map of the area [4]. Jubaland was incorporated into Somalia in 1926.

Italy was revenged for Adowa in 1936 when its forces invaded and occupied Ethiopia. Stamps inscribed "Etiopia", portraying Victor Emmanuel III, were soon followed by those inscribed "Africa Orientale Italiana" (Italian East Africa). In 1940 Italy declared war on Britain but by 1941 British troops had not only occupied Somalia and Eritrea but also liberated Ethiopia. British stamps overprinted "E.A.F." (East African Forces) were used in the former Italian territories [12], followed by stamps overprinted for Eritrea or Somalia under British military administration [13] and latterly under civil administration [14]. Somalia reverted to Italy in 1950 as a UN trust territory but gained its independence in 1960.

10

A Hard-won Struggle

Within ten years of their incorporation in Ethiopia, the Eritreans had risen in revolt and started a war that lasted 30 years. Two years before its independence was finally recognized by the world at large, Eritrea established a postal service, complete with stamps, in 1991. Stamps inscribed in English but printed in Italy reflect the support given to the new country by its former colonial rulers.

BRITISH TERRITORIES

British penetration of the area began in the 1880s as part of the Anglo-Egyptian Sudan, and Indian stamps were used until 1903 when the protectorate was transferred from India to the British government. Indian stamps overprinted "British Somaliland" [15] were used pending a supply of stamps more correctly inscribed "Somaliland Protectorate" [16]. Pictorial stamps were introduced in 1938 and continued until 1960, when the protectorate joined the newly formed Somali Republic [17].

ETHIOPIA

One of the oldest civilizations in Africa, Ethiopia was ruled by emperors who claimed descent from Solomon and the Queen of Sheba. The country retained its unique Coptic Christian culture and held aloof from the outside world until the late 19th century. It emerged from its isolation under Emperor Menelik II, portrayed on the stamps introduced in

1894. The country continued to make progress under his daughter, the Empress Zauditu (Judith) and her successor, Prince Ras Tafari, who was crowned emperor, with the title Haile Selassie, in 1930.

Many Ethiopian stamps of the early 20th century portrayed the members of the imperial family, along with exotic wildlife. Haile Selassie [18] reigned twice (1930–6 and 1941–74), steering his vast country into the modern world. Accusations of corruption levelled at the emperor, together with strikes and economic hardship arising from a severe drought, led to the abolition of the monarchy following a military coup, and Ethiopia became a republic [19]. In 1976 the ruling military junta proclaimed Ethiopia a socialist state, but in 1991, following a change of regime, Ethiopia emerged as a federal republic. Oddly, none of these political upheavals was reflected in any change of title on the stamps.

As a result of the new constitution of 1991 the province of Eritrea, which had fought a long and bitter civil war, was formally granted autonomy, and in 1993, following a plebiscite, it voted for outright independence from Ethiopia. Distinctive stamps appeared in 1991 to celebrate autonomy and the 30th anniversary of the armed struggle, followed by definitives showing the national flag and map. Most Eritrean stamps have been printed in Italy, the former colonial power.

Below: In 1995 Eritrea issued a set on the theme of the Council for Mutual Economic Assistance in Africa. The top value shows the emblems and flags of the member countries.

11

12

13

14

15

16

17

18

19

1

2

3

4

5

6

7

8

9

10

11

EAST AFRICA

This region, now comprising the republics of Kenya, Uganda and Tanzania, was colonized by the British in the 1890s and absorbed the former German East Africa (Tanganyika) during World War I. The postal services of this new British East African territory (later renamed the East African Posts and Telecommunications Corporation) were unified, although the component countries had political autonomy. This situation continued for some years after all three countries became independent republics within the Commonwealth. Nationalism developed rapidly after World War II in the "wind of change" that was blowing across the African continent. Kenya won its independence in 1963 after a long period of guerrilla warfare, and the other two republics soon followed.

Left: The architect of Kenyan independence was Jomo Kenyatta. Imprisoned by the British during the Mau Mau campaign in the 1950s, while in detention he was elected president of the national Kenya Africa Union party, becoming prime minister in 1963 and president of the republic a year later. His moderate policies and statesmanship conciliated the white community and made Kenya one of the most stable countries in Africa.

KENYA, UGANDA AND TANGANYIKA

East Africa was opened up by the Imperial British East Africa Company, which issued its own stamps [1] from 1890 to 1895, when it was taken over by the British government. In the same period a protectorate was proclaimed over Uganda, whose stamps featured a portrait of Queen Victoria by Baron Heinrich von Angeli [2]. The postal services of both territories were combined in 1903 and stamps portraying Edward VII [3] were introduced; the same frames were later used for stamps showing George V. The neater title of Kenya and Uganda was adopted in 1922 when British East Africa was transformed from a protectorate into a crown colony [4]. The former German colony of Tanganyika joined the postal union in 1935 and stamps bearing the names of all three countries were issued from then onwards.

It is important to note that, although collectors refer to this group as "Kenya, Uganda and Tanganyika" (KUT), the authorities were at pains to vary the order of the inscriptions so that no single territory assumed a dominant position. The inaugural series was in the prevailing colonial fashion for bicoloured pictorials, with a portrait of George V inset, and the series was re-issued in 1938 with the portrait of George VI substituted [5]. Stamps bearing the names of the three countries [6] continued until the 1960s, after they had become independent politically and even had their own stamps. From 1965 to 1975 stamps inscribed with the names of Kenya, Uganda and Tanzania were produced by the East African Posts and Telecommunications Corporation [7].

KENYA

Achieving independence in December 1963, Kenya became a republic a year later. The inaugural series inscribed "Uhuru" (Swahili for "independence") showed a mixture of subjects [8] but stamps since then have favoured natural history [9–10], handicrafts [12] and other subjects likely to attract tourists. They have also featured many universal organizations, such as Rotary, whose founder Paul P. Harris was portrayed on a stamp of 1994 for the 50th anniversary of the Mombasa club [11].

UGANDA

Distinctive Ugandan stamps were re-introduced in 1962, beginning with a set marking the centenary of the discovery of the source of the Nile [13]. Recess-printed, with a profile of Elizabeth II, these stamps were a far cry from the gaudy issues of later years, although the tyrant Idi Amin did not leave his mark on Ugandan stamps.

In later years stamps had a global outlook [14] but more recently Uganda has jumped on the thematic bandwagon with numerous sets – including the ever-popular Disney stamps [15] – aimed at collectors.

TANZANIA

Germany colonized Tanganyika in the 1890s and issued stamps inscribed "Deutsch-Ostafrika" [16] from 1893 to 1916, when the colony was occupied by British imperial forces. In this period stamps of the Indian Expeditionary Force were overprinted for use by troops on Mafia Island [17] blockading the Rufiji delta. From November 1917 German East Africa was under British administration and used stamps of East Africa and Uganda overprinted "G.E.A." [18]. Distinctive stamps featuring a giraffe [19] were introduced in Tanganyika in 1922 and continued until 1935, when the unified series was adopted. Though it was the last of the three countries to join the Commonwealth, Tanganyika was the first to gain independence, in 1961. Pictorial stamps inscribed "Uhuru" were issued in December that year.

Below: Lions of the Serengeti featured on one of Tanganyika's independence set of 1961 (left), and Sultan Kalif bin Harub on the Zanzibar definitive series of 1952 (right).

Missionary Mail

Uganda in the late 1880s was in a religious ferment as Muslim, Catholic and Protestant factions fought each other for converts. After the Anglo-German agreement of 1890, in which Britain exchanged Heligoland for a free hand in Uganda and Zanzibar, British influence increased and its missionaries were able to continue their work unhindered. One of these, the Reverend Ernest Millar at Mengo, organized the first postal service in March 1895, using sermon paper to produce stamps of a very basic design on his typewriter. Gum was supplied by the resin of a nearby tree.

The offshore island of Zanzibar, formerly centre of the Arab slave trade in Africa, had been a British protectorate since 1895 and originally used Indian stamps suitably overprinted. Later issues portrayed the sultans, dhows and distinctive Arabic architecture of the island. It gained full independence in December 1963 but only a few weeks later an African-inspired revolution toppled the sultan. Shortly afterwards Zanzibar joined Tanganyika to form the United Republic of Tanganyika and Zanzibar, soon shortened to Tanzania, but continued to issue its own stamps until 1967. During this period, despite the apparent unity represented by the stamps, Zanzibar was very much a law unto itself, with a Marxist regime that had its stamps printed in the German Democratic Republic and used strident images on them to promote its extreme left-wing politics [20].

12

13

14

15

16   17

18   19

20

1

2

3

4

5

6

7

8

9

10

11

CENTRAL AFRICA

A British expedition sponsored by the imperialist and financier Cecil Rhodes led the "scramble for Africa" in the late 1880s and resulted in the annexation of 1.25 million sq km/0.5 million sq miles of southern and central Africa in the name of the British South Africa Company. Out of Rhodes's ambition to create a British empire that stretched from the Cape to Cairo came the Bechuanaland protectorate (now Botswana in southern Africa) and three countries, formerly Northern and Southern Rhodesia and Nyasaland, but now known as Zambia, Zimbabwe and Malawi respectively.

Left: Cecil Rhodes made a fortune from the Kimberley diamond mines before entering politics and becoming prime minister of Cape Colony. At the same time his imperial ambitions led him to found the British South Africa Company as well as endowing Rhodes scholarships for Americans, Germans and colonials at Oxford University.

COMPANY RULE

Stamps inscribed "British South Africa Company" were introduced in 1892 [1], followed by two later sets also featuring the company arms. A shortage of stamps during the Matabele rebellion of 1896 was met by overprinting stamps of the Cape of Good Hope [2]. Although stamps continued to bear the company name until 1909, the name "Rhodesia" was adopted in 1895. Cecil Rhodes thus joined the elite band of those, including Amerigo Vespucci, Christopher Columbus and Simon Bolivar, who had countries named after them, the only difference being that he chose the name himself.

Sadly Rhodes did not live long enough to see his name on the stamps for he died in 1902, worn out by his exertions in the defence of Kimberley during the Boer War. In April 1909 existing stamps of the British South Africa Company were overprinted "Rhodesia" [3], pending a supply of stamps with this name engraved at the foot, although the company name continued to appear at the top. The inaugural series of 1910 is popularly known as the Doubleheads, on account of its side-by-side portraits of George V and Queen Mary. This bicoloured series was not only very beautiful but also rich in its philatelic variety.

It was superseded by the Admirals, so-called because the series portrayed the king in naval uniform.

Further north, an expedition led by Sir Harry Johnstone occupied Nyasaland in 1893 to prevent the Portuguese from joining Angola to Mozambique. Sir Harry not only founded British Central Africa but even designed its stamps [4]. Stamps of this territory included a provisional issue in 1898 that utilized the upright oval designs normally embossed on cheques to create 1d stamps during a shortage of that denomination.

COLONIAL RULE

Following a proposal in 1923 by the British government to detach the main area of white settlement from company territory and join it to South Africa, the white settlers voted to become a separate crown colony with self-governing status. In 1924, therefore, the company's territories were divided into Northern and Southern Rhodesia and thereafter used stamps thus inscribed.

In both territories definitives portrayed the reigning monarch [5]. The Victoria Falls featured in several issues of Southern Rhodesia, including sets celebrating the silver jubilee of George V in 1935 [7] and the coronation of George VI in 1937. British Central

Illegal Stamps

The regime of Ian Smith in Rhodesia defied the British government by the illegal act of UDI (unilateral declaration of independence). When a stamp celebrating this event was issued, the British declared it invalid for postage, and any mail arriving in the UK with such stamps affixed was treated as unpaid and surcharged accordingly.

Africa was renamed the Nyasaland protectorate in 1907, and stamps portraying the reigning monarch were subsequently produced. A first tentative essay in pictorialism was the series of 1934, which showed a leopard on a rock, derived from the badge of the protectorate, with the profile of George V inset. The same motif, with a profile of George VI, was in use from 1938 to 1944 but then gave way to pictorial definitives [8]. In Northern Rhodesia small-format stamps managed to combine royal portraiture with a vignette of African wildlife [6].

FEDERATION

With the intention of creating an independent dominion, the three British territories in central Africa formed a federation in 1954 and introduced a joint issue of stamps inscribed "Rhodesia and Nyasaland" [9], followed by a small-format pictorial series [10]. Political disagreements emerged between the predominantly black countries and Southern Rhodesia, so this merger proved unworkable. When the federation broke up in 1964 each country resumed its own stamp issues. The only thing they had in common

was a penchant for small horizontal stamps, but whereas Southern Rhodesia [12] and Nyasaland [14] favoured a wide variety of subject, Northern Rhodesia produced a standard design showing the national emblem [13].

CHANGES OF NAME

Both Nyasaland and Northern Rhodesia attained independence in 1964 and reverted to names long used by their indigenous peoples. Thus Nyasaland became Malawi and Northern Rhodesia was renamed Zambia. Both celebrated their independence with stamps: Malawi portrayed Hastings Banda and the sunrise [11] while Zambia chose jubilant dancers [16]. Definitives under the new names continued existing patterns [15].

Most Zambian stamps since 1964 have been designed by Gabrielle Ellison [17]. This has given them an integrity that the stamps of many other African nations now lack, and until very recently they concentrated on subjects specific to the peoples of the country and their way of life, with attractive genre scenes [18–19]. Another unifying element in many stamps was the incorporation of a band of metallic ink alluding to the copper industry.

Southern Rhodesia merely dropped the "Southern" and retained the name of its founder, becoming a bastion of white supremacy. While affirming allegiance to the Crown, as exemplified in its Churchill stamp of 1965 [20], it was drifting apart from the mother country. In November that year it unilaterally declared independence. Stamps with an "Independence" overprint were followed by definitives omitting "Southern" [21]. Black majority rule eventually prevailed and in 1980 Rhodesia changed its name to Zimbabwe [22]. Stamps since then have either been thematic, with the usual themes of fauna and flora, or have highlighted the apparent technological progress of Zimbabwe [23]. In place of a portrait, these stamps feature the secretary bird, its national emblem, carved in soapstone.

1

2

3

4

5

6

7

8

9

10

11

WEST AFRICA

Four of the five countries on the west coast of Africa south of the Sahara were formerly British colonies, while the fifth, Liberia, shares with the others a common language (English) and a parallel history. Sierra Leone (1787) and Liberia (1822) were created by Britain and the USA respectively as homes for freed slaves, while the Gambia was, from 1808, a base for the Royal Navy in pursuit of slave-traders. The Gambia formed part of Sierra Leone until 1843, when it became a separate colony with a protectorate extending inland along the banks of the Gambia River.

The Gold Coast, which was first settled in 1821, was likewise administered by Sierra Leone until 1886. Nigeria first came under British influence in 1853, when a base was established at Lagos for the suppression of the slave trade. Later protectorates were proclaimed over the Oil Rivers and the Niger Coast. A chartered company penetrated the hinterland, which, in 1900, was formed into the separate colonies of Northern and Southern Nigeria; these were united in 1914.

Liberia had the distinction of being the first black African independent republic and it was from there that the concepts of nationalism and independence spread to the Gold Coast, the first of the British colonies to break away and become a dominion in 1957, assuming the name Ghana from an ancient African empire of that name.

Left: Dr Kwame Nkrumah (1909–72) was prime minister of Ghana from 1957 to 1960 and president from then until 1966, when he was ousted by a military coup while on a visit to China. Educated at Lincoln University in the USA, he is shown here posing in front of the Lincoln Memorial in Washington, DC.

THE GAMBIA

The first stamps are known as the Cameos, from the embossed profile of Queen Victoria [1]. From the 1920s pictorial stamps were recess-printed in the restrained two-colour settings fashionable until after World War II [3], giving way to multicolour photogravure with definitives following a single theme [4]. Since independence the Gambia has developed as a popular tourist destination [5]. It achieved autonomy in 1963, independence in 1965 and became a republic within the Commonwealth in 1970 [6].

GHANA

The first stamps of the Gold Coast were issued in 1875 and thereafter followed the prevailing colonial fashions for royal portraits. In 1928, however, it became the first British colony to adopt photogravure, for a small-format series featuring Christiansborg Castle, a former Danish trading post in Accra, the capital [2]. Later definitives (1938–58) were recess-printed and reflected the British influence on the country [7]. Under Kwame Nkrumah [8], Ghana soon adopted an independent policy championing non-alignment and the cause of African freedom and unity [9], ideals maintained by his successors.

SIERRA LEONE

Sierra Leone introduced stamps in 1859, the first territory in West Africa to do so. They were confined to royal portraiture until 1932 when pictorial definitives were adopted [10–11]. Intaglio was employed from then until after independence was achieved in

1961. Since then a high proportion of the stamps have been colourful and exciting but seldom relevant to the country itself.

NIGERIA

Stamps were introduced at Lagos in 1874, portraying Queen Victoria [12]. Separate issues were discontinued in 1906 when Lagos joined Southern Nigeria. Ordinary British stamps were used in the Oil Rivers region pending the introduction of stamps overprinted after the territory was declared a protectorate in 1892 [13].

The protectorate was extended into the hinterland and renamed the Niger Coast Protectorate in May 1893, adopting stamps portraying the elderly Victoria the following January [14]. In 1900 Southern Nigeria was declared a crown colony and protectorate [15], while Northern Nigeria became a protectorate [16]. In January 1914 they were amalgamated to form Nigeria [17], which became an independent federation in 1960. Most stamps since then have been printed by the Nigerian Security Minting and Printing Company [18–19].

In 1967 the eastern region seceded from the federation under the name of Biafra and distinctive stamps were issued in 1968–9 before the area was overrun by federal forces. The stamps celebrating the first anniversary of independence depicted atrocities allegedly committed by the Nigerian army.

Below: Few charity stamps are as specific as this one from Liberia, which names a particular charity and shows Seán Devereux in action.

Free-form and Self-adhesive
Sierra Leone made philatelic history in 1964 when it produced the world's first self-adhesive stamps, die-cut in the shape of the country itself, with commercial advertisements on the backing paper.

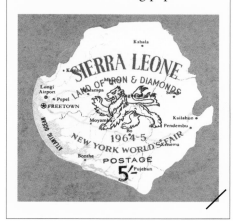

LIBERIA
The first stamps appeared in 1860 and featured the seated figure of Liberty alongside a sailing ship, uncannily like the reverse of the British copper coinage of the period. By the 1880s pictorial designs were featuring scenery, wildlife and native types as well as presidential portraits in the American style. From 1894 onwards stamp designs [20] leaned heavily on the famous Cape Triangulars. Separate stamps for registered mail [21] were produced from 1893 to 1923, many bearing the names of individual towns. The earlier stamps even provided a space for the manuscript insertion of the registration serial number, but by 1919 a more pictorial approach had been adopted.

By the 1930s Liberia had virtually become the private fief of the Firestone Rubber Company and many stamps from then onwards had an American slant. The very prolific issues since the 1980s seldom allude to the chronic civil wars affecting the country, but more often express its indebtedness to the USA [22]. Although it is not a member of the Commonwealth, Liberia has even participated in colonial omnibus issues commemorating the British royal family.

1

2

3

4

5

6

7

8

9

10

PORTUGUESE AFRICA

The Portuguese had a head start on all other European nations in opening up the "Dark Continent". In the 15th century their seamen, encouraged by Prince Henry the Navigator, pushed far down the west coast of Africa, establishing the trading posts that would become the nuclei of colonies. In 1498 Vasco da Gama rounded the Cape of Good Hope and sailed up the east coast of Africa as far as Mombasa, Kenya, before striking east to India. The major Portuguese territories in West Africa ranged from Cape Verde in the north-west to Guinea and the Congo in the centre and Angola in the south. On the east coast the main colonies were in Mozambique and Nyassa. The rise of nationalism in the 1960s led to long-running warfare on both sides of the continent before Portugal granted independence in 1975. With the exception of Portuguese Guinea (now known as Guinea-Bissau), the former colonies have not changed their names since the grant of independence.

Left: Stamps for general use in the Portuguese colonies and protectorates in Africa were issued in 1898 for the quatercentenary of Vasco da Gama's discovery of the sea route to India.

ANGOLA

The earliest stamps of Angola, introduced in 1870, conformed to the prevailing keyplate types used throughout the colonial empire, only the name and currency being distinctive. Even as late as the 1930s special issues followed an omnibus pattern [1], but in the 1950s special issues [2] and individually styled definitives were coming into use. The first multicoloured set appeared in 1955 and featured a map of the colony [3]. Since independence, stamps of Angola have adopted a more frankly thematic approach, although few issues have been as minimalist as the birds series of the 1990s [5]. A set of 2000 featured post offices around the country [6]. The Portuguese Congo, now the province of Cabinda north of the River Congo, had its own keytype stamps [4] from 1894 to 1920, when it was absorbed by Angola.

CAPE VERDE

The Cape Verde archipelago consists of ten islands off the west coast of Africa. Discovered in 1456, they were colonized four years later by Diogo Gomes. They became a Portuguese overseas province in 1951 and an independent republic in 1975. Standard colonial designs [7–8] were used until 1948 and new issues since then have been relatively moderate. The first full-colour stamps appeared in 1952, appropriately honouring the Portuguese navigators who used the islands as a staging post [9]. Tourism, wildlife and concern for the environment are recurring themes of more recent stamps [10].

GUINEA

The first stamps of Guinea consisted of those of Cape Verde overprinted in 1881. Thereafter, stamps of the key-plate types were inscribed for use until 1946, when a pictorial definitive series was adopted. In the 1960s stamps became more colourful and included an eye-catching diamond-shaped set devoted to indigenous snakes [11].

A revolt led by Amilcar Cabral against colonial rule erupted in 1963 and a decade later the republic of Guinea-Bissau was proclaimed. Its independence was recognized by the revolutionary government in Lisbon a year later, the first step towards the granting of independence to all the other African colonies. Stamps since then have been predominantly thematic in nature, from fire engines [12] to cats and dogs [13].

MOZAMBIQUE

At one time the provinces of Inhambane [14], Quelimane, Tete [18] and Zambezia had their own stamps in the prevailing keytypes. Lourenço Marques, Mozambique's chief port, also issued colonial keyplate stamps, as well as a solitary stamp in 1952 [15]. During World War I Portuguese troops invaded German East Africa and occupied the district of Kionga; stamps of Lourenço Marques were overprinted for use there [20].

Separate issues were made by two chartered companies for territory under their control. The Mozambique Company was chartered in 1891 and issued stamps featuring the company arms, followed by pictorial definitives in 1918 [16] and a series designed and printed in England in 1937 [17]. The Nyassa Company was chartered in 1894. Pictorial stamps appeared in 1901, followed by a series of 1921 [19], both printed by Waterlow of London. Nyassa reverted to Mozambique in 1929. The stamps of Mozambique proper followed the colonial pattern, apart from some charity tax stamps during and after World War I, until 1944. Even thereafter, most issues

formed part of the Portuguese colonial omnibus series, but from 1951 attractive thematic sets appeared [21]. A restrained issue policy has been pursued since the country's independence. In 1995 Mozambique became a member of the Commonwealth.

ST THOMAS AND PRINCE

These two islands in the Gulf of Guinea were discovered by the Portuguese in 1471 and were used as a penal colony from 1493 onwards, accommodating common criminals as well as Jewish children forcibly taken from their parents and baptized. By the mid-16th century the islands were covered with sugar plantations. Continual raiding by the French and Dutch destroyed the islands' prosperity in the 17th and 18th centuries and the colony began to recover only after the introduction of cocoa cultivation in 1890.

The islands used the various Portuguese colonial types from 1870 to 1948, but in 1951 they attained the status of an overseas province with considerable autonomy, and a more liberal policy was inaugurated. Although many of the stamps in the ensuing period honoured Portuguese explorers and politicians there were also sets featuring wildlife, ships, military uniforms and other popular subjects.

The islands became a wholly independent republic on 12 July 1975. Since 1977, however, the country has produced prolific "bandwagon" issues of little indigenous relevance.

Below: Stamps portraying President Carmona of Portugal (left) were released to mark his visit to the African colonies in 1970. Even before joining the Commonwealth, Mozambique celebrated British events (right).

11

12

13

14

15

16

17

18

19

20

21

1

2

3

4

5

6

7

8

9

10

SOUTHERN AFRICA

Three countries adjoining, or even landlocked within, South Africa were formerly known as the High Commission Territories because they continued to be administered by the British High Commissioner in South Africa after that country became an independent dominion in 1910 and subsequently a republic outside the Commonwealth. Lesotho (formerly Basutoland) and Swaziland are enclaves within South Africa, while Botswana (formerly Bechuanaland) lies between South Africa and Zimbabwe.

Left: The position of these three countries in relation to South Africa and their other neighbours was vividly illustrated by this stamp of 1990, which celebrated the tenth anniversary of the Southern African Development Coordination Conference and showed the countries' boundaries and flags.

BRITISH INVOLVEMENT

The British developed an interest in the essentially tribal territories of southern Africa in the second half of the 19th century. British Bechuanaland was declared a crown colony in 1885 and at first used the stamps of the Cape of Good Hope with a distinctive overprint [1]. Two years later British stamps, similarly overprinted, were adopted and continued to be used in that region until 1895, when it was annexed by the Cape and subsequently became part of South Africa.

Tribal territory to the north of British Bechuanaland was made a protectorate in 1888. The British stamps that had previously been overprinted for use in British Bechuanaland were now additionally overprinted with the word "Protectorate" to denote their use in this area [2]. British stamps overprinted "Bechuanaland Protectorate" continued to be used there until 1932, when a series portraying George V showed cattle at a water-hole [3]. The "thirsty cattle" design was subsequently used for the definitives of George VI and Elizabeth II until 1961. Even the stamps celebrating the 75th anniversary of the protectorate showed thirsty cattle flanked by Queens Victoria and Elizabeth [5]. Sterling currency was replaced by South African rands and cents in 1961. At first, existing stamps

were overprinted pending a pictorial series featuring birds [4]. Most countries hail independence with a sunrise but here again the importance of water in a semi-arid region was reflected in the stamps of 1965 marking internal autonomy [6].

Up to 1933 Basutoland used the stamps of South Africa distinguishable only by the postmark, but in that year it followed Bechuanaland with a series portraying George V over a picture of a crocodile and the Drakensberg Mountains [7]. This motif was retained for the George VI series but in 1954 a pictorial series with different themes was adopted. All three territories adopted South African decimal currency in 1961. The inauguration of the Basuto National Council in 1959 was marked by three stamps and for the first time the indigenous name of "Lesotho" was inscribed alongside the European name [8].

BOTSWANA

Bechuanaland became an independent republic in 1966 and adopted the older form of the name. Early issues, such as the set of 1970 marking the centenary of the death of Charles Dickens [9], reflected continuing cultural ties with Britain. Later stamps, however, faithfully recorded every aspect of the life and culture of the country, from occupations [10] and dress to the distinctive fauna [11] and flora [12] of the region. The countries of Southern Africa have enjoyed relative stability since independence, with strict observance of democratic principles [14].

LESOTHO

The kingdom of Lesotho has been ruled since gaining independence by Moshoeshoe II, apart from a five-year period (1990–5) when he was deposed and replaced by King Letsie, who later abdicated in his favour. Moshoeshoe II was portrayed on the 1988 definitives showing birds [15]. Latterly Lesotho has veered away from traditional subjects and become more aware of the themes that sell well, though there is no doubting the genuine feeling of affection in the country for the late Diana, Princess of Wales [13].

SWAZILAND

The tribal kingdom of Swaziland was placed under the joint protection of Britain and the South African Republic (Transvaal) in 1890 and stamps of the latter, overprinted "Swazieland" (*sic*) were then introduced [16]. Britain handed over sole control to the Transvaal in 1894 and ordinary stamps

Below: Swaziland stamps show a Kudu horn trumpet (top) and publicize the national AIDS campaign (bottom).

Royal Tour

In 1947 the British royal family toured Southern Africa and stamps celebrating their visit were issued by the various countries. The High Commission Territories had an omnibus issue, each releasing a set of four stamps in standard designs.

of that country (and later of South Africa) were used until 1933. Stamps portraying George V flanked by shields over a map of the country and mountain scenery [17] were then introduced and, as in the other territories, remained in use until the 1950s, with a portrait of George VI substituted.

In 1967 Swaziland became a protected state and stamps portraying Sobhuza II marked the occasion [18]. Full independence was granted the following year. Since then stamps have retained their primary interest in Swazi subjects, with portraits of Sobhuza II and his grandson, Mswati III.

Unusually, many of the early issues following the attainment of independence were lithographed in Bogota, Colombia, breaking with the usual tradition of obtaining stamps from the British security printers. Stamps from 1968 onwards chronicled Swaziland's entry into the United Nations and its membership of the Commonwealth. Material progress was the subject of the annual independence anniversary sets. At the same time the British connection was continually emphasized (especially in the Apartheid era in neighbouring South Africa), with stamps honouring the queen's silver jubilee [19], the Duke of Edinburgh's Award Scheme and Princess Diana, among other subjects.

11

12

13

14

15

16

17

18

19

1

2

3

4

5

6

7

8

9

10

11

12

SOUTH AFRICA AND NAMIBIA

The Union of South Africa was created in 1910 as an amalgamation of two British colonies (Cape Colony and Natal) and two Boer republics (the South African Republic, or Transvaal, and the Orange Free State). The passage around the coast was discovered by the Portuguese in 1498 but it was the Dutch who settled the Cape in the 17th century. Cape Colony was captured by the British during the Napoleonic Wars and it was to escape from British rule that the resident Dutch farmers (the Boers) trekked northwards from 1836 onwards, creating a number of ephemeral states that eventually formed the Transvaal and Orange Free State.

The discovery of gold and diamonds in these areas led to British attempts to take them over. The Transvaal was briefly annexed but won its independence in the first Boer War (1880–1), but the second Boer War (1899–1902) resulted in British victory. A resurgence of Afrikaner nationalism in the 1940s and 1950s led to South Africa becoming a republic and leaving the Commonwealth in 1961. In the ensuing years the policy of apartheid (literally, "separateness") was pursued relentlessly, and several African "homelands" were established as part of the process. It ended in 1993 with the election of Nelson Mandela, recently released from prison, as president. On 1 June 1994, South Africa rejoined the Commonwealth.

Left: One of the truly great men of the 20th century, Nelson Mandela spent 26 years in prison for political offences, directing the African National Congress campaign of defiance against the Afrikaner regime. His magnanimity did much to unite black and white.

COLONIAL TIMES
The Cape of Good Hope was the first part of Africa to issue stamps: its famous Triangulars, introduced in 1853 [1], showing the seated figure of Hope. Later stamps showed the standing figure of Hope [2] and a view of Table Bay with the colonial arms [3]. Natal followed suit in 1857. Its first stamps, embossed on coloured paper, were followed by a series bearing the Chalon portrait of Queen Victoria [4].

The Transvaal, then known as the South African Republic, adopted stamps in 1869 [5], later stamps being printed in Holland [6]. Stamps portraying Victoria were briefly used in the Transvaal when the British took over to rescue it from bankruptcy. The Orange Free State introduced stamps in 1866 and from then until 1902 the orange tree emblem was used exclusively [7].

Following the second Boer War, the Orange Free State and the South African Republic came under British administration, with their names changed to the Orange River Colony [8] and the Transvaal [9]. Separate issues were made by the short-lived Boer states of Stellaland and the New Republic as well as for the tribal areas of Griqualand West and Zululand [10].

SOUTH AFRICA
The former Boer republics and the two British colonies came together in August 1910 to form the Union of South Africa with dominion status. Pending the introduction of a unified definitive series in 1913 [11], stamps of the four provinces could be used throughout South Africa and collectors now prize examples of these "interprovincials" with legible postmarks of

provinces other than the territory of original issue. The opening of the Union parliament in November 1910 was celebrated by a large stamp portraying George V in ceremonial robes, with the emblems of the provinces in the corners. Like the definitives, this stamp was inscribed in English and Dutch, but from 1925 onwards Afrikaans replaced Dutch. A few stamps from then onwards were inscribed in both languages but in general stamps from 1926 were issued in bilingual pairs, inscribed alternately in English or Afrikaans [12]. This ceased in 1952 and from then until the 1970s inscriptions were provided in both languages [13]. From 1966 design was greatly improved by the reduction of the country name to its initials, "RSA" [15], following its change of status to a republic. Interestingly, the name "South Africa" with its Afrikaans equivalent returned to favour in 1993.

A pictorial series was introduced in 1926 and continued for a quarter of a century, undergoing numerous changes of printing and providing a rich field for philatelic study. Originally printed in England by letterpress, stamps were later produced in Pretoria using an early form of rotary photogravure. Apart from a few airmail sets the vast majority of South African special issues from 1938 onwards were charity sets marking the anniversary of the Boer trek of a century earlier. Although these stamps were increasingly nationalistic, they were balanced by stamps celebrating British royal events, from the silver jubilee of 1935 to the royal visit of 1947 [12] and the coronation in 1953. Many stamps from 1961, when South Africa declared itself a republic and left the Commonwealth, reflected the politics of the period, giving way to a more liberal policy since 1993.

BLACK HOMELANDS

Apartheid was taken to its illogical conclusion by the Bantu Homelands Constitution Act, passed in the 1970s, which established a series of "black homelands". These were theoretically

Africa's First Commemorative Stamp

The honour of producing Africa's first commemorative, in 1895, fell to the Transvaal, which issued a stamp celebrating the introduction of a 1d postage rate. The national arms were flanked by a mail coach and a mail train.

independent states within the frontiers of South Africa, but the intention was that black workers could be deported back to them at will and were therefore denied the full rights of citizenship within the republic itself. This system never achieved international recognition but the stamps of the homelands were accepted as valid on mail.

Bophuthatswana [16], Ciskei [17], Transkei [18] and Venda [19] issued stamps, beginning with Transkei in 1976, while Venda did not join in until 1981. All four homelands ceased to exist in April 1994 when they were re-incorporated in the republic.

NAMIBIA

Formerly German South West Africa, using the German keyplate stamps, this territory was occupied by Union forces in World War I and was subsequently mandated to South Africa. South African stamps overprinted "SWA" were often used, although distinctive stamps also appeared, including the pictorial definitive series from 1931 onwards [14]. The territory gained independence in March 1990, taking its name from the Namib desert. Its stamps at first portrayed President Sam Nujoma, the map and flag [20]; more recently scenery [21] has featured.

13

14

15

16

17

18

19

20

21

ASIA

The first adhesive stamps in Asia were used in the Indian province of Scinde (now part of Pakistan) in 1852, preceding the general issue of India by two years, but in some other regions progress was slow. Afghanistan and Persia both released stamps in 1870; Japan joined in 1871 and China in 1878.

LEBANON, IRAQ AND SYRIA

1

2

3

4

5

6

7

8

9

The three countries lying between Turkey and Arabia and stretching from the Mediterranean to the Persian Gulf have a common history and culture, diverging in only one respect. Having been part of the Ottoman Empire until 1918, Lebanon and Syria were mandated to the French while Iraq was mandated to Britain. As well as the resulting use of French or English in their stamps, each of the three countries adopted the form of government used by the controlling power, so Lebanon and Syria became republics whereas Iraq was a kingdom. Ironically, the Emir Faisal of the Hejaz, who had led the Arab Revolt against the Turks with the aid of Colonel T.E. Lawrence (Lawrence of Arabia), was originally installed as king of Syria, but he was promptly ejected by the French and consequently the British made him king of Iraq instead.

Left: Between February 1958 and September 1961 Syria was joined with Egypt to form the United Arab Republic (UAR). Stamps thus inscribed were used in both countries, distinguishable only by the currency – milliemes in Egypt and piastres in Syria.

LEBANON

The French added a considerable area, including Beirut, now the capital, to the traditional territory of Lebanon. Under the name "Grand Liban" (Greater Lebanon) stamps were introduced in 1924. At first contemporary French stamps were overprinted [1], followed in March 1925 by distinctive stamps [3]. The Lebanese Republic was proclaimed by the French in May 1926. The previous stamps were overprinted accordingly [2] and included overprints for airmail in 1928 [4].

The salient feature of Lebanese stamps has been the depiction of landmarks that date from Greek, Roman and Crusader times [5], a feature shared with those of Syria and Iraq. Definitive issues from 1937 onwards depicted the country's cedar trees, prized for their timber since classical times [6–7]. In 1941 Lebanon became an independent republic, following a takeover by the Free French from the Vichy administration, and most stamps since then have been simply captioned "Liban" [8–9].

IRAQ

Soon after the outbreak of World War I British and Indian troops occupied the port of Basra, at the head of the Persian Gulf, to protect the oil pipeline. From there they advanced up the rivers Euphrates and Tigris. Turkish stamps were issued for the occupation of Baghdad (1917) and Mosul (1918), followed by overprints for Iraq as a whole [10]. In April 1920 the League of Nations granted a mandate to the British, who installed the Emir Faisal of Syria as King Faisal I of Iraq. The British mandate expired in 1932 and thereafter Iraq was a completely independent republic. Later stamps

Tradition Triumphant

The vast majority of Syrian stamps in recent years have maintained the tradition of blending military symbolism and portraits of President Hafez al-Assad with images drawn from the region's long and colourful history. A series of 1980 illustrated tales from the *Arabian Nights*, including Sinbad the Sailor (curiously captioned as Sindibad).

portrayed King Ghazi who, when he was killed in a car crash in 1939, was succeeded by his four-year-old son Faisal II [11]. Later definitives showed the boy king grown to manhood.

Faisal II's reign was brutally terminated when he was murdered on 14 July 1958. Stamps portraying him were overprinted to signify the republic [12] that installed General Karim Kassem, leader of the coup, as president [13]. Kassem eventually came to a sticky end when he was overthrown by Colonel Salem Aref in 1963. He in turn was ousted by the revolution of 1968, masterminded by Saddam Hussein, who had fled to Egypt after attempting to assassinate Kassem in 1959. Most stamps of Iraq in this turbulent period glorified the army [14–15], a trend that increased during the Saddam regime.

SYRIA

In 1919, following the Arab Revolt, the entire area of Syria and Lebanon was assigned to the French, who issued stamps overprinted to signify their military occupation [16]. A mandate by the League of Nations came into effect in September 1923, and stamps inscribed "Syrie" were then introduced,

of which the vast majority featured landmarks from Greek, Roman and Crusader times [17; 19]. In 1934 Syria became a republic under French control. Separate issues were made for the territory of the Alawites [18], which became the Republic of Latakia in 1930 but was absorbed by Syria in 1937 when the latter became a wholly independent republic.

The later history of Syria is one of revolutions and military coups. In 1958 Syria joined with Egypt to form the United Arab Republic and stamps were overprinted "UAR" pending the release of stamps thus inscribed. The union was dissolved in September 1961 and since then stamps have been inscribed for the Syrian Arab Republic, often denoted simply by the initials SAR.

Below: Syrian stamps were overprinted for use in Latakia in 1930 (top); the revolution of 30 March 1949, was celebrated by stamps portraying President Hushi el-Zaim (middle); and stamps were overprinted "UAR" in 1958 following Syria's union with Egypt (bottom).

1

2

3

4

5

6

7

8

9

10

MIDDLE EAST

The land at the eastern end of the Mediterranean was part of the Ottoman Empire until World War I. The Egyptian Expeditionary Force (EEF) under General Allenby advanced along the coast and took Palestine, while T.E. Lawrence organized the Arab Revolt, which liberated much of Arabia and the land east of the Jordan. Britain was granted a League of Nations mandate over Palestine and Transjordan. The British mandate over the latter ended in March 1946 when it became an independent kingdom. The mandate in Palestine ended on 14 May 1948, the day the State of Israel was proclaimed.

Left: Stamps of the EEF were overprinted in Arabic alone (far left), or in Arabic, Hebrew and English, for use in Transjordan and Palestine respectively.

JORDAN

Abdullah, son of the king of the Hejaz (later part of Saudi Arabia), was made Emir of Transjordan, becoming king when the mandate ended. Stamps of Saudi Arabia were overprinted in 1924 to signify "Government of the Arab East AH 1343" [1] while Abdullah's portrait appeared on stamps of 1927–44 [2]. When the British withdrew from Palestine the neighbouring Arab states declared war on the infant Jewish state. Jordan gained territory on the west bank of the river (including part of Jerusalem) and as a result the country was renamed the Hashemite Kingdom of Jordan. Abdullah's son Hussein succeeded in 1952 [3] and played a prominent part in the Arab League [4], where he was a useful counter to Egypt's Nasser (who tried several times to have him assassinated).

Many Jordanian stamps from the 1960s onwards were printed by Harrison's of England [5]. An interesting feature of the stamps after 1964 was their emphasis on Jordan's custody of the Christian holy places, notably the set of 14 in 1966 showing the Stations of the Cross [15]. Jordan played a major role in defusing tension in the Middle East. A set of ten devoted to Builders of World Peace (1967) included Pope John XXIII and Presidents Kennedy and Johnson as well as Hussein himself [6].

PALESTINE

During the British mandate, stamps featuring prominent landmarks such as King David's Citadel and the Dome of the Rock [9] were issued. The Hebrew version of the name Palestine terminated in the letters *aleph yud*, meaningless to anyone but the Jews, who realized that they were the initials of Eretz Yisrael (land of Israel). Yet when the first stamps of Israel appeared in May 1948 [8] they were merely inscribed "Do'ar Ivri" (Hebrew Post). By the time the Jewish New Year was celebrated that September, the inscription "Israel" was in use.

During the war of 1948 both Jordan and Egypt seized parts of Palestine, on the West Bank and the Gaza Strip respectively, and overprinted stamps for use in their occupied territories [10–11]. Egypt later released a number of stamps inscribed specifically for Palestine [7]. An Indian stamp overprinted "UNEF" (United Nations Emergency Force) was used by peacekeepers in Gaza. Victory in the Six Day War (1967) gave Israel possession of both territories.

ISRAEL

Although Israeli stamps are inscribed in Arabic as well as Hebrew, no stamps portrayed an Arab Israeli until 2004. The vast majority of Israeli stamps have either emphasized the country's military might [12] or drawn heavily on Jewish culture, often from Europe. A very few have portrayed Britons who played a part in the creation of the state, such as Lord Balfour or Orde Wingate [16]. Several issues have extolled the bravery of women, including Haviva Reik, a British agent killed by the Gestapo.

A unique feature of Israeli stamps is the tabs along the bottom row of the sheet, which often bear an apt Biblical quotation, as seen in the issue marking the 50th anniversary of the Balfour Declaration [14], or form an extension of the design of the stamp.

THE PALESTINE AUTHORITY
Control of Gaza and Jericho passed from Israel to the Palestinian Authority under Yasser Arafat in May 1994 and stamps printed in Berlin have been used there ever since. The first series was denominated in mils, the currency of Palestine up to 1948, but later issues have been valued in fils, the currency of Jordan. Most Palestinian stamps have, as in Jordan [15] previously, emphasized the Christian aspects of the Holy Land [17]. Stamps are regularly issued for Easter and Christmas [13].

Below: Israel issued a stamp in 1994 to mark the centenary of the "Dreyfus Affair". It shows the public disgrace of Captain Dreyfus, who was wrongfully convicted of treason. Emile Zola, whose newspaper article exposed French anti-semitism, appears on the tab below.

Wishful Thinking?
In 1964 Jordan issued a set of five stamps to publicize the Arab Summit Conference, which it hosted in Amman. The stamps portrayed King Hussein and a map of Palestine as it was in 1920, but unless you could read the minuscule Arabic inscription at the side you would be forgiven for thinking that the map represented an enlarged Jordan and that Israel simply did not exist.

Personalities featured on Palestinian stamps include Mother Teresa and the German politician Hans-Jurgen Wischnewski, who have appeared on annual issues made under the title of Friends of Palestine, invariably portrayed with Yasser Arafat.

Below: Every year Israel remembers its war dead with a stamp showing a different war memorial.

11

12

13

14

15

16

17

1

2

3

4

5

6

7

8

9

10

ARABIA

Four-fifths of the Arabian peninsula is occupied by Saudi Arabia, an absolute monarchy created in 1932 by Abdul Aziz Ibn Saud, Sultan of Nejd, who conquered most of eastern and central Arabia in 1923 and then occupied the kingdom of the Hejaz in 1924–5. The combined territories were renamed by him seven years later. To the south lay the kingdom and imamate of the Yemen. The whole of Arabia was nominally under Turkish rule but it broke up in the aftermath of the Arab Revolt during World War I. At the south-western tip of Arabia lay Aden, a British crown colony since 1839, together with the eastern and western Aden protectorate comprising a number of small sultanates. In 1963 they became the Federation of South Arabia, but four years later left the Commonwealth to form the Yemen People's Democratic Republic in November 1967.

Left: The designs for the first stamps of the Hejaz in 1916 were suggested by Lawrence of Arabia and were derived from carvings on doors or prayer niches in Cairo mosques, or stucco work over the entrance to Cairo railway station. The stamps were printed at the Survey of Egypt, Cairo.

SAUDI ARABIA

The ruler of the Hejaz was Hussein, Emir of Mecca, in whose reign stamps were introduced by T.E. Lawrence. True to Islam, they were non-figurative and relied heavily on quotations from the Koran [1]. In 1923 the Wahabis of Nejd, under Ibn Saud, began rapid expansion. In 1925 Hussein was forced to abdicate and go into exile in Cyprus, but his son Faisal was later made king of Transjordan. In 1924–5 the Wahabis of Nejd invaded and took over the Hejaz. Stamps for the joint territories showed the *toughra* of Ibn Saud [2]. Early Saudi Arabian stamps continued this tradition [3] but by the mid-1940s pictorialism was making a tentative appearance [4]. Pictorial definitives since 1960 have included the cartouche of the monarch in lieu of a portrait [5]. The first portrait stamp marked the installation of King Faisal in 1964 [7]; since then the palm tree and crossed swords emblem has usually been the only form of identification [8].

YEMEN

Imam Yahya became the spiritual ruler of the Yemen in 1904 and transformed it into a monarchy in 1918 when Turkish rule was overthrown. Stamps were introduced in 1926 and were non-figurative until 1946 [9], but a scenic definitive series appeared in 1951 [6] and thereafter stamps followed the western tradition. His successor, Imam Ahmed, died in September 1962 and his son Mohammed al-Badr proclaimed himself imam, but his palace was bombarded and rebels proclaimed a republic. The imam escaped to the mountains of the north-west and for several years there were two rival states: the Mutawakelite kingdom [10] and Yemen Arab Republic, often abbreviated to YAR on its stamps [11].

SOUTH ARABIA

The nucleus of South Arabia was the seaport of Aden at the south-western tip of the peninsula. It was originally occupied by the British in 1839 and used as a base to stamp out piracy, but following the opening of the Suez Canal in 1869 it became an important coaling station. It used Indian stamps, identifiable by their postmarks, until 1937, when a series featuring an Arab dhow flanked by curved daggers was introduced [12]. The series was re-issued in 1939 in an elongated format

Opposing States with a Common Goal

The royalist and republican factions in the Yemen fought a ferocious civil war, but both had an eye to the main chance when it came to stamps, often commemorating the same events and personalities. This common purpose was vividly demonstrated by the stamps issued by both sides in 1964 in memory of the late John F. Kennedy.

to incorporate a portrait of George VI, with other vignettes added. An entirely new pictorial set portraying Elizabeth II appeared in 1953–63 and was re-issued in 1964 overprinted to mark the grant of a revised constitution that paved the way for the creation of the Federation of South Arabia. In the colonial period Aden produced no distinctive commemoratives but issued a number of sets in the prevailing colonial omnibus designs.

Aden controlled the eastern and western Aden protectorates, several of which issued stamps. Initially these consisted of the Kathiri State of Seiyun [14] and the Qu'aiti State of Shihr and Mukalla [15], but the latter changed its name to Hadhramaut in 1955 [13]. In 1966 both states began issuing multi-coloured stamps following prevailing fashions for Churchill [16], the Olympic Games and the World Cup. The Mahra State of Qishn and Socotra and the State of Upper Yafa briefly had stamps in 1967 showing their state flags [17], but these states were taken over by the National Liberation Front on 1 October 1967, and their stamps withdrawn from use.

The stamps of Aden and its protectorates were gradually phased out from 1963, being superseded by issues of the Federation of South Arabia [18]. Apart from the definitive series featuring the national flag or federal crest, the special issues of the federation were confined to the various colonial omnibus issues, from the Red Cross series of 1963 to the UNESCO anniversary set of December 1966, on which the queen's portrait was replaced by the federal emblem.

The federation became wholly independent in 1967, taking the name of the People's Republic of Southern Yemen [19]. Its title was changed at the end of 1970, when the word "Southern" was dropped and the style was changed to the Yemen People's Democratic Republic or People's Democratic Republic of Yemen [20]. The Yemen PDR and YAR amalgamated in May 1990 and since then stamps have been inscribed "Republic of Yemen".

Below: Stamps inscribed simply "Republic of Yemen" celebrated the merger of the two Yemeni republics in May 1990.

11

12
13

14
15

16

17

18

19

20

1

2

3

4

5

6

7

8

9

10

GULF STATES

A number of small states on the western side of the Persian Gulf, nominally under Turkish rule, came under British influence in the 19th century. Bahrain, Kuwait and Muscat had Indian post offices to facilitate external trade but following the establishment of the dominion of India in 1947 control of the Gulf post offices passed to Britain. In the 1960s the sheikhdoms introduced local posts and eventually also took over their external mails. Britain continued to give military aid, both in quelling local rebellions and in dealing with aggression from Iraq.

Left: Following the Iraqi invasion and occupation of Kuwait in August 1990, an international coalition liberated it in February 1991. The first stamps of Kuwait, released in May, celebrated the liberation.

COLONIAL ISSUES

Bahrain [1], Kuwait and Muscat [2] used Indian stamps suitably overprinted until 1947, when British stamps overprinted and surcharged in Indian currency [3] were substituted. British stamps with no name but denominated in annas and rupees [4] were used in Qatar.

INDEPENDENT STATES

Bahrain took over its own postal services in 1966, most stamps from that date including a portrait of the ruler Shaikh Isa bin Sulman al-Khalifa [5]. The usual range of popular themes is covered but a strong feature is the chronicling of the material progress of the state, especially public projects [6].

Kuwait assumed responsibility for its postal services in 1959 and stamps have since followed a pattern very similar to that of Bahrain. Portraits of the rulers [7] tend to be confined to the definitive issues, while a poster style is used for an extraordinary range of stamps released for Mother's Day, Family's Day [8] and many other annual events.

The sultanate of Muscat and Oman began issuing its own stamps in 1966, using the state emblem in lieu of the ruler's portrait in strict observance of Koranic law [9]. When Sultan Qabus succeeded in 1970 he decided that the name of the country should be short-

ened and since then stamps have been inscribed "Sultanate of Oman" [10]. He had no compunction about using his portrait.

Overprinted British stamps were used in Qatar until 1963. Distinctive stamps were issued from 1961 for internal mail, and were later extended to overseas mail. The majority portray the ruler alongside subjects that range from the extraordinary progress of the sheikhdom to international events [11].

UNITED ARAB EMIRATES

The southern coast of the Gulf was formerly known as the Pirate Coast. The British took strenuous measures to stamp out piracy and concluded a treaty with the ruler of Dubai to extend British influence in the Gulf. From this arose the collective name of the Trucial States for the seven sheikhdoms and emirates. British stamps surcharged in Indian currency were also used in Dubai till 1961, when stamps inscribed "Trucial States" were introduced [12]. In 1963 Dubai took over responsibility and began issuing stamps bearing its own name [13]. Later issues charted the phenomenal rise of Dubai as an oil-rich international trading centre [14].

Distinctive stamps spread to the other states in 1963–4 and over a seven-year period output assumed piratical proportions. The stamps

Big is Beautiful

Sharjah was not only prodigal in its own right but churned out numerous "regional" stamps for its dependency Khor Fakkan. Like the other Trucial States, Sharjah had a penchant for Americana, but outdid them all with this triptych for the New York World Fair in 1964.

11

12

13

14

15

16

17

shown here represent the more legitimate end of the spectrum, but by 1970 the various rulers had signed agreements with philatelic agents (some with two different agents simultaneously) and stamps poured off the world's presses at an astonishing rate, covering all the fashionable topics of the period but especially reproductions of European paintings (many of them

Below: A scene from the film Casablanca *featured on a stamp of 1969 from Umm al Qiwain (top). Mosques and desert forts are perennial subjects for stamps of the United Arab Emirates (bottom).*

nudes that would have been frowned upon had any of these stamps ever appeared in their respective states).

At their best, the stamps of Abu Dhabi showed the traditional way of life. One of Ajman's earliest sets celebrated the centenary of the Gibbons catalogues [15]. Few of Fujeira's unduly prolific stamps after 1966 have attained catalogue status [16]. From the assassination of the Kennedy brothers onwards, all of the Trucial States produced a prodigious number of stamps devoted to Americana. Ras Al Khaima's Apollo XI set was one of the few issues in the world to portray President Nixon [17]. In Umm al Qiwain the gift of a 16mm projector was sufficient to trigger off a set of 48 stamps featuring stills from famous films.

This philatelic whirlwind ended in 1973, when the seven states combined to form the United Arab Emirates, whose stamp policy has been a model of conservatism, combining traditional scenes with issues publicizing a wide range of international conferences.

At first Harrison and Sons in England enjoyed a monopoly of stamp production, but from 1984 onwards contracts were awarded to many other printers, from Questa and De La Rue to Enschede of Holland and Cartor of Normandy. Very occasionally they are lithographed at the Oriental Press in Bahrain, but are invariably designed locally, with a penchant for symbolism.

1

2

3

4

5

6

7

8

9

AFGHANISTAN AND IRAN

The neighbouring Islamic republics of Afghanistan and Iran lie in southwest Asia. Afghanistan is completely landlocked whereas Iran, lying to the west, has access to the Caspian Sea (north) and the Persian Gulf (south). Iran, three times the size of Afghanistan with more than three times its population, was one of the world's great empires from the 6th to the 4th centuries BC, and in the 20th century, when the country changed its name from Persia to Iran, attempts were made to capitalize on its ancient glories. Afghanistan, by contrast, was always a relatively poor country, its mountainous terrain making communications difficult and encouraging division. Afghanistan was, in fact, conquered by Darius I of Persia and subsequently endured conquest by Alexander the Great, Genghis Khan, Tamerlane, the Mughals and the British, though none of them ever succeeded in controlling it for long, as the Russians learned to their cost in the 1980s. The great Persian Empire had been in decline for many years when an obscure Cossack captain seized power in 1925 and began its transformation. The work was completed by his son, the last Shahinshah.

Left: In 1970–1 Iran celebrated the 2,500th anniversary of the Persian Empire with no fewer than eight sets of stamps harking back to the glories of Darius and Xerxes. The final issue glorified the Pahlavi era, portraying Shah Mohammed Riza at the height of his power.

AFGHANISTAN

The kingdom of Afghanistan was instituted in 1747, although the writ of the Amir did not run beyond Kabul. In 1871 Amir Sher Ali set up a postal service using circular stamps with the head of a lion surrounded by a Farsi text [1]. Similar stamps, introduced in 1877, were printed in different colours according to the province in which they were used. The stamps were among the most primitive in the world well into the 20th century, a circular armorial design being used for official correspondence [2]. A scenic definitive series was released in 1939–47 [3].

Crudely typographed or lithographed stamps continued until 1958, when the State Printing Works was granted a contract to produce stamps by photogravure [4]. Even so that year's Atoms for Peace stamps plagiarized stamps issued previously by the USA. An agreement with a philatelic agency in the USA in 1961 resulted in a deluge of stamps from Afghanistan over the ensuing three years [5]. Since then they have been much more restrained and generally thematic in content [6]. Annual issues marked "Pakhtunistan Day" are part of a propaganda exercise to wrest the land of the Pathans from neighbouring Pakistan [7].

In 1975 King Mohamed Zahir Shah was deposed and Afghanistan was declared a republic [8]. In 1978 Afghanistan became a Democratic Republic [9], a move that provoked Soviet invasion the following year and led to a war lasting until 1987. In that year Afghanistan became a republic again but as the Russians withdrew the Taliban regime took over. In more recent years, before the US invasion, Afghanistan's stamps had taken on a much more commercial tone, as seen in the stamps sponsored by the Ferrari motor company in 1999 [10].

PERSIA

The earliest stamps of Persia, introduced in 1868, were almost as primitive as those of Afghanistan. Although they were engraved by Albert Barre of Paris, they were printed in Tehran and the resulting impressions were very coarse [11]. Portraits of the Shah appeared from 1876 onwards, when stamps were printed in Vienna and later by Enschede of Haarlem [12]. Fine European printing contrasted with the numerous issues produced locally and their bewildering array of provisional overprints [13]. The coronation of Shah Ahmed in 1915 was celebrated by 51 stamps, the higher values with metallic gold frames [14].

IRAN

In October 1925 cavalry captain Riza Khan Pahlavi deposed Shah Ahmed Mirza and seized power; in December he was crowned Shahinshah of Persia and immediately began modernizing the tottering empire. Two-colour photogravure was adopted for the airmail series of 1930 [15] and stamps generally adopted a more westernized

Below: Many Iranian stamps celebrated the 2,500th anniversary of the Persian Empire (top), and a stamp of 1979 (bottom), designed by children, marked the International Year of the Child.

Mutilation Cancellation
Until the early 20th century the stamps of Afghanistan were cancelled by the postmaster or letter receiver by tearing a chunk out of them before mail went forward to its destination.

character. In 1935 Shah Riza changed the name of the country to Iran, an ancient term literally meaning "land of the Aryans". Despite westernization, Iranian stamps went through a phase when they were inscribed entirely in Farsi, including the set of 1939 celebrating the marriage of Crown Prince Mohammed Riza to Princess Fawzieh, sister of King Farouk of Egypt [16].

Shah Riza intrigued with Nazi Germany and was ousted in favour of his son in 1941. From the late 1940s the stamps of Iran contrasted the glories of the ancient empire of the Medes and Persians with the achievements of the Pahlavi regime in modernizing such a vast and disparate country. On the whole, however, the stamps of the reign of Shah Mohammed looked back to ancient Persia, culminating in a veritable orgy of celebration for the 2,500th anniversary of the empire [17]. Stamps of 1968 marked the centenary of the first stamps with reproductions of the lion and sun design [18].

In January 1979 the Shah went to America for medical treatment and in his absence Ayatollah Khomeini returned from exile and began the revolution that transformed the westernized empire into a fundamentalist Islamic republic. Stamps in the era of the ayatollahs reflected their uncompromising religious fanaticism.

10

11

12

13

14

15

16

17

18

1

2

3

4

5

6

7

8

9

10

BANGLADESH, PAKISTAN AND BURMA

These three countries have had a common history, having been part of British India for very many years. The territories of Bangladesh and Pakistan came under the dominion of the Mughal emperors in the Middle Ages and thus passed into the hands of the East India Company in the 19th century. Burma was also part of British India, of which it was the largest province as well as the most easterly. It had been a powerful kingdom in its own right, but when its king invaded Bengal in 1825 the British retaliated and annexed Lower Burma in 1926. Two further Burmese wars, in 1852 and 1885, led to the entire country coming under British rule. It was granted autonomy in 1937, suffered Japanese occupation in 1942 and after liberation in 1945 adopted a nationalist government that attained full independence in 1947 and left the Commonwealth. Pakistan was created in the same year and consisted of the two predominantly Muslim parts of British India. However, as these were separated by India and ethnically different from each other, it was inevitable that they would split up. When West Pakistan resisted the secession of East Pakistan and tried to put down the revolt, the Indian Army

intervened on the side of the rebels, whose independence as Bangladesh was confirmed in 1971.

Left: Stamps of 1955–6 showed maps of West and East Pakistan, the latter marking the first session of the Pakistani parliament in Dacca, the capital of Bengal. This was the region that seceded in 1970–1 to form Bangladesh. Stamps were usually inscribed in English and Arabic but this set was exceptionally inscribed in Bengali instead of English in an attempt to appease Bengali nationalism.

BURMA

Ordinary Indian stamps were used in Burma until April 1937, when it was separated from India and placed under direct British administration. Indian stamps were then overprinted for use there [1] pending a distinctive series released in 1938–40 [2]. Burma was the only country in the British Empire to celebrate the centenary of adhesive postage stamps, with an overprinted stamp issued in May 1940 [3].

The Japanese invaded Burma in 1942 and blotted out the portrait of George VI with a peacock emblem. In 1943 they set up a puppet government, which issued its own stamps. At the end of World War II the country was placed under military administration [4] prior to the creation of the Union of Burma as a completely independent state [5]. While very few stamps were released in the ensuing years, they tended to emphasize the unique character of the people [6].

Following a referendum in December 1973 the military junta that had seized power in 1962 made way for a one-party socialist republic. Stamps with inscriptions reflecting this change were in use from 1974 [7] until the government changed the name of the country in 1990: "Myanmar", which had always been used in Burmese script, was adopted as the western form as well [8]. The country now holds the world record for the fewest new stamps, only about 20 having been issued since 1990, usually for the anniversary of independence.

Martyrs for the Cause

In 1991 Bangladesh celebrated the 20th anniversary of independence by embarking on a long series of stamps portraying Martyred Intellectuals – doctors, lawyers, politicians and teachers who lost their lives when Pakistan attempted by force to prevent the secession. These stamps were issued in sheets of ten different designs. A total of 240 different stamps were released, 30 at a time, up to 1999.

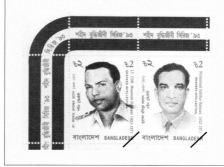

PAKISTAN

When the Islamic Dominion of Pakistan was created in August 1947 overprinted Indian stamps [9], many of them handstruck locally, were in use pending the supply of distinctive stamps in 1948 [10], recess-printed by the new Pakistan Security Printing Corporation, which has been responsible for the vast majority of stamps ever since. One of the earliest special issues marked the centenary of the Scinde Dawks, Asia's first stamps [11], as the formerly Indian province of Scinde now forms part of Pakistan.

In 1956 Pakistan became an Islamic republic [12] and thereafter stamps became more Muslim in character and content. By the early 1960s stamps were inscribed in English, Bengali and Urdu in a bid to placate the secessionist tendencies of East Pakistan [13]. A recurring theme was the quarrel with India over Kashmir, which had a mainly Muslim population but had remained in Indian hands [14]. From time to time the philatelic propaganda campaign has erupted into border incidents that have almost brought India

and Pakistan to open warfare. More recent stamps have reflected Pakistan's involvement in world affairs, including an issue publicizing its expedition to Antarctica [15]. One thing Pakistan has in common with India is a policy of issuing mainly single stamps, often portraying personalities little known by the rest of the world, although a 1990s series celebrated Pioneers of Freedom.

BANGLADESH

In time-honoured fashion the new country made use of overprinted Pakistani stamps before adopting distinctive stamps. The first series of these, issued in July 1971, showed a map of the new country [17] and portrayed the leader of the struggle for independence, Shaikh Mujibur Rahman [16]. Over the past 30 years the stamps of Bangladesh have been printed as far afield as Vienna and Melbourne. Many of them provide public service messages to the population [18] but the majority emphasize the distinctive cultural heritage of the country [19].

Below: The Bagha mosque of Rajshahi (top) was part of the 1997 Historic Mosque set, and a 2000 stamp (bottom) marked the tenth anniversary of the uprising for the restoration of democracy.

11

12

13

14

15

16

17

18

19

1

2

3

4

5

6

7

8

9

10

11

12

INDIA

The subcontinent of India has fostered civilizations for thousands of years and is home to almost a billion people of many languages, cultures and religions. The only factor common to all educated Indians is the English language, but in the scramble for India the British were late starters. The Portuguese got there first, in 1498, followed by the French and the Danes. The British founded the Honourable East India Company in 1600 to trade with India and the Far East, establishing its first settlement at Surat in 1612. Bombay was ceded by Portugal as part of Catherine of Braganza's dowry when she married Charles II in 1662. By 1700 Britain also had control of Madras and further expansion came at the expense of the French, who were defeated by Robert Clive in 1757. Over the ensuing century the East India Company gained control of the whole of India by bribery or force, ruling directly or through the feudatory princes. The Sepoy Mutiny (1857) led to the administration of India being handed over to the imperial government.

Indian nationalism grew after World War I, under the charismatic leadership of M.K. Gandhi. Britain agreed to independence in principle in 1931 but implementation was delayed by disagreement between the Hindu and Muslim factions. India eventually gained independence in August 1947, but was partitioned between India and Pakistan, with great bloodshed and ethnic cleansing, creating the greatest upheaval of population.

Left: Mohandas Karamchand Gandhi, architect of Indian independence, was assassinated by a Hindu fanatic on 30 January 1948, because he had failed to prevent the secession of Pakistan. The first of many stamps portraying him were released on 15 August 1948, the first anniversary of India's independence.

BRITISH INDIA

In 1852 India had the distinction of issuing the first stamps in Asia, the Scinde Dawks (derived from the name of the province and *dawk*, the Hindi word for posts). They were embossed and bore the emblem of the HEIC [1]. Stamps for the whole of India were introduced in 1854 [2] and from 1855 to 1926 were printed by De La Rue in England [3]. The inscription "East India" continued in use until 1877, when India was declared an empire with Victoria as Empress. Later definitives portrayed the reigning monarch [4] until 1947 and included the George VI series showing the many forms of mail transport in use [5]. India's first commemorative stamps appeared in 1931 to celebrate the inauguration of New Delhi as the nation's capital [6].

REPUBLIC OF INDIA

A set of three stamps was released on the day independence was proclaimed. The communal violence, which created an immense refugee problem, induced the Indian government to issue compulsory tax stamps in aid of refugee relief [7]. The same device was used in the 1970s to help refugees from the former East Pakistan.

Most definitives, such as those publicizing the Five Year Plan of 1955 [8], have retained the small size used under the British Raj. When the currency was decimalized in 1957 stamps showing the map were released [9]. Later sets were often didactic, educating the Indian public by focusing on social and economic matters from good husbandry to family planning. The latest series portrays prominent figures [10].

Most special issues are single stamps portraying historic personalities. Relatively few, such as Nehru [11], are known outside India. Subhas Chandra Bose was the leader of the Free India movement [12] who collaborated with the Japanese during World War II. The conquest of Everest in 1953 was marked by stamps showing the mountain, but it has also featured in several later issues [13]. Very few non-Indians have been portrayed, although they include Lord Mountbatten (the last Viceroy), Annie Besant (the founder of the theosophist movement), Abraham Lincoln [14] and Martin Luther King [15]. Philatelic tributes to the great and good of the past [16], as well as the religions and mythology of the subcontinent [17], are aimed at making Indians more aware of their diverse cultural heritage.

HIMALAYAN KINGDOMS

Nepal, the world's only Hindu kingdom, was welded into a single state in the late 18th century when the Gurkha ruler conquered a number of independent mountain principalities. Nepal had its own stamps from 1881 [18] but they were confined to internal mail until 1959, when Nepal joined the Universal Postal Union, and until then Indian stamps were used on mail going abroad. Everest, which lies partly in Nepal, features prominently on the modern stamps [19].

The kingdom of Bhutan also had stamps for internal use [20] until 1969, when it joined the UPU. Even before that date, however, it had embarked on prolific issues aimed at the international philatelic market.

EUROPEAN COLONIES

In the 17th and early 18th centuries France rivalled Britain for possession of India, but by the Treaty of Paris, which ended the Seven Years War, France relinquished all her territory except for Pondicherry and four other small outposts. These constituted the French Indian Settlements until 1954 when they were taken over by the Republic

World Leader in Gimmickry
Bhutan has produced more innovations in stamps than the rest of the world put together, including the first scented stamps (with flower motifs), stamps printed on textiles or steel plates, and even talking stamps in the form of phonograph records that play the national anthem. It also pioneered 3D stamps (see below), either laminated prismatic stamps or plastic stamps in high relief.

of India. The French colonial keytypes, suitably inscribed, were introduced in 1892, followed by bicoloured pictorials in 1914 showing the god Brahma and a temple near Pondicherry. These stamps were overprinted "France Libre" in 1941 when the settlements joined the Free French, and subsequently a set of stamps produced in England was released [21]. A postwar series featured various Hindu deities.

The Portuguese territories of Goa, Damao and Diu on the west coast were all that remained of the territory acquired by Portugal from 1510 onwards, following Vasco da Gama's discovery of the sea route to India. Distinctive stamps, designed and printed in Goa, were introduced in 1871, and the local issues were superseded by colonial keytypes from 1877 to 1945, followed by a set portraying historic figures [22]. Portuguese stamps were withdrawn in 1961 when the territory was annexed by India.

13

14

15

16

17

18

19

20

21

22

INDIAN OCEAN

Dotted around the Indian Ocean are a number of archipelagos and individual islands, all of which are, or were, colonized by Britain or France. Some, like Sri Lanka, have a civilization dating back thousands of years, which saw the Portuguese and the Dutch come and go before falling into British hands. At the other end of the ocean, Mauritius was settled by Arabs and Malays before passing to the Dutch, then the French, before it fell to Britain during the Napoleonic Wars. Madagascar was contested by Britain and France before the latter triumphed. Other islands were gradually snapped up by the two major colonial powers in the 19th century. Relatively undeveloped, their mainstay was fishing and coconut cultivation until the advent of tourism in more recent years.

Left: Sri Lanka, formerly Ceylon, is arguably the foremost preserver of Buddhism, as reflected in numerous stamps. This one of 1959 marks the inauguration of the Pirivena universities.

SRI LANKA

Formerly Ceylon, Sri Lanka was taken from the Dutch in 1802 and became a British crown colony, adopting stamps in 1857. They followed the prevailing British colonial patterns, using various portraits of Queen Victoria until 1900. Following the switch from sterling to a decimal system based on the rupee in 1872, Ceylon acquired an unenviable reputation for its enormous number of provisional surcharges throughout the 1880s and 1890s. After the Edwardian series the colonial keytypes were adopted for the stamps of George V, followed by scenic pictorials in 1935 with the king's portrait inset. The same designs were retained under George VI with his portrait substituted [1].

Although Ceylon became a dominion in 1948, ties to the British Crown remained strong, exemplified by stamps for the coronation and royal visit of 1954 [2]. It became the Republic of Sri Lanka in May 1972, and most stamps since that time have featured local personalities and institutions, with a strong Buddhist flavour [3–4].

MAURITIUS AND DEPENDENCIES

Although to this day French influence has remained strong in the language and customs of Mauritius, it was one of the few British colonies to celebrate the diamond jubilee of Queen Victoria with stamps [5]. After achieving self-government in 1967 the island became a republic within the Commonwealth in 1992 [6]. It continues a modest policy regarding new issues, which publicize tourism and an unchanging way of life [7–8].

The Seychelles were formerly a dependency of Mauritius and used its stamps, distinguishable only by their postmark, until they adopted distinctive stamps in 1890. Many stamps issued since gaining independence in 1975 have featured the wildlife of the islands, a major tourist attraction [9]. The Seychelles Outer Islands (Les Iles Eloignés Seychelles), comprising several outlying islands, had their own stamps from 1980 to 1992 and were served by a ship acting as a floating post office. During that period three different forms of the name in the local phonetic patois were tried.

The Chagos archipelago, formerly administered by Mauritius, became a separate crown colony in 1965 under the name of the British Indian Ocean Territory [10]. It included the Seychelles Outer Islands, but when the Seychelles became independent these outliers reverted to them.

MALDIVE ISLANDS

Lying to the south of Ceylon (Sri Lanka), this archipelago was a British protectorate and used stamps of Ceylon suitably overprinted before adopting distinctive stamps in 1933. In 1953 it briefly became a republic, but reverted to a sultanate later the same year. Since then it has become one of the most prolific stamp-issuing countries in the world. The vast majority of Maldives stamps have no bearing on the islands but are aimed at the world philatelic market [11–12].

MADAGASCAR AND DEPENDENCIES

An independent kingdom until the late 19th century, Madagascar's mail services were operated by the British consul (overseas post) and a syndicate of businessmen (inland mail), both using distinctive stamps [13]. These posts were suppressed by the French when they subjugated the island in 1895. French colonial stamps [15] were in use from then until 1958, when Madagascar attained independence as the Malagasy Republic, but it reverted

to its original name in 1992. Since then, like the Maldives, it has gone overboard on stamps that are more relevant to the USA than to the Indian Ocean, including a lengthy series cashing in on the *Titanic* craze.

North-west of Madagascar lies the Comoro archipelago. Each island in the group at first issued its own stamps, using the French colonial standard design with the name at the foot [14], but a general series was substituted in 1950 [16]. When the Comoros became an independent state, Mayotte was detached and became an overseas department of France. French stamps were used until 1997, when distinctive stamps were adopted.

Réunion, east of Madagascar, had its own stamps as long ago as 1852 but from 1891 used the French colonial keytypes. It used distinctive stamps from 1907 [17] as well as a Free French issue during World War II. Réunion became an overseas department of France after the war and the majority of its stamps were French, inscribed or overprinted in colonial francs. In 1975 it adopted the French metropolitan currency and separate stamp issues were then discontinued.

Below: The stamps of present-day Mayotte reflect the exuberance of the people (top). The Free French stamps of Réunion showed local produce (bottom).

9

10

11

12

13

14

15

16

17

1   2

3

4   5

6

7

8   9

10   11

INDOCHINA

The French conquered Indochina in the late 19th century, the name being given from 1888 onwards to the colonies and protectorates of Cochin-China, Annam and Tongking (Vietnam) and Cambodia, to which were later added Laos (1893) and Kouang-Tcheou (1900). With an area greater than France itself, inhabited by peoples of diverse races with civilizations dating back many centuries, it is not surprising that colonial rule was resisted to a greater or lesser degree.

Resistance was greatest in north and central Vietnam, where Nguyen Ai Quoc (later known as Ho Chi Minh) campaigned for independence from the 1920s. Japan occupied Indochina in 1942–5 but allowed the Vichy administration to continue. During this period anti-Japanese resistance was organized by Ho. When French power was restored in 1945 France created the United States of Indochina, giving limited autonomy to each region. The Viet Minh waged war to unite the Vietnamese regions. In 1950 France tried to retain overall power in the area by giving greater autonomy to Vietnam and the kingdoms of Cambodia and Laos, but by that time its action was too little and too late.

Left: Ho Chi Minh (1892–1969), prime minister (1954–5) and president (1955–69) of North Vietnam, led the Viet Minh resistance movement from 1941 against the Japanese and later the French. "Uncle Ho" was also the driving force in the war between North and South Vietnam in the 1960s.

CAMBODIA

The French had produced stamps showing indigenous subjects for the whole of Indochina from 1889 to 1945 [1–2]. Stamps for the independent kingdom of Cambodia were introduced in 1951. King Norodom Sihanouk abdicated in 1955 in favour of his father Norodom Suramarit [3] but continued as president of the council of ministers. Stamps from this period concentrated on Cambodian culture [4]. When Suramarit died in 1960 Sihanouk refused the crown but ruled as chief of state. In 1970 he was deposed by the Khmer Rouge communist rebels, who established the Khmer republic [5] under Lon Nol.

In turn Lon Nol was overthrown by Pol Pot, who created Democratic Kampuchea. He abolished money, public transport and the postal service as well as murdering countless thousands of his own people. The country was liberated by Vietnamese forces, and the People's Republic of Kampuchea was proclaimed in 1969. The stamps of the ensuing period were apolitical and strongly thematic [6], a policy continued after the Vietnamese withdrawal in 1989 and reversion to the name of Cambodia [7]. The kingdom was restored, with Norodom Sihanouk once more on the throne.

LAOS

Compared with that of its neighbours, the history of Laos since independence in 1951 has been relatively stable. It remained a kingdom until 1975, when King Savang Vatthana abdicated and the Pathet Lao rebels proclaimed a people's democratic republic. Under the monarchy, most stamps were produced in France, mainly by intaglio [8] but latterly in multicolour lithography [9]. In the republican period they have been predominantly thematic [12].

VIETNAM

The Vietnam Democratic Republic was proclaimed by Ho Chi Minh [13] at Hanoi in September 1945 and was initially recognized by France, but relations deteriorated and erupted into guerrilla warfare. By 1947 the Viet Minh had withdrawn to northern Tongking [10]. In 1951 the French created Vietnam as an independent state within the French Union [11] but gradually the Viet Minh fought back. After they had decisively defeated the French at Dien Bien Phu in 1954 [14] a conference in Geneva partitioned the country at the 17th parallel.

The stamps of North Vietnam were extremely political, either attacking the USA directly for its support of the South, or praising those who protested against American policy, such as Norman Morrison, a Quaker who burned himself to death. Stamps supported Cuba and mourned the Marxist leader of Chile, Salvador Allende [15]. Separate issues were made in 1963–76 by the National Front for the Liberation of South Vietnam and these,

Below: A set of four stamps was issued by South Vietnam in 1968 to express thanks for international aid (top). Many recent issues of Vietnam feature wildlife (bottom).

Shooting Down the Enemy

During the Vietnam War the US Air Force carried out numerous air raids on North Vietnam and areas of the South controlled by the Viet Cong. A recurring theme of stamps in this period was the shooting down of American planes, often showing downed fliers as prisoners or anti-aircraft batteries in action, with the latest score.

if anything, were even more virulently anti-American [16]. By contrast, the stamps of South Vietnam highlighted the plight of refugees from the North [17] or promoted the solidarity of its allies in the long-drawn-out war.

Following the American withdrawal in 1975 the country was re-unified under the name of the Socialist Republic of Vietnam. Since then stamps have simply been inscribed "Viet nam" and have been devoted to the usual range of popular subjects.

KEEPING THE PEACE

In August 1954 the International Control Commission for Indonesia was created by the Geneva Declaration. It was chaired by India, regarded as the leading power among the neutral nations of the world, with Canada and Poland as the other members. Joint inspection teams of service personnel were provided with 1949 Indian definitives overprinted in Hindi, for separate use in Cambodia [18], Laos [19] and Vietnam. In 1960 the map series was overprinted for use in Laos and Vietnam [20]. They were replaced in 1965 by stamps overprinted "ICC" for use throughout Indochina [21].

12

13

14

15

16

17

18

19

20

21

1
2
3
4
5
6
7
8
9
10
11
12

CHINA

The world's largest country, China is inhabited by a quarter of the human race. The Manchu dynasty, which had ruled China since 1644, was overthrown by Sun Yat-sen in 1911 but the republic barely survived the trauma of World War I. Central government collapsed in the 1920s as China was polarized between communism and nationalism, led by Mao Zedong and

Chiang Kai-shek respectively. Breakaway provinces were ruled by warlords and the country was on the brink of anarchy. From 1931 onwards it was also prey to the aggression of the Japanese. At the end of World War II the Japanese returned Taiwan (which it had seized in 1895) just in time to provide the nationalists with a home after they were ousted from the mainland. The People's Republic of China was proclaimed in September 1949.

Left: Mao Zedong, the red flag and a military parade in Beijing were potent symbols used on many stamps from 1949 onwards.

EARLY POSTAL SERVICES

Although the Chinese emperors had a very sophisticated communications network for thousands of years, there was no countrywide postal service open to the public before 1897. The first stamps were issued in Shanghai in 1865, and were later overprinted to commemorate 50 years of international settlement [1]. The various towns with international communities under the terms of the Treaty of Nanking (1842) followed suit, and distinctive stamps were issued by Amoy, Chefoo [3], Chinkiang, Chungking, Foochow, Hankow, Ichang, Kewkiang, Nanking, Wei Hai Wei and Wuhu.

Several foreign powers operated postal agencies in China to facilitate the handling of overseas mail. Following the murder of German missionaries in Shantung, Germany occupied the port of Tsingtao and subsequently acquired a 99-year lease of Kiaochow, which had its own stamps [2], until the outbreak of World War I, when it was captured by the Japanese.

In 1863 Robert Hart was appointed Inspector General of the Imperial Customs and it was under this department that a new postal service was

introduced in 1878 [5]. Knighted in 1882, Sir Robert went on to organize the Chinese Imperial Post in 1897. The last issue of the empire appeared in 1909 and celebrated the first anniversary of the accession of the baby Emperor Hsuan T'ung. Appropriately it depicted the Temple of Heaven in the Forbidden City [4]. Deposed in 1912, Hsuan T'ung continued to live in the Summer Palace in seclusion but in 1932 he was plucked from obscurity by the Japanese to rule Manchukuo (formerly Manchuria) under the title of Kangde. Stamps of the puppet empire were issued from 1932 until 1945 [6].

NATIONALIST REPUBLIC

The first special stamps of the republic appeared in December and portrayed Sun Yat-sen, who had engineered the overthrow of the Manchu dynasty. Subsequently he appeared on most of the definitive sets down to 1949 [9]. An airmail series introduced in 1932 showed the Great Wall of China [7]. In addition to the mainstream issues of the republic, stamps were overprinted or surcharged for use in many of the provinces where the yuan fluctuated in value. From 1927, when war between nationalists and communists broke out, there were many local posts in areas under communist control.

War with Japan erupted in 1931 and escalated in the ensuing decade. The value of the yuan plummeted [8], as shown by the inflated value of this stamp, and China suffered hyperinflation from 1946 until the nationalists withdrew from the mainland three years later [10].

COMMUNIST INSURGENCE
By 1937 the Japanese had occupied most of China but both communists and nationalists put up a strong resistance. The communist guerrilla armies operated in Japanese-held territory and organized a somewhat nomadic postal service, with many issues that fluctuated as the tide of war ebbed and flowed. These stamps are among the most complex in the world, issued by armies constantly on the move rather than associated with postal services in the accepted sense. Often crudely designed and printed under difficult conditions, they include many rarities.

As the communists gained control of many provinces after the defeat of Japan in 1945 postal services became more settled, and separate issues that read like the points of the compass appeared in different parts of China. Nevertheless, there were still many different issues, including seven in North-east China and ten in North-west China alone. Typical of these provincial stamps of 1945–9 were motifs of Mao Zedong and banner-waving troops [11–14]. Even after the proclamation of the People's Republic in 1949, separate stamps continued in North-east China because of the different value of money there.

PEOPLE'S REPUBLIC
The earliest definitives showed the Gate of Heavenly Peace in Beijing [15] or Chairman Mao [16], both themes that recurred frequently. Special issues reflected the rhetoric of the period, celebrating the 25th anniversary of the People's Liberation Army [17] and inauguration of the New Constitution [18]. The currency depreciated during the early 1950s but in 1955 it was reformed. In the ensuing period a more thematic approach crept in, gradually replacing endless Five Year Plan sets and portraits of communist heroes with sets reflecting the arts and crafts of old China [19]. During the Cultural Revolution (1965–71) quotations from Mao's little red book predominated [20]. Since the 1980s, recurring themes have been history and culture, among them stamps illustrating scenes from folk tales and Chinese classics. China's spectacular material progress since the 1990s has also been recorded [21].

Below: Supporting the Front *by Cui Kaixi featured on a 1998 stamp for the 50th anniversary of the Liberation War (top) and spectacular scenery is shown on a stamp of 2004 (bottom).*

13

14

15

16

17

18

19

20

21

LUNAR NEW YEAR STAMPS

The Chinese calendar is based on the phases of the Moon and can be traced back 2,000 years to the time of the Eastern Han dynasty. The vast majority of China's predominantly rural people were illiterate, so astronomers worked out a dozen animal signs as readily identifiable symbols for the months, and these were also employed to describe the 12-year cycle of the years.

In Chinese culture the animal emblems are associated with the 12 earthly branches, representing nature or destiny. When combined with the five celestial stems or main elements – gold, wood, water, fire and earth – they produce a 60-year cycle known as a *chia-tzu*. Long after the construction of the calendar, the zodiac came to be applied to casting horoscopes, the reasoning being that every person born in a particular year would exhibit broadly similar character traits, governing their lives and affecting their future.

The 12-year cycle begins with the Rat (*Tzu*), which is followed by the Ox (*Chou*), Tiger (*Yin*), Rabbit (*Mao*), Dragon (*Chen*), Snake (*Szu*), Horse (*Wu*), Ram (*Wei*), Monkey (*Shen*), Rooster (*Yu*), Dog (*Hsu*) and Pig (*Hai*). These are the animals believed to have

been especially loyal to the Lord Buddha. According to Chinese folklore, their order of precedence in the zodiac follows the sequence in which they responded to the Buddha's summons to his power conference.

COMMEMORATIVE STAMPS

Although stamps marking the Lunar New Year were issued by Japan as long ago as 1936, this is a theme that developed only gradually from the 1950s onwards. By the 1980s they were regularly released by Japan, Korea, Taiwan, Hong Kong, Macao and Singapore, invariably featuring the relevant

animal in the Chinese zodiac. In recent years Japan's Lunar New Year stamps have been issued in two versions: a pair for ordinary postal use, and a matched pair in a longer format with serial numbers that are entered in a draw, the prizes being special miniature sheets.

In almost 70 years the Lunar New Year has spawned a formidable array of stamps, booklets, pre-stamped postcards and souvenir covers. Until fairly recently these were quite compact and manageable, being confined to the

Left: A rat and a snowman were shown on the New Year stamp from South Korea in 1995.

Below: Travelling pigs appeared on South Korea's stamp for the Year of the Pig, late 1994; the Hong Kong series (January 1995) showed pottery pigs.

Below: A stylized monkey is shown on a Macao stamp for the Year of the Monkey (2004); the 33c US stamp by Yuan Lee marked the Year of the Rabbit in 1999.

Below: Courting pigs from French Polynesia marked the Year of the Pig, 1995; Yuan Lee designed this 37c US stamp for the Year of the Goat, 2003.

Above: To mark the Year of the Dragon (2000) Micronesia released this $2 miniature sheet (left), reproducing a traditional Chinese image. Japan uses miniature sheets (right) as prizes in its annual New Year lottery.

countries of South-east Asia, but in the past few years the concept has spread like wildfire.

GOING WORLDWIDE

The United States, which has the largest Chinese population outside Asia (about six million), started the ball rolling with a 29c stamp in December 1992 to mark the Year of the Rooster (1993) and this has since become the theme for an annual issue. It spread to Canada in 1997 when the Year of the Ox was marked by a 45c stamp accompanied by a miniature sheet in the shape of a Chinese fan – this was a major innovation, as miniature sheets up to that time had invariably been rectangular in shape.

In recent years the concept has spread to every part of the globe, yielding Lunar New Year stamps as far afield as Ireland, the Marshall Islands and the Netherlands Antilles, and from Sweden to New Zealand and South Africa. Among the most attractive, and certainly most humorous, are those designed by Victor Ambrus for Jersey in the Channel Islands. They are in the form of £1 miniature sheets with the appropriate motif projected into the sheet margins. The Republic of China (Taiwan) has been issuing Lunar New Year stamps since 1969 (Year of the Dog). Latterly these issues have taken the form of two stamps showing different artistic interpretations of the appropriate animal.

Sweden seems about as unlikely a country as any to celebrate the Lunar New Year, but in recent years the event has been cleverly combined with tributes to children's literature. New Zealand likewise adopted an oblique approach to the Lunar New Year. In 1997 a set of six stamps featured different breeds of cattle, but the interpane gutters included the Chinese zodiacal symbol for the Year of the Ox. This established a precedent that is now followed every year.

For some years Ireland has produced stamps early in the year, primarily for Valentine's Day greetings. In January 1995 a booklet of four 32p stamps depicted various symbols of love, but the stamps were released simultaneously as a miniature sheet celebrating the Year of the Pig, with appropriate motifs and symbols for the Lunar New Year in the sheet margin. This established a pattern that has been maintained ever since.

A number of issues from the countries in the Inter-Governmental Philatelic Corporation group have also celebrated the Lunar New Year. These made their debut in May 1994, well into the Year of the Dog, and consisted of a number of sets depicting different canine breeds, but these stamps incorporated a tiny symbol in one corner inscribed "Year of the Dog", flanking the appropriate Chinese symbol.

More relevant were the issues of April 1995, designed by the leading Chinese-American artist Yuan Lee and featuring different aspects of pigs. Recent issues have tended to be more modest, confined to sheetlets of four and a matching souvenir sheet, with artwork by Yuan Lee predominating.

Below: One of the four stamps issued by Hong Kong for the Year of the Horse in 1990 (top) and the stamp from French Polynesia for the Year of the Dragon in 2000 (bottom).

1

2

3

4

5

6

7

8

9

CHINESE TERRITORIES

In addition to China proper there are a number of territories that were at one time part of China (such as Mongolia) or, conversely, were European colonies but have now reverted to China (Hong Kong and Macao). Tibet, once autonomous, has been absorbed by the People's Republic, whereas Taiwan, which was occupied by Japan from 1895 to 1945, later became the

refuge of the Chinese Nationalists and survives to this day under the name of the Republic of China. The former British and Portuguese colonies of Hong Kong and Macao have enjoyed phenomenal economic growth in recent years; though now part of China again they are guaranteed autonomy for 50 years.

Left: The high-rise commercial buildings of Victoria, Hong Kong's capital, include several of the tallest structures in the world. Set against this background, the Peak Tram, opened in 1888, continues to transport tourists and commuters alike.

HONG KONG

In 1839 the Chinese tried to suppress the opium trade from India, but Britain retaliated and in 1841 forced China to cede Hong Kong island, which thereafter became the centre of drugs trafficking. The Kowloon peninsula was ceded in 1860 and a 99-year lease on the New Territories was granted to Britain in 1899. When it expired in 1997 Hong Kong's status was no longer viable and it was returned to China. Since then it has been a special administrative region and retains its own currency and stamps.

Hong Kong adopted stamps in 1862 and for almost a century most definitives were identical apart from the monarch's portrait. Although it actually produced the first commemorative stamp in Asia – the 2c definitive overprinted in 1891 to celebrate the 50th anniversary of British rule – a further half century would elapse before the first distinctive series appeared. This was a set of bicoloured pictorials marking the centenary of the colony in February 1941 [1], shortly before it was occupied by the Japanese.

Hong Kong participated in the various colonial omnibus issues from 1935 to 1966, an exception being the Victory pair of 1946: these utilized a design sketched by W.E. Jones in a

Japanese prison camp, showing a phoenix rising from the flames to symbolize the eventual re-emergence of Hong Kong after enemy occupation. Royal events, such as the wedding of Charles and Diana in 1981, and a visit of 1989 [3], were also covered.

Postwar commercial development and the influx of refugees from the People's Republic of China totally transformed the crown colony. Many stamps of this period presented a view of Hong Kong as a little bit of Britain in the Far East, with features such as Georgian pillar-boxes [2], but increasingly its Chinese heritage came to the fore. Numerous sets of recent years have featured costumes [4] and other aspects of the applied and decorative arts. Tourism is a major subject, reflected in scenery and local events such as the dragon boat races [7]. Since 1997 stamps have been inscribed "Hong Kong China", including a set celebrating the centenary of its waterfront trams [5]. The People's Liberation Army [8] took over the former British bases but generally keeps a low profile.

MACAO

The oldest European settlement in the Far East, Macao was settled by the Portuguese in 1557. As Portuguese colonial power declined in the 19th century Macao became a backwater, preserving its distinctive Iberian architecture. In 1999 it became a special administrative region of China and, like Hong Kong, retains its own stamps and currency. The early stamps from 1884 conformed to the Portuguese colonial designs, and distinctive motifs did not appear until the 1930s. After World War II they became much more colourful and thematic [6], but have latterly concentrated on indigenous art and culture, with numerous sets featuring the rapidly vanishing way of life [11]. Recent stamps, inscribed "Macau China", include a pair celebrating the first Chinese astronaut [9].

TAIWAN

The early issues of the Republic of China (ROC) were often inscribed entirely in Chinese, even when they related to international organizations [10], but later the name was rendered in English. When the nationalists fled from the mainland they took the vast bulk of the Chinese art treasures from Peking (Beijing) and these have been a fertile source of stamp illustrations ever since [12]. Many stamps from the 1960s to the 1980s highlighted Taiwan's siege mentality, but in the more relaxed atmosphere of recent years the emphasis has shifted to nostalgia, as in the old railway station series [13], and a revival of the penchant for illustrating the arts [14] and customs such as puppetry [15], folk tales [16] and children's pastimes [18].

Below: Damdinsuren's Camel Caravan *was one of several paintings on a 1969 Mongolian set for the tenth anniversary of the Co-operative Movement.*

Boxer Rebellion

When the Boxer rebellion laid siege to the foreign legations in Peking (1900), twelve countries, including the USA and Japan, formed a coalition to relieve them. Indian stamps overprinted "C.E.F." were used by the China Expeditionary Force which quashed the uprising.

MONGOLIA AND TIBET

Landlocked in central Asia, between Russia and China, is Mongolia, one of the oldest countries in the world. When at the height of its power in the 13th century Mongolia, under Genghis Khan, conquered the whole of China and expanded as far west as Poland and Hungary. After the Manchus conquered China in 1644 they absorbed Mongolia in 1681.

Following the Chinese revolution of 1911, Mongolia asserted its independence, which it attained in 1921 under the leadership of Sukhe Bator [17]. A people's republic from 1924, it overthrew its communist regime in 1990 and became the State of Mongolia. Since the 1930s, stamps have been an important source of hard currency.

Tibet was at various times tributary to China and its earliest stamps were those of China overprinted. Distinctive stamps appeared in 1912 and continued until 1950, when the Chinese invaded and annexed Tibet. The world's only theocracy has struggled ever since to regain independence, and stamps portraying the Dalai Lama and showing monasteries and the Potala Palace in Lhasa [19] have been produced by the government in exile.

1

2

3

4

5

6

7

8

9

10

11

KOREA

As a kingdom, Korea dates its origins to 2333 BC, and this is the starting point of its calendar. The country's history is well documented from 57 BC. The Yi dynasty had an unbroken record from 1392 until it was overthrown in 1910. In 1637, however, Korea was defeated by the Manchus and was a tributary of China from then until 1895. It was completely cut off from the outside world until 1876, when it was compelled to allow trade with Japan. In 1897 King Kojong proclaimed an empire. In 1905 Japan took over the postal service and five years later forced the emperor to abdicate. Korea was then annexed and remained part of the Japanese empire until 1945. Shortly before the war ended Russia declared war on Japan, and Soviet troops invaded North Korea. This proved to be the opening round of a conflict that has lasted ever since. The country was divided into Soviet and American zones of occupation by a line drawn across the peninsula at the 38th parallel.

Left: One of many tributes to its allies in the Korean War, a miniature sheet portraying General MacArthur and the Korean, UN and US flags was issued by South Korea in 1965.

UNITED KOREA

A postal service was introduced in November 1884 but a riot at the post office in Seoul a few weeks later led to the suspension of the service and the gradual infiltration of Japanese agents. The first stamps [1] are plentiful in mint condition but of the greatest rarity used, which is hardly surprising since they were in use for such a short time. A second attempt, in 1895, was more successful. The last series was designed and printed in Paris and bore the name of the Korean Empire in French. Under United States military government in 1945, distinctive stamps were revived [2].

SOUTH KOREA

The Republic of Korea, under Syngman Rhee, was proclaimed in August 1948, but in June 1950 it was invaded from the north. By September the enemy had overrun most of the country, but an American-led UN force landed at Inchon and the war raged back and forth for two years. Eventually a truce was reached and a demilitarized zone established, initially patrolled by Indian troops, who had their own stamps [3]. Many of the stamps of South Korea since that time have referred to the war [4] and paid tribute to the USA for its support [5].

President Rhee was elected to a fourth term in 1960 but ousted by a military coup a month later [6]. By the 1970s South Korea was enjoying unprecedented prosperity and this is reflected in the stamps, which were not only well designed and printed but covered a wide range of topics, from fauna and flora [7] to cartoons [9] and comic book characters [10]. South Korea enthusiastically embraced the American way, from Boy Scouts to Lions Clubs [11], but its unique culture was not forgotten [12]. High-speed trains [13], motor manufacture and jet liners are recurring definitive themes. The country gained international prestige by hosting the Olympic Games (1988) and the football World Cup (2002), both marked by numerous stamps.

Cult of the Personality

The overriding theme of North Korean stamps has been the glorification of the Comrade Great Leader Kim Il Sung and now his son and successor Kim Jong Il. Not content with merely portraying these figures, the stamps incessantly depict them as role models and paragons of every virtue, in scenes that range from showing the peasants how to plant their crops to exhorting the factory workers to even greater efforts. Every other issue from the North seems to portray the two Kims.

12

13

14

15   16

17

18

NORTH KOREA

The polarization of the two Koreas is vividly demonstrated in their stamps. The Russian occupation ended in September 1948 with the institution of the Korean People's Democratic Republic. The stamps of this period were often crude imitations of contemporary Soviet designs, and they included numerous references to the war, especially when it was going well for the communists [8]. Whereas the stamps of the South clung to the Korean chronology, the North adopted the Christian calendar. Many stamps alluded not only to victories and anniversaries of the Korean War but also commemorated earlier conflicts, from strikes and demonstrations [15] to outright guerrilla warfare against the Japanese [14].

More peaceful subjects began to appear in the late 1960s [16] but the onset of the Vietnam War gave North Korea more scope for its ongoing hatred of America. Anti-American propaganda included a stamp showing a monster in a GI helmet being skewered by bayonets [17]. In more recent years propaganda against the South has increased [18] although at the same time greater attention is given to popular themes [19]. Even UNICEF (if not the UN itself) gets some credit for relieving child poverty [20].

Below: This North Korean stamp was issued in 1998 to mark the 75th anniversary of Kim Il Sung's "250-mile journey for national liberation".

19   20

JAPAN

According to legend the empire of Japan was founded in about 600 BC by Jimmu Tenno, who was a descendent of the great sun goddess Amaterasu. All the emperors from that time until now have been in direct descent and their status as living deities explains why they are never portrayed on Japanese stamps, for to deface them with a postmark would be an act of sacrilege. Although the Portuguese first visited Japan in 1542 and Dutch traders subsequently got a toehold on Deshima, all foreign contacts were banned from 1630 until the visit of Commodore Perry of the US Navy in 1853. For 250 years the emperor was little more than a figurehead, while real power was vested in the shoguns, the xenophobic leaders of the military caste, but under Emperor Meiji, who ascended to the throne in 1868, Japan rapidly industrialized, the shogunate was abolished and the country adopted western dress, technology and warfare, as well as a postal system, complete with stamps.

Left: The founder of the modern postal service was Baron Maeshima, who has been portrayed on many definitive stamps and special issues since 1946.

EARLIEST STAMPS

Four stamps covering the basic postal rates, denominated in mon, were introduced in April 1871 [1], but a few months later the currency was decimalized, based on the yen of 100 sen. Japan was not slow to introduce special issues: the first, in 1894, celebrated the emperor's silver wedding with a motif of cranes (symbolic of fidelity and long life). Victories over China in 1895 and Russia in 1905 were celebrated by stamps [2], while the battleships *Katori* and *Kashima* were featured on stamps issued in 1921 to celebrate the return of Crown Prince Hirohito from a tour of Europe [3].

WORLD WAR II AND ITS AFTERMATH

Japanese militarism gathered momentum in the 1920s and 1930s. Censured for its invasion of China in 1931, Japan left the League of Nations and formed an alliance with Nazi Germany. Rivalry with the USA in the Pacific led to the unprovoked attack on Pearl Harbor in December 1941, the start of Japan's own "lightning war" in the Pacific. The first anniversary of that "day of infamy"

was celebrated by stamps showing the air raid on Pearl Harbor and Japanese tanks in action at Bataan in the Philippines [4]. Although the tide turned at Midway in 1942 it took three long, hard years, and the use of two atomic bombs to destroy Hiroshima and Nagasaki, to bring Japan to its knees. Wartime definitives reflect the militaristic outlook of the period, but in the immediate aftermath stamps were poorly printed, often without perforations, because the usual printing works had been destroyed [5].

MODERN JAPAN

In contrast with the bellicose nature of the years up to 1945, postwar Japan concentrated on conquering the world markets, developing especially in the fields of electronics and the automotive industry. The vast majority of stamps are printed in photogravure, latterly in full colour. Definitives concentrate on antiquities, fauna and flora [6]. Since 1936 Japan has produced hundreds of stamps extolling the beauties of its many national parks [7]. Stamps have also been produced for New Year greetings, while annual issues of more recent

Letter Writing Day

To encourage Japanese children to write more letters, stamps in many different shapes have been designed by the Dutch artist Dick Bruna in recent years.

times have been aimed at popularizing letter writing, especially to pen-pals abroad [8]. Stamps are captioned only in Japanese [9], which creates difficulties for foreign collectors lacking a fully illustrated catalogue, but in compliance with Universal Postal Union regulations the country name "Nippon" has been inscribed in the Roman alphabet since 1966 [12]. The vast majority of Japanese stamps concentrate on the unique culture of the country, including its architecture, costume [10], theatre [11], art and music. However, western influences shine through in sport [13] and, of course, in technology [15]. For the Millennium Japan began a series of ten sheetlets (one for each decade of the 20th century) and has since produced similar sheetlets for the UNESCO World Heritage Sites in Japan, art treasures, and popular cartoon and comic-book characters.

Japan is divided into 47 administrative regions known as prefectures. In 1990 it released a sheet of 50 stamps to publicize the PhilaNippon international philatelic exhibition of 1991. Three non-postal labels advertised the exhibition but the rest of the sheet consisted of 47 stamps of the ¥62 denomination, each featuring a different flower associated with a particular prefecture, from the sweet briar of Hokkaido to the coral tree of Okinawa. This sheet was analogous to the sheets of 50 that have been issued by the United States since 1976, featuring the flags, birds and flowers of the 50 states. Japan, however, took the concept a stage further in April 1989 when the first batch of stamps pertaining to specific prefectures was released. Each prefectural stamp [14] is valid for postage all over the country but is sold only within its own prefecture and the other prefectures in one of the eleven postal regions into which the country is divided. In the main, these stamps are issued in conventional sheets, although some have also been released in booklets of miniature sheets. The number of different stamps fluctuates, from 19 in the inaugural year to 13 in some of the later years. Most of them feature landmarks, scenery and wildlife, but some have been issued to mark a special event.

WARTIME OCCUPATION ISSUES

Between 1942 and 1945, when Japan occupied China, South-east Asia and many of the Pacific islands, it overprinted the stamps of the occupied territories. These are noted elsewhere but a selection of the distinctive stamps of the period is shown here, including stamps for Burma [16–17], Malaya [18], Dutch East Indies [19], North Borneo [20] and the Philippines [21]. After the war Australian stamps were overprinted for the use of British Commonwealth Occupying Forces. In 1945 a US military administration was imposed on the Ryukyu Islands, including Okinawa, and distinctive stamps were used there until 1972 when the islands were handed back to Japan [22].

1

2

3

4

5

6

7

8

9

10

11

12

INDONESIA AND THE PHILIPPINES

These two large countries of the south-western Pacific have much in common and a parallel history. Both are archipelagos covering vast areas, which made communications difficult and encouraged the development of numerous petty states before they were conquered by European powers – Indonesia by the Dutch and the Philippines by the Spanish. Neither colonial ruler ever exerted full control and there were numerous rebellions. The modern republics have inherited many of these problems. In World War II both were overrun by the Japanese, who exploited latent nationalism. Both are nominally democracies, although in their recent past they have both been subjected to authoritarian rule.

Left: Achmed Sukarno founded the Indonesia National Party in 1927. Imprisoned and exiled by the Dutch, he was given power by the Japanese in 1942 and became president in 1945. In the 1960s luxury hotels contrasted with chaos and poverty and in 1965 an abortive communist coup led to his downfall.

DUTCH EAST INDIES

Portuguese traders discovered the spice islands in the 16th century but it was the Dutch who took over in 1602 and eventually ruled over an archipelago of 13,000 islands spread across 5,000 km/3,000 miles. Stamps were introduced in 1864, bearing a full-face portrait of William III, but from 1870 onwards the Indies, like other European colonies, conformed to the colonial keytypes. In 1902 stamps were overprinted specifically for use in Java [1] and six years later the same series was overprinted "Buiten Bezit" (outer possessions) for the outlying islands.

Airmail stamps were introduced in 1928 and charity stamps for child welfare became an annual feature from 1930 onwards, following the example of the mother country. Other early charity sets raised funds for a leper colony (1931), the Salvation Army (1932) and the YMCA (1933). A pictorial definitive series, with a standard design showing rice cultivation, appeared in 1933, while short sets depicting indigenous peoples and their customs appeared in the 1930s and early 1940s [2].

Although the Netherlands were overrun by the Germans in 1940, the colonial empire continued to function, being administered by the Dutch government in exile. In this period a charity set raised funds for the Dutch forces fighting with the Allies. The Netherlands Indies itself was under Japanese occupation (1942–5) and the nationalists then took over [3], but with the aid of British and Japanese troops Dutch rule was restored in Java. In 1950 the Dutch bowed to the inevitable and handed power over to the nationalists. Stamps portraying Queen Wilhelmina were overprinted "Indonesia" [4].

INDONESIA

A period of chaos followed in which different stamps were issued in Java, Sumatra and Madura and a series printed in Vienna was never put on sale [5], although it was at one time very common on the world stamp market. The various factions united in August 1950 to form the Indonesian Republic [6]. Until 1965 Sukarno, the founder of the country, remained firmly in control [7] but he gradually handed over to General Suharto. In turn Suharto was ousted in 1997, and Indonesia experienced true democracy for the first time in half a century.

The stamps of Indonesia have the usual themes [8] but also endeavour to bring together the country's many different ethnic groups [9]. Tourism is still a major industry, reflected in many sets featuring scenery and wildlife [10].

Separate stamps were issued in 1954–65 for the Riau-Lingga islands, whose currency was tied to the Singapore dollar [13]. After the Dutch handover to Indonesia they held on to West New Guinea and issued distinctive stamps [14], but from 1950 onwards Indonesia laid claim to this territory. To settle the dispute, it was placed under UN administration in 1962 and stamps were accordingly overprinted [11]. It was handed over to Indonesia in May 1963 and renamed Irian Barat, or West Irian [12].

The island of Timor in the Sunda group was partitioned between the Dutch and the Portuguese. Stamps of the Portuguese colonial type were used in east Timor from 1885 to 1975 [15]. Civil war erupted but when the Fretilin faction proclaimed independence Indonesian troops invaded and occupied the area. The oppressive regime was overthrown in 2003 and stamps inscribed "East Timor" are now used.

PHILIPPINES
Fernando Magellan was killed in the Philippine islands in 1521 during his voyage round the world. They were colonized in 1542 and named for the king of Spain. Stamps were introduced in 1854 [16], the last issue, during the Spanish-American War, portraying the young Alfonso XIII [17]. The indigenous population had fought a guerrilla war against the Spanish since 1873 and declared a republic in 1897, with distinctive stamps in 1898–9 [18].

The islands were ceded by Spain to the USA and placed under military administration. US stamps were overprinted [19], but were soon followed by stamps bearing the name of the

Good Relations
The close ties that exist between the USA and the Philippines have given rise to numerous stamps over the past century portraying American historical figures, but the Philippines alone produced a stamp showing not just John and Robert Kennedy but the entire Kennedy clan. The contract for the stamps, produced by an American agency with the agreement of the Filipino government, was cancelled at the last moment, and the stamps had no postal validity although they were on sale in the USA.

United States as well as the Philippines. Under the Commonwealth of the Philippines, established in 1935, the islands were granted autonomy. At first the previous pictorial definitive series was overprinted "Commonwealth" [20] and an entirely new series was just in the process of being released in 1941 when the islands were invaded.

After wartime occupation by the Japanese the Philippines became an independent republic in 1946, and the prewar overprinted series was reissued, overprinted "Victory". Many of the stamps from that time hark back to the heroic struggle of the war period [21], including several issues portraying General MacArthur, who was field marshal of the Filipino army from 1935 onwards and returned to liberate the islands in 1944. The modern stamps [22] reflect the unique cultural mixture of the Philippines, an amalgam of Spanish, American and Malay influences and of Catholicism and Islam, as well as the great diversity of landscape.

13

14

15

16

17

18

19

20

21

22

1

2

3

4

5

6

7

8

9

10

11

SOUTH-EAST ASIA

The Malay peninsula at the south-easterly tip of Asia is shared by three countries – Thailand, Malaysia and the tiny island republic of Singapore. Historically and culturally interlinked, their mutual interdependence was formalized when the menace of communism was at its height in the 1970s. Politically, Malaya consisted of three components: the Straits Settlements (a British crown colony consisting of Malacca, Penang and Singapore), the Federated Malay States (Negri Sembilan, Pahang, Perak and Selangor) and the independent states of Johore, Kedah, Kelantan, Perlis and Trengganu, all of which issued their own stamps at various times. A Malayan Postal Union, created in 1934, co-ordinated the postal services and issued postage due labels, but the issues of the various states continued. The Malay states

were overrun by the Japanese in 1941–5, and at the end of World War II they came under British military administration until 1948. It was in this period that plans for closer integration and greater autonomy were formulated, leading to the creation of the Federation of Malaya in 1956.

Left: The Association of South-East Asian Nations (ASEAN) has expanded since its formation in 1977, as this 30th anniversary stamp from Brunei, showing the flags of the member states, demonstrates.

SINGAPORE

Founded by Sir Stamford Raffles in 1819, Singapore grew from a fishing village into one of the world's largest ports, a major centre for world trade. With Malacca and Penang, it formed the Straits Settlements, administered by the East India Company, which originally used Indian stamps surcharged in cents [1]. British influence over the Malay peninsula developed in the 19th century and after World War II Singapore was part of the Federation of Malaya [2], but in 1965 it seceded to form an independent republic within the Commonwealth. Its stamps reflect its astonishing urbanization [3], its multi-ethnic character [4] and its military preparedness [5].

MALAYSIA AND BRUNEI

Britain gradually brought the various Malay sultanates under its protection. Some of these were grouped together in the Federated Malay States [6] but each of the unfederated states had its own distinctive stamps [8–9] until the

late 1940s. Thereafter uniform designs were used, differing only in the names of the states and the portraits of their rulers [7]. Labuan [10] and British North Borneo [11] combined to form the state of North Borneo [12], which subsequently joined the Malay Federation under the name of Sabah. In 1947, following Sarawak's transfer to the governance of the British colonial administration, its stamps were overprinted with the crowned cipher of George VI, pending a pictorial definitive series in 1950 with a portrait of the king inset. A new series, with Elizabeth II inset, was released in 1955 and continued until 1964, when Sarawak joined the Federation of Malaysia [13].

Stamps inscribed in Malay signified the Federation of Malaya [14], which was unique in having a king elected from the various sultans. The Federation changed its name to Malaysia in 1963. Apart from the states issues the national definitives have featured birds, fruits, fish and, most recently, butterflies [15], augmented by

The Land of the White Rajahs

For ridding his domain of pirates, the sultan of Brunei granted the Englishman James Brooke the title of rajah of Sarawak in 1842. Now a state of Malaysia, Sarawak has had its own stamps since 1869. After Japanese and British military occupation it was returned to the Brooke family in 1946, but the last rajah ceded it to Britain soon afterwards. All three white rajahs were portrayed on the stamps intended for the centenary in 1942 but delayed until 1946 as a result of the Japanese invasion.

short thematic sets ranging from birds of prey to marine life. Many of the recent stamps have shown the extraordinary development of the region, including one of the world's tallest landmarks, the Petronas Towers in Kuala Lumpur, depicted in a stamp marking the inauguration of the Putra light railway system in 1998 [16].

Closely associated with Malaysia is the sultanate of Brunei. Once an insignificant petty state in North Borneo, it is now one of the world's wealthiest countries due to the discovery of oil. Stamps showing a fishing village were current from 1907 until 1952, making them one of the world's longest running series [17]. Even today, Brunei operates one of the most conservative new issue policies in the world, with an average of 20 stamps a year, almost all of which are entirely pertinent to the country itself. Since his accession in 1967 Sultan Sir Hassanal Bolkiah has been portrayed on the vast majority of Brunei's stamps.

THAILAND

A postal service restricted to the royal court functioned in the mid-19th century, but an external service operated at the British consulate in Bangkok from 1858. Straits stamps overprinted "B" were introduced in 1882 [18] but were withdrawn in 1885 when Thailand joined the Universal Postal Union and introduced its own stamps [19]. Stamps bore the name of Siam until 1940, when the present name was adopted. Thailand has strong Buddhist and monarchical traditions, which have featured on numerous stamps [21]. Its military forces are highly trained and well equipped [22]. Most special issues are singles, with occasional longer sets.

JAPANESE OCCUPATION

During World War II the Malay peninsula was under enemy occupation from December 1941 until 1945. The conquerors began by overprinting stamps of the Malayan Postal Union, Malay states, Straits Settlements, North Borneo, Brunei and Sarawak with Japanese characters [20], but in April 1943 they produced a series of pictorials, printed by a Dutch company in Batavia.

Thailand was allied to Japan and was rewarded with the transfer of the northern Malay states (Kedah, Kelantan, Perlis and Trengganu), which had traditionally been under Thai influence. From October 1943 to September 1945 Thailand issued special stamps for use in these states, before they were returned to British administration.

Below: A tin dredger appears on one of the pictorials issued in Malaya during Japanese occupation in 1943 (left). The Thai war memorial featured on the stamps issued in 1944 during the Thai occupation of northern Malaya (right).

12

13

14

15

16

17

18

19

20

21

22

AUSTRALASIA

This term encompasses Australia, New Zealand and their dependencies in the Indian Ocean and Antarctica as well as the islands of the south, central and western Pacific. Adhesive stamps spread to Australia in 1850 and New Zealand in 1855, while the first stamp of New Caledonia appeared in 1860.

AUSTRALIA

Probably sighted by the Chinese in the early 15th century and visited by the Spanish and Portuguese a century later, Australia was partly explored by the Dutch in the 17th century and charted in 1769–70 by James Cook, who annexed it to the British Crown. It is the smallest continent in the world, and the only one that forms a single country. The British colonized Australia piecemeal and eventually created six colonies, beginning with New South Wales in 1788. Originally allocated to the former territory, Van Diemen's Land (later renamed Tasmania) became a separate state in 1825, followed by South Australia in 1836, Victoria in 1851 and Queensland in 1859. Western Australia was settled by 1829. The British parliament approved a federal constitution in 1900 and the following year the Commonwealth of Australia came into being.

Left: A set of three appeared in 1938 to mark 150 years since the first settlement of New South Wales. All the stamps were of a common design showing the landing at Sydney Cove on January 26, 1788.

1

2

3

4

5

6

7

8

9

10

11

AUSTRALIAN COLONIES

Each of the six colonies issued its own stamps, adopting a highly individual approach to the matter. In fact, New South Wales beat the mother country to it by introducing prepaid letter sheets, embossed with the colonial seal, in November 1838, 18 months before Britain adopted the Mulready wrappers. However, adhesive stamps were not introduced in New South Wales until January 1850. From 1851 stamps of New South Wales [1] generally portrayed Queen Victoria, with the exception of the centennial series of 1888. Other colonies followed suit [2–3]. Stamps inscribed "Van Diemen's Land" [4] were used in Tasmania from 1853 to 1857, and in 1899 Tasmania was the only colony to adopt a wholly pictorial definitive series [5]. Victoria likewise favoured portraits [7], whereas stamps of Western Australia [6] featured its emblem, the black swan.

The different postal rates in each colony meant that their distinctive stamps continued in use until 1913.

COMMONWEALTH ISSUES

From the outset the issue of stamps was a political tool. Labour were in power when stamps were introduced, hence the national motif of the kangaroo on a map of the country [8], but when the Conservatives returned to power soon afterwards the kangaroo gave way to the king [9]. When Labour returned to power, so did the roo, and so it continued through the 1920s and 1930s. Less controversial was the 6d stamp of 1914 showing a kookaburra [10].

Special issues, which appeared infrequently from 1927 onwards, marked the inauguration of the federal parliament in Canberra and the Sydney Harbour Bridge [11], while the trio celebrating the silver jubilee of George V in 1935 showed him in field marshal's

Australian Innovations

A self-adhesive booklet issued in 2004 took a rather whimsical look at some of Australia's ideas and inventions. These ranged chronologically from Racecam TV sports coverage, introduced in 1979, to the Baby Safety Capsule of 1984 and the world's first polymer banknotes, which were issued in 1988 for the bicentennial celebrations.

12   13

14

15   16

17

18

19   20

21

uniform mounted on Anzac [12], the horse named in honour of the Australian and New Zealand Army Corps, which had fought at Gallipoli in World War I. Fine intaglio printing continued until the early 1950s. The set honouring Australian Imperial Forces [13] was the only special issue of World War II until February 1945, when stamps marked the arrival of the Duke of Gloucester as governor-general [14]. From 1938 definitives were more pictorial, but continued the tradition of blending wildlife with royal portraits [15]; by the late 1950s less fussy designs were favoured [16].

Stamps for international occasions, such as the 75th anniversary of the UPU in 1949, were given an Australian slant [17]. Monochrome intaglio gave way to multicolour photogravure in the 1960s [19]. Annual stamps mark Australia Day [18] as well as the queen's birthday [20], indicating a strong monarchical feeling despite the rise of republicanism in recent years. Modern stamps reflect the laid-back, often irreverent, attitudes of Australians, whose off-beat humour is often expressed in both definitives and special issues. Not surprisingly, given the nation's many achievements in sport, this remains an immensely popular philatelic theme.

In recent years Australia has adopted a number of technical innovations, such as the use of holograms to convey the impression of Australian opals [21]. In 1994 Australia also led the way in developing self-adhesive stamps, in coils or special booklets. The Melbourne international philatelic exhibition of 2000 introduced personalized stamps, with adjoining labels bearing people's own snapshots, a technique that is now used worldwide. Stamps portraying the Australian gold medallists at the Sydney Olympics were on sale in their home states within 48 hours.

1

2

3

4

5

6

7

8

9

10

NEW ZEALAND

Slightly larger than the British Isles but with a 20th of their population, New Zealand is often referred to by the British as the Antipodes (literally, the place lying at the opposite side of the world). Its climate and scenery are similar to those of Britain, if on a much grander scale. The North and South Islands were first populated by the Maori, Polynesians who sailed their canoes across the ocean from Hawaii between the 10th and 14th centuries. The islands were discovered by the Dutch in 1642 and charted by James Cook in 1769. The haunt of whalers in the early 19th century, New Zealand was annexed by the British in 1840, becoming briefly a dependency of New South Wales. It attained self-government in 1852 and, after refusing to join the Commonwealth of Australia in 1901, became a dominion in 1907.

Left: The centennial of annexation was marked by a long series of 1940 charting the country's history from the arrival of the Maori in 1350 onwards. This stamp shows the Treaty of Waitangi being signed by Captain Hobson and Maori chiefs.

EARLY STAMPS

Although a postal service was organized in 1840 it was not until 1855 that New Zealand adopted adhesive stamps. To mark the centenary the original design was revived, with a portrait of Elizabeth II replacing the Chalon portrait of Victoria [1]. Thereafter, most stamps were produced by the Government Printer in Wellington, although the dies were sometimes engraved in Australia. The first 1/2d stamp, introduced in 1873 when a low rate for printed matter was conceded, was a blatant copy of the contemporary British 1/2d stamp.

All stamps until 1898 bore portraits of Victoria, the last series portraying images of the queen from her teens to the Jubilee and Veiled Head portraits of 1887 and 1893 respectively. In 1893 the definitives were issued with advertisements printed on the back and these stamps, popularly known as "Adsons", are much sought-after. In 1898 New Zealand was one of the first colonies to issue pictorial stamps, featuring scenery, wildlife and a Maori war canoe [2]. The advent of the 1d rate to any part of the British Empire was marked by a stamp in 1901 that underwent numerous changes over the ensuing decade before the words "Dominion of" were

added, along with a series portraying Edward VII, who also appeared on the 6d [4]. Royal portraiture was the norm for the low values until 1935, when New Zealand returned to pictorials featuring scenery, wildlife and people [3; 7]. Pictorial and portrait definitives alternated until the 1960s.

BRITAIN OF THE SOUTH SEAS

The white settlers of New Zealand were predominantly from Britain and, until the 1960s, regarded that as "home", an attitude reflected in many stamps. A 1920 set marking victory in World War I used motifs from London statuary [5], setting a precedent for the Peace issue of 1946, which included a view of St Paul's Cathedral in the Blitz, with Churchill's assertion, "This was their finest hour" [8]. The Coronation set of 1953 showed not only the Crown Jewels and state coach, but also Westminster Abbey and Buckingham Palace [9]. Special issues also covered local landmarks and even incorporated Maori art in their borders [6], but the overwhelming impression is of stamps that were better at featuring the United Kingdom than British stamps were.

Sir Charles Kingsford-Smith pioneered air routes linking Australia and New Zealand and from 1931 onwards

Health Stamps

New Zealand's world-famous Health stamps began in 1929 with a stamp raising funds for the anti-tuberculosis campaign. It was reissued the following year with the caption altered to "Help Promote Health". Stamps have since been issued annually to raise funds for holiday camps, giving urban children in need the chance of a spell in the country. A recurring theme is the younger members of the British royal family, now extending to the third generation.

special stamps were produced for airmail. Few commemoratives were produced before World War II but the centennial of annexation in 1940 was the pretext for a long set reviewing the country's history and development. A long set of 1946 marked the return to peace, many of the stamps contrasting scenes in peace and war. From 1948 onwards many sets celebrated the centenaries of the settlement of various parts of New Zealand and later the charters of the various towns and cities.

New Zealand began issuing Christmas stamps in 1964, the first stamp appropriately marking the 150th anniversary of the first Christmas sermon, preached by the Reverend Samuel Marsden to a largely Maori congregation in 1814 [10].

MODERN NEW ZEALAND

Britain's entry into the EEC in 1973, and subsequent restrictions on trade between Britain and New Zealand, forced the latter to reassess its position as a country whose chief interests now lay in the Pacific region. This was increasingly reflected in stamps from this time onwards. The definitive series

of 1975 portrayed the queen on the 10c stamp but all other values had local subjects [11]. New Zealand sent troops to Vietnam [13] and developed closer ties with other countries of the Pacific Rim. Since 1988 New Zealand has issued a series of circular stamps showing its national bird, the kiwi. Designed in New Zealand, engraved in Canada and recess-printed in Australia, the Round Kiwis have continued intermittently to the present day [12].

RECENT DEVELOPMENTS

Most New Zealand stamps are now lithographed by Southern Colour Print of Dunedin. New Zealand is justifiably proud of the fact that it granted women the vote in 1893 and was the first country to do so [14]. Rugby football has been depicted on numerous stamps since the 1960s, even stamps for individual teams [15]. By contrast with the historical set of 1940 for the centenary, the 150th anniversary triggered off several sets devoted to the country's heritage, followed by the decades of the 20th century [16]. Scenery continues to predominate [18–19], interspersed with sets devoted to historic buildings [20] and antique farming equipment, but recent sets have also poked fun at typically Kiwi phenomena such as hokey-pokey (toffee crunch), jandals (flip-flops or thongs) and fish and chips, or some of the wacky letterboxes that dot the countryside. Special stamps were issued for the Government Life Insurance Department from 1891 to 1989, featuring lighthouses [17].

Below: A Burrell traction engine on a stamp of 2004 was part of a series showing vintage farm machinery.

11

12

13

14

15

16

17

18

19

20

1

2

3

4

5

6

7

8

9

FIJI, KIRIBATI AND TUVALU

The indigenous inhabitants of the native kingdom of Fiji are thought to be a mixture of Melanesians and Polynesians. Incessant tribal warfare induced King Cakobau to cede Fiji voluntarily to Britain in 1874. The import of Indian indentured labourers to work in the sugar and cotton plantations (developed after trade between Britain and the Confederate States was cut off during the American Civil War) eventually led to the native Fijians being outnumbered by Indians, a matter that caused considerable conflict in the 1970s following Fiji's attainment of independence.

The Gilbert and Ellice Islands became a British protectorate in 1892 and a crown colony in 1915. Between December 1941 and November 1943 the Gilberts were overrun by the Japanese and were latterly the scene of some of the bitterest fighting of the Pacific campaign. Self-government was granted in 1971 and five years later the Ellice Islands seceded to form Tuvalu. Subsequently the Gilberts adopted the Polynesian phonetic spelling of their name, "Kiribati".

Left: The Battle of Tarawa in 1943, one of the decisive actions of World War II and the most important event in the history of the Gilbert Islands, has been the subject of many stamps in recent years.

FIJI

The first attempt at a mail service in Fiji was organized by a local newspaper, the *Fiji Times Express*, followed by a nationwide post under the auspices of King Cakobau, whose crowned monogram was featured on the stamps [1]. The monogram of Queen Victoria was substituted after Fiji was ceded to Britain, but subsequently Fiji used the standard colonial keytypes [2].

Pictorial stamps were introduced in 1938, with some denominations reappearing in 1954 with the portrait of Elizabeth II. An entirely new series appeared in 1962–7, with the usual medley of fauna, flora and native customs [3], and this policy was continued with the series of 1968, which was amended for the change to decimal currency in 1969–70. The relatively few special issues tended to commemorate the discovery and exploration of the islands [4].

Since becoming an independent member of the Commonwealth in 1970, with the British monarch as head of state, the stamps of Fiji have become more colourful and issues rather more frequent. Landmarks were the theme of the series of 1979–94 [5] but wildlife continues to be a popular subject [6]. For the annual Christmas stamps, however, from 1996 onwards Fiji switched from Old Master paintings to motifs with a local accent [7].

GILBERT AND ELLICE ISLANDS

This protectorate, later a crown colony, was an artificial creation that linked two widely differing groups of islands scattered across the central Pacific. New Zealand operated postal agencies in Fanning and Washington, two of the Line Islands, and stamps bearing these postmarks are now highly regarded. In 1911 stamps of Fiji were overprinted for use in the Gilbert and Ellice Islands, pending the supply of a series featuring a pandanus pine two months later [10]. This issue was short-lived and from 1912 to 1939 the colonial keytypes portraying George V were employed [11]. A pictorial series appeared in

Man Overboard!

Nowadays, with a much faster pace of stamp issues, design errors are not uncommon. Back in 1938, when stamps might take months to engrave, mistakes were rare, so it was disconcerting to find that two major errors occurred in the Fiji pictorials of that year. Several stamps featured a map of the islands but omitted the important numerals "180", marking the International Dateline. Much more glaring, however, was the 1½d stamp showing an outrigger canoe under full sail with no one at the helm. The stamp was hastily re-engraved and a man inserted.

1939 and continued until 1955 [8]. Apart from the various omnibus sets from 1935 onwards, the islands had no distinctive commemorative stamps until 1964 [9]. Fine intaglio gave way to rather crude lithography in 1965: this series was surcharged in decimal currency [12] and then reissued with values in dollars and cents.

KIRIBATI

Following the break-up of the crown colony of the Gilbert and Ellice Islands at the end of 1975, stamps inscribed "The Gilbert Islands" were used from 1976 to 1979 [13], but when the islands gained independence they adopted the local spelling of their name, Kiribati (pronounced Kiribas). Since then stamps have pursued the same policy as before, apart from bearing the national arms in place of the royal portrait. Although the majority of stamps have continued to reflect the scenery and culture of the islands, Kiribati has participated in a number of international philatelic events and supported them with special stamps. In connection with the 150th anniversary of the Penny Black and the London international stamp exhibition of 1990, Kiribati produced a set reproducing stamps used in the islands from 1912 onwards [14]. Not surprisingly, marine life of the Pacific forms a major source of stamp illustrations [15]. To mark the 15th anniversary of independence Oliver Ball designed a set showing a family silhouetted on the beach [16]. Kiribati has also taken part in a few joint issues, notably the *Sesame Street* series of March 2000.

TUVALU

At first the stamps of Tuvalu, formerly the Ellice Islands, also followed a moderate policy, but since independence in 1978 the tempo has increased from year to year, with an increasing number of "market-led" stamps in more recent years, catering to every passing craze. As in the stamps of Kiribati, the national arms have replaced the queen's profile although the subject matter reflects continuing strong ties with Britain [17–18].

Below: Traditional dancing on a Tuvalu Christmas stamp of 1997 and one of the Dolphin series of 1998.

10

11

12

13

14

15

16

17

18

INSCRIPTIONS

Most stamps can be identified by their inscription, language and expressions of value, but there are some that baffle even the collector of long standing. Below is a list of key-words and abbreviations found in inscriptions and overprints, with their country, state or district of origin.

A & T Annam and Tonquin
Acores Azores
Afghanes Afghanistan
Africa Portuguese Africa
Akahi Keneta Hawaii
Amtlicher Verkehr Württemberg
AO (Afrika Ost) Ruanda-Urundi
Allemagne/Duitschland Belgian occupation of Germany
A Payer Te Betalen Belgium (postage due)
A Percevoir postage due Belgium (francs and centimes); Egypt (paras, milliemes)
Archipel des Comores Comoro Islands
Avisporto Denmark
Azad Hind Free India (unissued stamps prepared for use in India after Japanese "liberation")
B (on Straits Settlements) Bangkok
Bani (on Austrian stamps) Austrian occupation of Romania
BATYM Batum (now Batumi)
Bayer, Bayern Bavaria
BCA British Central Africa (now Malawi)
Belgique/Belgie/Belgien, also **Belge** Belgium
Böhmen und Mahren Bohemia and Moravia
Bollo delta Posta Napoletana Naples
Bosnien Bosnia
Braunschweig Brunswick
C CH Cochin China
Cechy a Morava Bohemia and Moravia
CEF (on India) Chinese Expeditionary Force

CEF (on German colonies) Cameroons under British occupation
Centesimi (on Austria) Austrian occupation of Italy
Centimes (on Austria) Austrian POs in Crete
Centrafricaine Central African Republic
Ceskoslovensko Czechoslovakia
Chiffre taxe France
Chine French POs in China
Comunicaciones Spain
Confed. Granadina Granadine Confederation (Colombia)
Cong Hoa Mien Nam National Liberation Front for South Vietnam
Congo Belge Belgian Congo
Continente Portuguese mainland
Coree Korea
Correio Brazil, Portugal
Correos Spain, Cuba, Porto Rico, Philippines
Côte d'Ivoire Ivory Coast
Côte Française des Somalis French Somali Coast
Danmark Denmark
Dansk Vestindien Danish West Indies
DDR German Democratic Republic
Deficit Peru
Deutsch Neu-Guinea German New Guinea
Deutsch Ostafrika German East Africa
Deutschösterreich Austria
Deutsch Südwestafrika German South West Africa
Deutsche Flugpost/Reichspost Germany
Deutsches Reich Germany
Dienstmarke Germany
Dienstsache Germany
Diligencia Uruguay
DJ Djibouti
Drzava, Drzavna Yugoslavia
EEF Palestine
Eesti Estonia
EE UU de C Colombia
EFO French Oceania
Eire Republic of Ireland
Elua Keneta Hawaii
Emp. Franc. French Empire
Emp. Ottoman Turkey

Equateur Ecuador
Escuelas Venezuela
España, Espanola Spain
Estados Unidos de Nueva Granada Colombia
Estensi Modena
Estero Italian POs in the Levant
Etablissements de l'Inde French Indian Settlements
Etablissements de l'Océanie French Oceanic Settlements
Etat Ind. du Congo Congo Free State
Filipinas Spanish Philippines
Franco Switzerland
Francobollo Italy
Franco Marke Bremen
Franco Poste Bollo Neapolitan provinces and early Italy
Franqueo Peru
Franquicia Postal Spain
Freimarke Württemberg, Prussia
Frimerke Norway
Frimaerke Denmark
G (on Cape of Good Hope) Griqualand West
G & D Guadeloupe
GEA Tanganyika
Gen. Gouv. Warschau German occupation of Poland, World War 1
General Gouvernement German occupation of Poland, World War II
Georgie Georgia
Giuba Jubaland
GPE Guadeloupe
GRI British occupation of New Guinea and Samoa
Grossdeutsches Reich Nazi Germany
Guine Portuguese Guinea
Guinea Ecuatorial Equatorial Guinea
Guiné French Guinea
Gultig 9 Armee German occupation of Romania
Guyane Française French Guiana
Haute Volta Upper Volta
Hellas Greece
Helvetia Switzerland
HH Nawab Shah Begam Bhopal
Hrvatska Croatia
HRZGL Holstein
IEF Indian Expeditionary Force

IEF 'D' Mosul
Imper. Reg. Austrian POs in Turkey
Impuesto de Guerra Spain (war tax)
Inde French Indian Settlements
India Port. Portuguese India
Irian Barat West Iran
Island Iceland
Jubilé de l'Union Postale Switzerland
Kamerun Cameroons
Kaladiit Nunat, Kalaallit Nunaat Greenland
Karnten Carinthia
Karolinen Caroline Islands
KGCA Carinthia
Kgl. Post. Frim. Denmark, Danish West Indies
Khmere Cambodia
Kongeligt Post Frimaerke Denmark
KK Post Stempel Austria, Austrian Italy
KPHTH Crete
Kraljevina, Kraljevstvo Yugoslavia
Kreuzer Austria
KSA Saudi Arabia
K.u.K. Feldpost Austrian military stamps
K.u.K. Militärpost Bosnia and Herzegovina
K. Württ. Post Württemberg
La Canea Italian POs in Crete
La Georgie Georgia
Land-Post Baden
Lattaquie Latakia
Latvija Latvia
Lietuvos Lithuania
Litwa Srodkowa Central Lithuania
Ljubljanska Pokrajina Slovenia
L. McL. Trinidad (Lady McLeod stamp)
Lösen Sweden
Magyar Hungary
MAPKA Russia
Marianen Mariana Islands
Maroc French Morocco
Marruecos Spanish Morocco
Marschall-Inseln Marshall Islands
Mejico Mexico
Militär Post Bosnia and Herzegovina
Mocambique Mozambique

Modonesi Modena
Montevideo Uruguay
Moyen-Congo Middle Congo
MViR German occupation of Romania
Nachmarke Austria
Napoletana Naples
NCE New Caledonia
Nederland Netherlands
Ned. Antillen Netherlands Antilles
Ned./Nederl. Indie Dutch East Indies
NF Nyasaland Field Force
Nippon Japan
Nieuwe Republiek New Republic (South Africa)
Norddeutscher Postbezirk North German Confederation
Norge, Noreg Norway
Nouvelle Calédonie New Caledonia
Nouvelles Hébrides New Hebrides
NSB Nossi-Be (Madagascar)
NSW New South Wales
NW Pacific Islands Nauru and New Guinea
NZ New Zealand
Oesterr., Oesterreich, Österreich Austria
Offentligt Sak Norway (official stamps)
Oltre Giuba Jubaland
Orts Post Switzerland
OS Norway (official stamps)
Ottoman, Ottomanes Turkey
P, PGS Perak (Government Service)
Pacchi Postale Italy (parcel stamps)
Pakke-Porto Greenland
Para Egypt, Serbia, Turkey, Crete
Parm[ensi] Parma
Pesa (on German) German POs in Turkey
Piaster German POs in Turkey
Pilipinas Philippines
Pingin Ireland
Poblact na hEireann Republic of Ireland
Poczta Polska Poland
Pohjois Inkeri North Ingermanland
Port Cantonal Switzerland (Geneva)

Porte de Conduccion Peru
Porte Franco Peru
Porte de Mar Mexico
Porteado Portugal and colonies
Porto Austria, Yugoslavia
Porto-pflichtige Württemberg
Post & Receipt/Post Stamp Hyderabad
Postage and Revenue United Kingdom
Postas le n'ioc Republic of Ireland
Postat e Qeverries Albania
Poste Estensi Modena
Poste Locale Switzerland
Postes (alone) Alsace and Lorraine, Belgium, Luxembourg
Poste Shqiptare Albania
Postgebiet Ob. Ost German Eastern Army
Postzegel Netherlands
Preussen Prussia
Provincie Modonesi Modena
Provinz Laibach Slovenia
PSNC Pacific Steam Navigation Co., Peru

Qeverries Albania
R Jind
Rayon Switzerland
Recargo Spain
Regno d'Italia Venezia Giulia, Trieste
Reichspost German Empire
RF France and colonies
RH Haiti
Repoblika Malagasy Malagasy Republic
Republica Oriental Uruguay
Répub. Franc. France
République Libanaise Lebanon
République Rwandaise Rwanda
Rialtas Sealadac na hEireann Provisional Government of Ireland
RO Eastern Roumelia
RSA Republic of South Africa
Rumanien (on German) German occupation of Romania
Russisch-Polen German occupation of Poland
Sachsen Saxony

Scrisorei Moldavia and Wallachia
Segnatasse Italy
Serbien Austrian or German occupation of Serbia
SH Schleswig-Holstein
SHS Yugoslavia
Shqipenia, Shqipenie, Shqypnija, Shqiptare Albania
Sld., Soldi Austrian Italy
Slesvig Schleswig
Slovensky Stat Slovakia
SO Eastern Silesia
SPM St Pierre and Miquelon
S. Thome e Principe St Thomas and Prince Islands
Suidwes Afrika South West Africa
Sul Bolletina, Sulla Ricevuta Italy
Sultunat d'Anjouan Anjouan
Suomi Finland
Sverige Sweden
SWA South West Africa
TAKCA Bulgaria
Tassa Gazzette Modena

Te Betalen Port Netherlands and colonies
TEO Cilicia. Syria
Terres Australes et Antarctiques Françaises French Southern and Antarctic Territories
Territoire Français des Afars et les Issas French Territory of the Afars and Issas
Tjanste Frimarke Sweden
Tjeneste Frimerke Norway
Tjeneste Frimaerke Denmark
Toga Tonga
Toscano Tuscany
UAE United Arab Emirates
UAR United Arab Republic (Egypt)
UG Uganda
UKTT United Kingdom Trust Territory (Southern Cameroons)
Uku Leta Hawaii
Ultramar Cuba. Porto Rico
UNEF Indian Forces in Gaza
UNTEA Western New Guinea

Vallées d'Andorre Andorra
Van Diemen's Land Tasmania
Venezia Giulia (on Italian stamps) Trieste
Venezia Tridentina Trentino
Viet Nam Dan Chu Cong Hoa North Vietnam
Vom Empfanger Einzuziehen Danzig (postage due)
YAR Yemen Arab Republic
YCCP Ukraine
YKP. H. P. Ukraine
Z Armenia
ZAR South African Republic (Transvaal)
Z. Afr. Republiek South African Republic (Transvaal)
Zeitungsmarke Austria, Germany (newspaper stamps)
Zil Eloine Sesel Seychelles Outer Islands
Zuid West Afrika South West Africa
Zulassungsmarke German military parcel stamp

GLOSSARY

Stamp collectors have a language all of their own, which can be puzzling to a newcomer. Some of the more commonly used terms are given below. References to glossed terms appear in bold.

Adhesive Stamp issued with **gum** on the reverse for sticking on mail, as opposed to one printed directly on the envelope, card or wrapper. *See also* Self-adhesive.
Aerogramme Specially printed air letter sheet on lightweight paper.
Airgraph World War II forces mail sent by micro-film, then enlarged for dispatch to the addressee.
Alphabets The different styles of lettering printed in the corners of British stamps 1840–87.

Backstamp Postmark on the back of an envelope, usually applied in transit or arrival.
Bantams South African stamps printed as a reduced format in World War II to save paper.
Bilingual pairs Stamps printed alternately in two different languages, as seen in issues from South Africa (1926–50) and Ceylon (1964).
Bisect Stamp cut in half for use at half the usual value, in times of shortage. Bisection may be made horizontally, vertically or diagonally.
Blind perforation Perforation in which the paper is merely dented, owing to blunt teeth in the perforating machine.
Block Four or more stamps joined together; also used in continental Europe as a synonym for a **miniature sheet**.

Bogus Label purporting to be a genuine stamp but without any validity or even a reason for issue other than to defraud collectors. Bogus overprints may be found on genuine stamps for the same reason.
Booklet One or more panes (small blocks) of stamps, usually held together with card covers. **Cachet** Mark applied to cards and covers, other than the postmark, and often private or unofficial in nature.
Cancellation Postmark applied to stamps to prevent their re-use. Often hand- or machine-struck from steel or brass stamps, but may also be applied from a rubber, cork or wood stamp, or even by pen and ink.
Cancelled to order (CTO) Stamps postmarked in bulk, usually for sale to philatelists

below face value; usually recognized by still having the gum on the backs.
Cantonals The earliest issues of Switzerland (e.g. Basle, Geneva and Zurich).
Carriers Stamps issued by private carriers, mainly in the United States, 1842–59.
Centred A stamp whose design is equidistant from the edges of the perforations is said to be well centred. Off-centre stamps have perforations (or scissor cuts if imperforate) cutting into the design on one or more sides.
Chalk-surfaced paper Security paper used for many British and colonial stamps to prevent re-use by cleaning off the cancellations. Can be detected by means of a silver pencil.

Chalky paper Special paper with a glossy surface used for many modern British definitive stamps, and also widely used for multicoloured stamps.
Chalon heads Name given to some early stamps of British colonies, e.g. Bahamas, Ceylon, New Zealand, Tasmania. reproducing a full-face portrait of Queen Victoria by Edward Chalon, RA.
Classics The earliest stamps of the world, 1840–1870.
Cliché Stereo or electro unit used in letterpress printing. These are assembled in a **forme** to form a printing plate.
Coils Stamps issued in reels or coils and often collected in **strips**. Can often be identified by being **imperforate** on two opposite sides.

Colour trials Impressions, or **proofs**, created in various colours prior to issue, for the purpose of determining the most suitable colours in actual production.

Combination cover Cover bearing stamps of two or more postal administrations, mainly from the early period when stamps had no franking validity beyond the frontiers of the country of issue.

Comb perforation Perforation on three sides of a stamp made at one stroke of the perforator, resulting in perfectly even corner teeth, compared with **line perforation**.

Commemorative A stamp sold in limited quantities for a period of time, often honouring a person, place, or event, but also used to promote current events.

Compulsory Stamp Charity stamps, issued at one time by countries such as Portugal and Yugoslavia, for compulsory use on mail.

Controls Letters and numerals found on British sheet margins, 1881–1947, for accounting purposes.

Cork cancellation Obliterators cut from corks, usually with fancy devices; widely used by 19th-century American postmasters. Also used in Britain to obliterate incorrect datestamps.

Corner block Stamps taken from the corner of a **sheet**, adjacent to marginal paper showing **controls**, **cylinder numbers**, plate numbers or printer's imprint.

Corner letters Double alphabet sequence of letters found in the corners of British stamps, 1840–87, indicating the position of the stamp in the **sheet**.

Cover Envelope or wrapper with stamps affixed or imprinted. Stamps are said to be "on cover" when the envelope is intact, as opposed to "on front" or "on piece".

CTO Widely used abbreviation for "**Cancelled to order**".

Cut to shape Imperforate stamps of unusual shapes, with margins trimmed accordingly.

Cylinder number Tiny numeral printed in the sheet margin to denote the cylinder(s) used in production.

Dandy roll Wire gauze cylinder used in the manufacture of paper and impregnation of **watermarks**.

Definitives Stamps in general use over a period of years, as opposed to **commemoratives**, charity or semi-postal stamps and other special issues.

Demonetized Obsolete stamps declared invalid for postage.

Die The original piece of metal on which the stamp design is engraved.

Die proof Impression pulled from the **die** to check its accuracy.

Dominical labels Small labels attached below Belgian stamps, 1893–1914, instructing the postmen not to deliver the letter on Sunday. Where no objection was raised the labels were detached. **Dumb cancellation** Postmarks with the town name erased for security reasons in wartime, and also special anonymous obliterations produced for the same purpose.

Engine-turning Intricate pattern of spiral lines forming the background to the earliest British and colonial stamps. This security device was copied from banknotes.

Entire Complete envelope, card or wrapper.

Entire letter Complete envelope or wrapper, with the original contents intact.

Embossed Stamps, or a portion of their design, die-struck in low relief, often colourless against a coloured background. Widely used for postal stationery.

Error Stamps deviating from the normal in some respect: missing or inverted colours, **surcharges** and **overprints** or mistakes in the design which may later be corrected. Usually worth more than normals, although in some cases (e.g. the Hammarskjold issue in the United States), the postal authority may take steps to minimize the rarity of the original.

Essay Preliminary design, not subsequently used.

Fake Genuine stamp that has been tampered with in some way to make it more valuable: e.g. fiscally used high-value stamps with the pen markings erased and a postmark substituted, or a stamp converted to a valuable rarity by the addition of an overprint.

First Day Cover or FDC Envelope bearing stamps used on the first day of issue.

First Flight Cover Cover carried on first airmail by a new route, or new aircraft.

Fiscal Stamp intended for fiscal or **revenue** purposes.

Flaw Defect in the printing **plate** or **cylinder**, resulting in a constant blemish on the same stamp in every sheet; plate flaws are useful in sheet reconstruction.

Forme Printer's term for the frame clamped around stereos or **clichés** to make a printing **plate** in the letterpress process.

Frank Mark or label indicating that a letter or card can be transmitted free of postage. Widely used by government departments. Military franks have been issued by France, Vietnam etc for use by personnel.

Gum Mucilage on the back of unused stamps. British stamps changed from gum arabic (glossy) to polyvinyl alcohol gum (matt, colourless) and later PVA Dextrin gum (with a greenish tint).

Gutter Area between panes of a sheet. Stamps from adjoining panes with the gutter between are known as gutter or interpanneau pairs.

Half tone Black-and-white photographic image appearing on a stamp; often a feature of early 20th-century **essays** where they were created by a simplified form of the photogravure process.

Healths Stamps issued by New Zealand since 1929 and Fiji (1951 and 1954), with a premium in aid of children's health camps.

Imperforate Stamps issued without any means of separating them, thus requiring them to be cut apart with scissors. Stamps with no perforations on one or more sides may come from **booklets** and those with no **perforations** on two opposite sides are from **coils**.

Imprint Inscription giving the name or trademark of the printer. **Imprint block** Block of four or more stamps with marginal paper attached bearing the imprint.

Intaglio Printing process where the design is engraved in "recess", or below the surface of the printing plate.

Issue New stamp or stamps issued by a postal authority.

Jubilee line Line of printer's rule reinforcing the edges of the plate and first used on the British "Jubilee" series of 1887. Appears as bars of colour in the margin at the foot of the sheet.

Key plate Printing plate used to generate the design of the stamp. Used in conjunction with a duty plate, which prints the value.

Keytype Collectors' term for stamps of the British, French, German, Portuguese and Spanish colonies which used identical designs, differing only in the name of the colony and the denomination.

Kiloware Originally sealed kilogram bags of stamps on paper, but now applied to any mixtures sold by weight.

Line perforation Perforation where holes are punched out on one side of a stamp at a time, with the result that two sets of perforated lines do not register at the corners of the **sheet**.

Lithography Surface printing method where a design is photographically transferred to a zinc or aluminium **plate**. *See also* Offset lithography.

Locals Stamps whose validity is restricted to a single town or district and cannot be used for sending national or international mail.

Marginal markings Marks on the margins of sheets include **controls**, **cylinder numbers**, "traffic lights", printers' imprints, **jubilee lines**, sheet serial numbers, arrows showing the middle of the sheet, values of rows or sheets, ornament and even commercial advertising (France, Germany).

Meter marks Marks applied by a postage meter used by firms and other organizations. They comprise the indicium (or imitation "stamp" with the value), the town die (with the date) and an advertising slogan, or may combine these elements in a single design. Invented in New Zealand (1904) and used inter-nationally since 1922.

Miniature sheet Small sheet containing a single stamp or a small group of stamps, often with decorative margins.

Mint Unused stamp with full, original **gum** on the back.

Obsolete Stamp no longer on sale at the post office but still valid for postage.

Obliteration Post-marking of stamps to prevent re-use. *See also* cancellation.

Offset lithography Printing process whereby an image is transferred from an aluminum or zinc plate to a rubber blanket, and then from the rubber blanket to the paper.

Omnibus issue Commemoratives issued by several countries simultaneously, using similar designs.

Overprint Printing applied to a stamp some time after the original printing, to convert it to some other purpose (e.g. **commemorative**, charity, or for use overseas).

Pane Originally a portion of a **sheet** (half or quarter) divided by **gutters**, but also applied to the blocks of stamps issued in **booklets**.

Patriotics Covers and cards with patriotic motifs, fashionable during the American Civil War, the Boer War and both World Wars.

Perfins Stamps perforated with initials or other devices as a security measure to prevent pilfering or misuse by office staff.

Perforation Form of separation using machines which punch out tiny circles of paper. *See also* Comb perforation; Line perforation.

Phosphor band Almost invisible line on the face of a stamp, created by the application of a chemical, to facilitate the electronic sorting process.

Photogravure Printing process where the design is photographed onto the printing **plate** using a fine screen which breaks the copy up into very fine square dots. The tiny depressions that form around the squares retain the ink.

Plate Flat or curved piece of metal from which stamps are printed.

Plate proof Impression of a **sheet**, **block** or **strip** of new issues, pulled from the **die**, usually in black ink, or sometimes in various colours.

Plebiscites Stamps issued in towns and districts, mainly after World War I, pending the vote of the population to decide which country they should join, e.g. Memel, Marienwerder, Carinthia and Silesia.

Postage dues Labels denoting the amount of postage unpaid or underpaid (often including a fine).

Postage paid impressions (PPIs) Marks printed on envelopes, cards or wrappers, often used in bulk business mail.

Postal stationery Envelopes, cards and wrappers bearing **imprinted** or **embossed** stamps.

Pre-cancels Stamps used in bulk postings, with marks previously overprinted to prevent reuse. Widely used by Canada, Belgium, United States and France, but now largely superseded by **meter marks** and **postage paid impressions**.

Printer's waste Stamps with defective, double or misaligned printing, usually

imperforate, and discarded during stamp production. Though usually strictly controlled, such material occasionally comes on to the market and is of interest to the specialist.

Proof Impression of a stamp design, pulled from the **die**. With perforated proofs, an overprint is often added to cancel the design and prevent it being used for postal purposes. *See also* Die proofs; Plate proofs.

Provisionals Stamps **overprinted** or **sur-charged** to meet a shortage of regular issues. Also used by emergent nations pending a supply of distinctive stamps, the stamps of the former mother country being overprinted.

Recess printing Term used in catalogues to signify **intaglio** printing.

Re-entry Portion of an **intaglio plate** which is re-engraved or re-entered by the transfer roller, usually detected by slight doubling of the lines.

Redrawn Stamps in which the basic design has been retained but various changes made in a subsequent edition.

Remainders Stocks of stamps on hand after an issue has been **demonetized** are sometimes sold off cheaply to the philatelic trade, with some form of cancellation to distinguish them from unused stamps sold at full value during the currency of the stamps.

Reprints Stamps printed from the original plates, sometimes long after the issue has ceased. They can be detected by differences in the paper, watermark and colour.

Retouch Repairs to letterpress plates and

photogravure cylinders to touch out a flaw may result in stamps that can still be detected as slightly different from the normal. The corrected versions are known as retouches.

Revenue Stamp intended for **fiscal** or revenue purposes.

Rouletting Form of separation in which serrated instruments cut or pierce the paper without actually removing any, as in **perforation**.

Secret marks Tiny letters, numbers, dates and other devices introduced into the design of some stamps (notably the United States and Canada) for security reasons.

Self-adhesive A stamp in a **coil** or **booklet** with backing paper from which it is peeled and affixed to mail without the necessity to lick or moisten the back.

Selvedge Stamp edging or sheet marginal paper.

Se-tenant Two or more stamps of different designs, values or colours, printed side by side.

Sheet A complete set of stamps taken from a single printing **plate**. This may then be cut into individual **panes** for sale at a post office.

Sheetlet Small sheet of stamps, of varying quantities depending the on country of issue.

Specimen Stamp perforated or overprinted thus, or its equivalent in other languages, for record or publicity purposes and having no postal validity.

Straight edge Stamps with no **perforations** on one or more sides, mainly found in **coils** and **booklets** but including **sheets** of stamps from countries such as Canada and the United States.

Strip Three or more stamps that have not been separated.

Surcharge An **overprint** that alters the face value of a stamp.

Tablet Adjoining section of a stamp that bears an inscription, advertisement or other design.

Tabs Stamps with marginal inscriptions alluding to the subjects depicted, widely used by Israel and also by Switzerland and the United Nations.

Tied Postmarks that overlap the stamp and the envelope or card, a useful feature in establishing the genuineness of **bisects**.

Toughra (also tughra) Calligraphic markings indicating the signature of the former Sultan of Turkey, prevalent on Turkish issues predating the Ottoman Empire's demise in 1920.

Typography Collector's term for letterpress printing, abbreviated in catalogues to "typo".

Unused Stamp lacking a cancellation, but in less perfect condition than **mint**.

UPU Universal Postal Union.

Used Stamp bearing a cancellation.

Variety Any variation from the normal issue, relating to its shade, **perforation**, **watermark**, **gum** or phosphorescence, usually listed in the more specialized catalogues.

Vignette The main motif or central portion of a stamp design, as opposed to the frame, value **tablet** or inset portrait or effigy of the ruler.

Watermark Translucent impression used as a security device in the paper from which stamps are printed.

Zemstvos Russian local postal network which prepaid postage from the many smaller towns to the nearest imperial post office.

INDEX

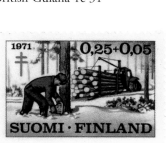

PICTURE ACKNOWLEDGEMENTS

All stamps illustrated in this book and on the jacket were supplied by Dr James Mackay, from his private collection, unless indicated below.

Royal Mail British Stamps © Royal Mail Group plc. All rights reserved. Reproduced with the permission of Royal Mail Group plc

Penny Black and the Penny Black stamp are the registered trade marks of Royal Mail Group plc in the United Kingdom. Anness Publishing Ltd would like to thank Royal Mail Group plc for allowing us to reproduce images of this stamp on the jacket spine and on the following page 44 (top left).